MW01109912

Wayne Bullard
time friend. He
ever known.

Each week he gives an intimate view of what is happening in the Allen community as well as commentary on national issues. Many of his columns are the kind that will be passed on from generation to generation.

Wayne's column shows how our community deals with local and national issues and he writes with wit and wisdom.

My mother once said the only reason she bought the newspaper was to read Wayne's column. I reminded her that I also wrote a weekly column and she replied, "I know."

In this book you will find Wayne explaining the unexplainable in a series of his columns and reading them will most often bring a smile to your face, and at times uncontrollable laughter. There are also those columns that will cause you to weep.

Faith, facts, fun and family....Wayne covers them all. There is no doubt this book will have a lasting place in Allen history.

Bill Robinson, Publisher

The Allen Advocate

One Pharmacist's View

One Pharmacist's View

By Wayne Bullard, Pharm D

Robinson
PUBLISHING
COMPANY, INC.

PUBLISHED BY ROBINSON PUBLISHING CO., INC.
HOLDENVILLE, OKLAHOMA

Cover Design: Diane Brannan
Interior Design: Dayna Robinson

PRINTED IN THE UNITED STATES OF AMERICA
JUNE 2015

ISBN 978-194327695-0

DEDICATION

I dedicate this book to my family, especially my partner and love of my life, Pat. I would never have had this good life, a college education or a professional career without her help and encouragement. The most precious gift perhaps God gives anyone is a good wife and children. We have four--all of whom made my life a joy and were a great help working hard in every respect and making our family an entity held together by mutual respect and love. I give my thanks and love to Pat, Ron, Traci, Lesli and Steve.

Our Family

Pat, Ron, Traci, Steve, Lesli, and Wayne

TABLE OF CONTENTS

Why this Book?

I've always liked to write. Not that I'm all that good at it. I enjoyed writing letters even as a child and didn't mind the writing classes in school. I was not much of a student but in spite of my blasé attitude toward my education, excellent teachers over at Stonewall made sure we were fairly literate, with teachers like Flossy Grogan seeing that we learned. Aboard the USS Lexington I assisted a pair of Yeoman with the daily newspaper they had to write. I would take news off the teletype for them and summarize it for them.

Years later, in Allen, I wrote my own advertising ads for my community pharmacy and enjoyed doing it. I also wrote a little weekly news article in which I handed out advice about medicine, health aids and the latest drugs. These included my viewpoints and sometimes I had a story to slip in. My customers encouraged me to write more stories and so it began. One guy said, "let off that pharmacy stuff and give us more of your story stuff." Of course advice like that just pushed me along.

By the time I sold my pharmacy in 1997, my "One Pharmacist's View" stories were an established item in The Allen Advocate and when I quit, my readers encouraged me to keep on writing them. I was torn and it wasn't until my publisher, Bill Robinson, paid a visit and encouraged me to continue that I considered it. My wife encouraged me and even helped shape the stories by proof reading for errors and content. I often claim my stories are 80% true and 20% parable thus when my little sister Sue questions a story, she calls Gerald to see if it's really true. So far, he has backed me up so my 80% estimate is more than safe.

Wayne Bullard, Pharm D

About the Author

Wayne Bullard grew up in rural settings. Born on Cleveland Street in Allen, Oklahoma, Bullard's family lived briefly in nearby Calvin and in 1938 moved to Centrahoma where his father was employed as a clerk in a grocery store. Soon after, the Bullard's moved into the back end of another grocery store and shortly thereafter Mr. Bullard's dad bought out the Brown Grocery Store. Wayne started 1st grade at Centrahoma School and between a lot of fellowship and the dynamic times of the depression and then World War II, he learned a lot about life--a hard-scrabble life.

In 1944 Wayne's dad bought a small movie theatre in Stonewall, just 12 miles up Highway 3 and the Bullard's made another move. Life was easier and somewhat different in the little oilfield boom town and Wayne migrated up to the projection room and showed what seemed like a million movies. He watched them all. Stonewall was a rough and tough little town and between the church life favored by his family and the bootleg culture that seemed to dominate at least parts of the community's culture, Wayne was infused with a unique mixture of survival, education and Christianity. Luckily for him, the influence of church and school was strong--that and a Godly mother continued to shape him.

The draft was still in effect and he chose to serve four years in the Navy where he served on an aircraft carrier and then a destroyer escort as an electronic technician. He finished his four years in 1958 and worked awhile for Chance Vought Aircraft in Dallas. In 1963 he earned his Pharmacy Degree from The University of Oklahoma. He worked at three stores and then bought a pharmacy in Allen - back where he started. He and his wife Patricia have been married nearly 57 years and are at home in the old Doctor Bentley house on Lee Street, Allen, a town he is quite at ease in.

01-03-01
Everyone Needs a Buddy Sometime

It wasn't rowdy, it wasn't too motivated and in fact it barely existed except on paper. It was, however, the 13 year old boy's class of First Baptist Church in Stonewall—such as it was. No one wanted to teach a class of dead-heads like us—a class of no shows. We had no teacher. But there was this one guy named Buddy Harper. He had never taught Sunday school and he was a member of the church so they asked him. Buddy liked working with kids and liked to play baseball and softball. He probably thought he would get to coach a team out of this and indeed he would. But there would be problems.

After a few Sundays I still remember Buddy flipping through his ring binder that contained about a dozen names. Only two of us were showing up. Glenn Elkins and myself. Glenn was a Methodist and after Sunday school walked the block over and attended church with his parents. Buddy wasn't licked yet—we'll just start a new class, he said. He informed us that we were to invite one kid to class for next week and he handed both of us a name. Mine was David Alexander. I told him, "Mr. Harper, David Ray isn't going to come. He doesn't go to church and none of his family go." "Give me an easier name out of the binder" "No, he replied, all these boys are on the roll and have shown no response to my invites."

Monday night after Buddy came in from work he called me. "You call David?" he asked. "Uh, not yet." "Did you see him today?" "Yes." "Get on it" he replied. "He won't come," I answered. "That's not your problem, all you have to do is invite him." The next afternoon he called again. "Get it done?" "Uh, not yet, didn't get a chance to," I replied. "How close do you sit to him?" "Uh, I sit right next to him I guess" I mumbled. "Get on it Wayne," Buddy said. I figured out eventually that if I wanted to get Buddy off my back (plus I really liked and looked up to Mr. Harper) I would just have to invite David Ray Alexander to Sunday school. I did. I said something to the effect

17

that I knew he wouldn't want to come but I had to invite him. He was there Sunday morning. Glenn's invitee showed too so we had a big class of 4. Buddy prevailed in having all of us again invite someone new. We were getting ready for a class of travel, softball and camping. The class quickly became a done thing.

We learned a lot of things that summer, much by example. I don't remember much about what Buddy taught in class or his coaching but I do remember the fellowship I had with all those kids and how we felt toward Mr. Harper. Buddy made some good talks around campfires that summer on trips to Wilburton and some other campouts. Decisions were made by some as the summer went along. When we would go to Stringtown (a boy's reformatory) to play ball and spend a night, we had to agree to share our faith with at least one boy and he began working on and with us about what we could say. Some of the boys had nothing to share and Buddy had a remedy for that too. We baptized a bunch of boys that summer and fall.

Families would come and attend their kid's baptisms and through this some of the parents and siblings started to church. Many later became Christians. The boys soon grew up and disappeared. I can't keep track of them but know some are still working in their churches and many of their family members (some still over at Stonewall) are still at it. Buddy ran into some opposition during his ministry from scoffers and some church members who said the boys were just there for the fun and games of it all. Buddy himself was a little rough around the edges and far from a perfect man, but the fact remains he took a bunch of 13 year olds and taught them a lot. Lessons about life, lessons about family and lessons God. Jesus pointed this out in Matthew, when he told of the man who had so much trouble getting folks out to the wedding and he had to resort to unorthodox methods to get people to attend—for you see, the ones who were supposed to come, wouldn't. Besides, I always feel that everyone needs a Buddy. So did a bunch of boys at the First Baptist Church in Stonewall once upon a time.

Wayne Bullard, DPh

04-22-04
The "Onion"

The "Onion" stood just northwest of Stonewall. Painted white with a big red flying horse painted on its south side, it made an enticing climbing target by 6th and 7th grade boys. Its large and gracious winding stairway promised easy access to a great view and its tall security fence sported an unlocked gate. Last fall I stood out on the new girls' softball field near where the old onion that had been built out there in the 1930s, and discussed the old Magnolia Park with former superintendent Gibson and how beautiful it had been—but my mind kept directing my eyes in the direction of the now vanished "Onion." Whenever I looked over there, shivers went up my back as I remembered certain events that took place back around 1946.

I first saw the big onion in October 1944 when I moved to Stonewall. I hadn't lived there very long before I tied up with one Bobby Dale Newport, an experienced oil derrick climber, original thinker and local daredevil. Bob and I had soon climbed a few old rusty oil derricks, explored the interiors of a few massive (but empty) storage tanks, reset the brakes on several railroad cars and did other dangerous and forbidden things, but it was out on the big onion that we discovered which of us was really brave and who wasn't.

It came to pass that on a certain day, several of us were atop the big onion (not an unusual happening) when Bobby ventured outside the safety railing. The top part of the onion was fairly flat but after you got out there about 8 feet, the incline was pronounced. The dare was who was going out further than the other. With urgings by our "chicken" (but wiser) friends, we ventured out quite a ways that day. It was so far that I thought that this was as far as I could get and not slide on over the edge, becoming impaled in the fence below.

The next day Bobby told me that we were going back out there and see how far we could go. I could tell he had given it some thought. We took a pair of pencils and a few fans to observe this, another great feat. Of course, I think all the others just wanted to see us fall and be able to report first hand, the gory details of our violent deaths. And this is just what Bobby Dale had in mind-putting on a show for the more conservative (smarter) members of the class. Some of the guys out there were David Alexander, Gilbert Miller, R.C. Adams and Darrell Sinclair. Bob and I (barefoot) went to the edge of the abyss to make our mark for glory and fame. Bobby went out about as far as he wanted to and put his pencil at the end of his big toe and made a mark and put a "B" by it. I went down and about ½" further and made a mark with a "W", hoping that Bob would chicken out as I had gone as far as I wanted to go. But, of course, Bobby went further and repeated his marking. I followed suit and beat him just a bit. This went on until finally, as I made my mark and was trying to write a "W" by it, I felt a little slip. I leaned back for better traction and down below the big security fence with its steel poles and 4 strands of barbwire on top waited for my fall. I lay there, sort of scrunching up and I told the "Dear Lord" that if he could possibly extract me from this precarious situation, that I would never ever do anything like this again. I lied, of course, but finally I gathered my wits and with a little help from the Almighty and his Angels I made it back up like a human fly.

I thought that might be the scariest moment of my life but no, when my best friend Bobby went down and placed his, and the final winning mark on the edge, I was real scared for him. I thought I was going to have to go tell Nora and Clyde that their youngest son was hopelessly impaled and dead on a tall fence post at the onion. Bobby took a long time, it seemed to me, working his way back up and looked up at me and said, "your turn." I said, "you win, there is no way I am going back there" and we adjourned.

Bobby continued in his daredevil ways, but I settled down after that and while I didn't enter the ministry in repentance, God endowed me with enough wisdom afterwards, so I never ever even climbed on that onion again. Bobby got older and broke several speed records on old Highway 3 between Ada and Stonewall, yearned for something faster and learned to fly an airplane. He finally, in search of something real fast, joined the U.S. Air Force and was commissioned an officer that was allowed to fly jet fighters.

My friend is gone now, victim of a highway broadside many years later (that wasn't his fault) and I miss him greatly. But whenever I remember the greatest and best times of my Stonewall childhood, Bobby Newport comes to mind.

Have a good week and don't forget to go to church this Sunday. And remember, if you ever climb an onion, stay away from the edge.

04-29-04
A Muddy Night for the Undertaker

There is a big two-storied house that sits on East Broadway that was built by Will Pegg a long time ago. And then lived in by several families since. James Arnold owns and lives in the stately old house now. For a while back in the 1930s the house sheltered an undertaker and his family. He lived upstairs and did his "work" downstairs. The late J. I. Jones, a good friend of mine who lived just next door to the undertaker related this story to me. Remember, all my stories are always true, or at least 80% true with 20% for parable purposes.

So it was back in the 30s here in Allen there was a real rainy spell. It was one Sunday morning at 2 a.m. that someone rang the bell at the funeral home. The undertaker came downstairs and was greeted by the wettest Indian he had ever seen who proceeded to tell the undertaker that "Grandpa died tonight and you need to come get him." He also told the undertaker that he would ride with him and show him the way. Business wasn't all that good and the financially challenged undertaker proceeded to get dressed. They went outside and got into the old Cadillac Hearse and the grieving young man directed him south on a poorly graveled road now known as Highway 48.

The cold rain, according to J. I. continued to pour and they worried about the creeks being up and over the roads. When their turnoff was reached (somewhere down near the Red Oak area) they headed down a bad rutted road and busted mud-holes but kept on powering their way through the mud. Then they came to a turnoff that ran down through the woods and led to the old house where the deceased grandfather waited in repose for their arrival. The hearse never made it. Some distance from the house they hit bottom and the vehicle stuck. The resourceful Indian said, "Stay here, I will go get my horse and pull you on down to the house."

The tired undertaker just sat there with his lights off, his heater running and in a little bit, dozed off. When he roused it was getting a little bit light outside. He realized some time had passed and his faithful guide had never returned. He grabbed his slick and boots and went out into the rain and continued afoot to the dead man's house to see what had happened to his faithful guide. And elderly Indian lady answered his wet knocks at the front door. They visited a moment about why he was there and about her grandson and the astonished lady told him: "Grandpa not dead." "He OK, grandson, he just need a ride home. He sleeping in back room.'

Grandma made the young man get up and see the wet and cold undertaker back to the hearse and drag it back to the main road with the horse.

I don't know if the undertaker ever got over his adventure but he did soon pull up and leave Allen—becoming the last undertaker (that I know of) to practice his needy art in Allen.

Be sure and go to church Sunday and remember if you need a ride home some rainy Saturday night, just walk or call a cab or something. Don't go fetch a hearse.

Wayne Bullard, DPh
waynebullard@sbcglobal.net

03-15-05
Chasing Robbers in Allen

It was one of those cold foggy nights in February and we had gone to Stonewall to celebrate my birthday. There was a roadblock near the edge of Allen and we stopped. After we stopped we found they were actually looking for us. They thought something had happened to the Bullards. You see, earlier that night Bill Carr, the guy who ran the OTASCO store next door to my drug store thought he heard a racket and went over to see what was going on. He had been working late. He found a bad guy who had a 357 magnum breaking into my store. Bill dropped his little 22 pistol and the guy marched him over to the retaining wall by the Farmer's State Bank. As Bill awaited his doom he heard his captor say: "Do you think you could stay here and not move, not look, not peek or anything while I walk over to my truck and leave, or should I just go ahead and blow your head off?" Bill was in favor of the guy going and leaving him alone and he assured him what had happened was confidential.

The robber left and went straight to my house where he looked around, and if he stole anything I couldn't figure out what. I had, you may remember, gone to Stonewall. Of course Bill Carr was lying. He sought help and they looked for me. They eventually drew the conclusion that the Bullards had been taken off. After a good search of my home they finally found me at the roadblock and another search ensued. I thanked one and all and said I wanted to go to bed. It was getting late.

Vernon Burright was there—armed to the teeth. He looked absolutely ferocious. And Vernon wanted to get this bad guy—tonight. We knew who he was, what he drove and by Jove, we needed to get him into custody. We tried to load up in the antiquated Allen police car but Bill Callaway said, "No let's take my new Ford, its real fast." So we did—the six of us—all armed with pistols and with shotguns.

J. D. Wilson and Welton Priest were there—at that time the entirety of the Allen Police Department. And of course Virgil Guy was there. We were looking for an old 55 Chevy pickup. About 1AM we found one. A solitary man driving and J. D. exclaimed: "That's it!" "I would know his pickup anywhere!"

We quickly caught the felon and didn't know what to do. Bill's car had no red lights. No siren. So we followed. A few minutes passed before Bill ran out of gas. We radioed with Welton's little hand held radio and had the Ada Police set up roadblocks. He wasn't getting away that easy! We finally got some gas from a nearby and somewhat terrified resident but before we could get underway the Ada Police radioed us that they had stopped an 84 year old Stratford peach farmer, a pillar of the community driving home from bingo in his 55 Chevy pickup. After throwing him to the ground and handling him roughly they had released him with the hope they wouldn't get sued. Welton answered, "I guess we will just go back to Allen and wait for tomorrow to apprehend this guy," "We would really appreciate that," the tired cop replied. And we did—wondering what the world would do without dedicated citizens such as us.

Have a nice day and go to church Sunday. And be cautious when grown armed citizens ask you to go with them in the middle of a cold, foggy night.

Wayne Bullard, DPh
waynebullard@sbcglobal.net

05-05-05
Red Ant Beds & Centrahoma

The little shack had few if any redeeming features. The unpainted hulk had two rooms and an ugly yard which contained the town's largest red-ant bed, tall weeds and an old dilapidated outdoor toilet that leaned to the East. A pair of trees made little shade since they were mostly dead. It was a pitiful place serviced by a dirt road and close to a neglected railroad track. A few old boxcars were parked on the nearby siding—something to climb on.

We were not on the "wrong" side of the tracks: we were living in Centrahoma in 1938 and there wasn't any good "side." We were down on our luck and my dad had been jobless, but now he was employed and we were to live a few months in this pitiful house. At least twice a day a passenger trolley (they called it the dinky) rattled by hauling passengers between Atoka, Ada and Oklahoma City. It had more crew than passengers and often jumped the rough rail which was to provide a lot of future entertainment for Gerald and me. They parked a crane on the siding to set the little tram back on the tracks and used it often.

The house hadn't been lived in for a while—it had been used as a barn to store hay and peanuts. I could tell by what was left there. Things were like that in 1938—it was called "The Great Depression." We never considered ourselves unlucky or looked to anyone like the government for help—it wouldn't have done any good if we had. We actually felt lucky. We had the next meal, a shelter and there was family around—and dad had a new job. Many dispossessed families literally lived in the woods under a tarp, or under a highway bridge. There was a "Hooverville" in every town of any size, full of plywood structures and tents, cooking pots and kids—just trying to survive. Hobos rode the trains sometimes jumping off to get a handout. Mom always kept something handy to give them to eat. It's a good thing none showed up those first few days.

Mom always liked a challenge and she liked to remodel homes—but she cried when she saw this place. She rolled up her sleeves and went to work and soon we were acting like this was the best house dear old dad had ever found. She scrubbed that place down with some of her mom's old homemade soap—breathtaking soap that would kill E-Coli fast. She papered the walls with sheets of "The Daily Oklahoman" to keep out the wind and dirt. She mixed up her own paste which gave the place a clean smell. She put up the beds, hung her curtains, fixed the doors and all was well. After a few minutes in the yard, not a weed had survived, she had Dad soak the ant bed with something and it disappeared.

My older brother Gerald had more taste than the rest of us. He cried when he saw our bedroom and mom responded by getting piles of funny papers and repapering our room with comics. This seemed to satisfy my somewhat uppity brother and certainly pleased me. That was about 73 years ago and while we didn't stay in that little house very long, we lived in Centrahoma until October of 1944 moving up SHW-3 to Stonewall—but I sometimes like to think of that time in the little two-room shack and what my mom did for us once upon a time 73 years ago.

Mom is now 96 and lives in a nursing home here in Allen. I don't think I could list all the houses she has lived in—every one of them quickly remodeled—since that time in Centrahoma. Time has stolen a lot of her memories, but she still likes to move her little bed from one side of her room to the other—and does frequently. Just remodeling. Have a good week and be sure to go to church this Sunday.

Wayne Bullard, Pharm. D.
waynebullard@sbcglobal.net

08-05-06
Will Armstrong, A large crowd and The Dust Bowl with Julia

Grandma Julia and W. W. Armstrong's marriage was not without its problems. Will thought he had to help his large family but Julia did impose some limits. When Will moved his invalid mama in with them it meant Julia had to take care of her. This meant a lot of work for Julia......laundry using an outdoor pot and carrying a bedpan. Lots of work. Two of his sons by his previous marriage were still around. Jim had taken up with a young teen named Josie who lived in a tent down on Mountain Creek. When Josie got pregnant Jim married her and found an old shack near Will and Julia and sort of lived off them.

Then there was George, W. W.'s oldest boy. His nickname was Boss and he had found a small abandoned shack near Will and like Jim just lived off his daddy. Boss and Jim brought their families visiting each mealtime and Julia cooked for them all. Boss eventually fouled his nest and good fortune one day as he was helping out by plowing with 2 of the pricey horses Julia brought into the marriage. Boss lost his temper and went to whipping the horses. The two hardworking and gentle horses didn't know how to respond and Boss just kept on whipping. The two were upside down and tearing up their harnesses when a "stirred up" Julia got to George. She took his whip and lashed him a few licks before making him pack up and get off the property. That was the end of George and his family as far as support went.

Jim on the other hand was never caught doing too much work. But he did like to dance and carry a six-shooter. Not a good combo at a wild dance in Eastern Oklahoma. He shot a man one night and was arrested. The man lived and Jim was sent away to prison—I guess at McAlester. Grandpa Will was very worried about Jim. Josie by now had moved into the house and was an aggravation to the little girls, Lora, Cora, Dora and Ruth, who had been brought into the marriage.

It was fairly tense and various other kin had also moved in from time to time.

Grandpa had no money so he hocked Julia's good farm, her horses and everything that was on that farm to hire a good lawyer to get Jim out. He did but was unable to pay back the note. They lost the farm. Somehow they made a move to Lula and became sharecroppers. It was the great depression and they didn't have a chance. The dust was thick and crops were thin. The family worked hard in Lula scratching a living from the dusty ground as best they could, raising pigs and chickens and keeping milk cows. Grandpa had always had talents as a Smithy and made a little cash repairing harnesses, shoeing horses and mules and fabricating metal farm tools. Basically they lived on the edge of poverty but didn't know it. Everyone else was just as poor but they felt lucky in that they had plenty of chickens, cows and pigs and grain to feed and all the food (milk, eggs, ham, chickens etc.) they wanted to eat.

After Julia passed away in 1941 Will moved to Centrahoma to be near us. His boys, Ezra and J. C. had military duties and he was otherwise alone. Out of his children the ones who kept in touch were of course Dora who lived nearby—Oma and Ruth who for years lived in the area and of course J. C. who literally moved in with him his last year or so to care for him. I remember Uncle "Buddy" (Marcus) who cared deeply about his dad's welfare. Grandpa went to visit Uncle Raymond in Wister a few times and probably would have visited others if he knew where they went. Uncle Ezra who may well have been the best of the bunch lived in California but made frequent trips to Oklahoma to check on family. Grandpa spent 2 or 3 summers out on Uncle John Roundtree's Red Bean Farm near Cortez, Colorado. John, married to Will's daughter Lula headed up a nice family and our visits out there were all pleasant. Grandpa always said he could breathe well out there in the high dry altitude. Wayne Bullard, DPh.

28

01-09-08
My Old Cousin, Isaac Brock

I enjoy writing stories about my family and today I will share a story about my late cousin Isaac Brock. While I claim my stories are nearly always 80% true and perhaps 20% parable, this story was published in the Gadsden, Alabama newspaper by staff writer Jerry Jones. Anyway, the first Isaac Brock came over from Germany, settled in Buncombe county, North Carolina and had two sons named Lloyd and Isaac. By the time of the 1850 census, son Isaac was living in Gadsden, Alabama—the key word here is living—cousin Isaac would eventually live to be 122 years old, the oldest man (at that time) in the USA.

Born in 1787, Brock didn't die until 1909—in Texas! He was married 3 times and except for the Revolutionary War, he served in all the nations' wars—joining the Confederate army at the age of 74. He lived another 44 years after that serving as a Texas Ranger when he moved to Texas.

A Blacksmith by trade, Isaac celebrated his 100th birthday by shoeing a kicking mule—after notifying the local press. By the skillful use of the pen and a constant appearance of his picture in the newspapers of that time (to advertise the "Cure-All remedy of the makers of a certain proprietary medicine) a sort of romance was thrown around Isaac as he grew famous in his old age. (Note to myself: Try to find the name of that medicine).

Isaac Brock's nephew, Josiah Brock lived on Lookout Mountain in Alabama and owned land in Etowah County. Josiah's son, Harvey Brock became the first circuit clerk of Etowah County. He has several relatives still living on Lookout Mountain that appear to be kin to just about everyone else up there—including the Bullards.

In 1909 Isaac Brock was to make what was to be his final appearance on the world stage: he was brought before the McLennan

County, Texas (Waco) Court—old and blind. At age 122 Isaac was tried for lunacy and was found sane but the court recommended his being placed in the county home for the poor. He died there on Sept 3, 1909 and was buried by the county as no family claimed his body.

A tombstone marks his grave in the China Springs cemetery in McLennan County, Texas and bears this inscription "Isaac Brock, born March 1, 1787, died Sept 3, 1909—age 122 years, 6 months, 2 days. "He died as he lived, a Christian."

Since you may not live to be 122 you probably should consider going to church this Sunday.

Wayne Bullard, DPh

waynebullard@sbcglobal.net

01-31-08
The Hungry Veteran

The thin pale veteran looked more like a walking ghost than a man. When he sat down by me he said in his soft voice: "Makes you appreciate what you got," as he looked at the young double amputee sitting in a wheel chair across from us. I was in the 4th floor waiting room up at the Veterans Hospital, waiting to get my blood pulled. I had noticed the man who was speaking when he first walked in . He was about the thinnest human being I had ever seen. He looked sick and pathetic and I wondered what he had to appreciate. I agreed with him about the guy in the wheel chair and after a few moments asked him where he lived. "Wichita Falls," he said. "I come up here on the veterans van. As to where I live," he continued, "I'm about as near being homeless as you can get. I live in an old 1972 model 22 foot motor home without any utilities. But I give thanks to God for that, for it keeps me dry. Me and my dog. I have a little heater and a 5 gallon bottle of propane which I light when I get too cold. I just light it now and then 'cause it has to last. But I appreciate what I got and am thankful I can walk around. I have a good sleeping bag to sleep in and I am thankful for my friends that come to see me sometimes. When they come, I get to eat."

I asked him if he had eaten today, and he said he couldn't: "Lab tests. I didn't eat yesterday, either, but that's OK," he said with a kind of sad grin. "Do you get any compensation?" I asked. "No, I guess I will, in time—I ain't able to work. They said I'm eligible but they haven't started any checks yet. The woman told me I needed to move to federal housing but that I can't take my dog, so I won't go. The dog's all I got for company. But no one need feel sorry for me cause there's a lot of people worse off than me—look at all these young veterans missing limbs. Makes me thankful for what I got."

"What are they testing you for?" I asked. "They say I got a baseball-sized object in my right lung." I asked him his name and he said "Jim."

I asked him some more questions about his living conditions. He said, "a man lets me live in his back yard and I power my 12" TV on an extension cord. I ain't got no cable," Jim said, "and I have to borrow a toilet. My personal hygiene is a concern of mine as it probably is to the people who have to be around me here and in church. But I do the best I can. Just me and my dog."

The nurse called my name about then and I went on in the lab to give my blood, but it was Jim I had on my mind. My own worries were forgotten as I could still see this little wisp of a man sitting out there in that waiting room, brave and proud. He had willingly served his country and was proud of that service and his country but he was now ravished by poverty, a tumor and loneliness. On my way out to my other appointment I stopped and shook hands with Jim and told him goodbye. I don't ever expect to see him again, but he let me have a glimpse into his life and soul that morning and I shared a little of the money I had on me with him. He looked surprised, but looked up at me and said "thanks." I told him, "Thank you" and meant it.

The rest of the day I couldn't help but notice that there were indeed many veterans creeping up and down the long halls up at veterans in Oklahoma City who were a lot worse off than I. Thanks to "Jim's attitude adjustment" I was seeing things differently than when I had arrived. While I am on the subject of the Veterans Hospital, let me say I think they are doing a great job serving our nation's veterans. At least in Oklahoma. They took real good care of me the other day and while I have to go back for more treatment, I am getting along pretty good. I especially appreciate the concern and prayers of my friends. Thanks.

I hope each of you have a good weekend and remember to go to church Sunday. And as old Jim said, "be thankful for what you got."

02-07-08
Gerald-Broken Leg-Dr. Cody

My main job was to just sit there and keep the flies off my sleeping brother. Mom had just laid a new linoleum she had bought over at Hudson's Big Country Store in Coalgate on the floor. New curtains had been hung on the windows and we were pretty proud of our "new" home. We had moved into the duplex there on 7th street in Centrahoma just a week before—an arrangement much better than the old shack we had been living in . It was freshly painted a gleaming white and had electricity. I was pretty pleased with our fortune. But that was then. It was 1938 and now there was fresh blood on the new linoleum.

Gerald was a second grader and we had summer school in Centrahoma. It was a summer day in Centrahoma when his class had gone on a walking field trip out in the woods. There was a cliff and a stream and some of the kids stood too close to the edge to get a good look. Without warning, a large chunk of earth turned loose, my brother found himself falling—doing a 360 degree mid-air loop before landing on his left leg. The impact caused a compound break in his femur. They brought him home in the back of a pickup; there was no hospital in Coal County. The protruding femur had caused a lot of bleeding and Gerald was bloody and pale as they laid him down on that new linoleum. Dr. Cody was summoned and he probably saved Gerald's life.

Gerald had suffered a major injury and the doctor gave him a shot of something and knocked him out—relieving him at least from the pain of this ordeal—and us from the hearing. Then the doctor and my mom struggled to clean up the mess and set the leg (she was a tough woman) while dad drove to the Palace Drug in Coalgate and bought a jar of Plaster of Paris. Later, Doc Cody and my dad spent what seems like forever, making and applying the cast—Dad must have been tough too. When Doctor Cody finally finished, he told us he had done the best he could but that my brother would likely have a limp and he wished that he was at Children's Hospital in Oklahoma City. But he might just as well have suggested a trip to the moon. We had no car and no money.

Doctor Cody left and returned several times over the course of the afternoon and night, checking on Gerald and even brought him a little black Emerson fan.

Jack and Pearl Downard, institutions in their own time were there too, helping out and Billy Moore had loaned dad his Chevy to go to Coalgate. As for me, I was fascinated by the quiet and efficient fan as I (with the able company of Garvin and Letha Moore) kept a close watch on my brother. I will always be grateful to Dr. Cody for what he did on that hot and humid summer afternoon in a little 3 room duplex in the tiny town of Centrahoma. It is now 70 years later and while my brother's leg might be a little bent, and he does have a trick knee, he doesn't limp—he was tough too. He just doesn't stand so close to the edges anymore. You did OK too, Doctor.*

Centrahoma is little more than a few buildings along an abandoned highway these days with it's main street just a memory and most buildings gone forever. The school was closed about 56 years ago and later burned to the ground. Centrahoma's former inhabitants have been dying out for years, taking their memories with them. The highway now passes south of the old town and passersby may not even know a town was ever over there. But there was.

Have a good week and don't forget to go to church this Sunday— and stay away from cliffs.

*details as recited by Dora Bullard and personal memories.

03-12-08
Bingo the Commando

Bingo came staggering out of the barn, made a few feeble steps and laid down. Bingo may not have known it, but had he expired his burial would have been swift. He was one sorry and sick looking dog. Bingo's ever-present smile was gone. It had been two weeks now since my mystified grandpa and dad had started doctoring Bingo. They both said he would die. We said he must have been hit by a car but we were lying.

Every Friday night there was a movie up at the Centrahoma School and we never missed. Since WWII had started, most movies were of the war. The latest had to do with army paratroopers. Billions of little guys came floating down from the sky with machineguns and when they landed did hand-to-hand combat. We were impressed. The next morning Gerald and I made little parachutes out of hanky's and kitchen towels. Gerald was really good at it. He quickly graduated from the hanky and pebble stage to a large pillowcase with a good weight on it. These we took to the beam of the barn roof and we watched in awe and wonder as they floated gently down.

Of course, Gerald found an old sheet which he affixed with heavier cord and it was tested with heavier loads. It worked fine. He soon brought me into his vision of greatness. He wanted me to jump. Of course, I was chicken as was Garvin Moore, our next door neighbor who was also a daredevil but without vision. His sister Letha Mae was equally unwilling to achieve fame from the roof of our barn so it was up to Bingo the little dog.

Up to this time Bingo was just happily dancing around smiling. He was glad we were out on this glorious day where he could play with us. Yep. Old willing and ready Bingo. He let us carry him up on the barn's roof but registered some concern with our work. He had played with us before and Bingo wasn't stupid. Eventually Gerald had made all the critical adjustments and we were ready. Bingo wasn't. He had wiped the smile off his face and when we tossed him over he panicked and managed in the short time before the chute could deploy to get on top of it, wad it up in a ball and stand on it as he smashed to the ground.

In due time, with careful nursing and prayer, Bingo survived, physically. But he was always an emotional wreck after that, being careful to stay away from us when we played near the barn. Gerald gave up parachute manufacturing and turned to other things. I may have become more philosophical because of this "war-time" incident and also continue to view my older brother with a jaundiced eye (PTSD?) if he wanted to get up on a roof or something.

Wayne Bullard, DPh

03-05-09
Unscheduled Stop in Weleetka

It was quiet—very quiet. All I could hear were the sounds of my '51 Old's dead engine—snapping and popping. It was 1957. There was very little traffic on the road that October morning just north of Wetumka, Oklahoma. I was in the Navy and a few moments ago I had been in a big hurry. Now I was just here, in a mess. The night before I delayed an early start back to my ship but I was young and knew I had a good reliable-fast-running car. And it was too, until now. At some point I became aware of a "Huck Finn" looking little boy standing at the edge of the woods, just looking at me. It turned out he lived just down the highway and walked me the quarter-mile to his house.

His disreputable looking daddy was out working on an old truck. He looked me over real good and spat in my general direction. "I need to use your phone," I said and of course he said he didn't have one. The 10 year said, "Pa, he's in the Navy" "How you know that, son?" he quarried. "His uniform is hanging in the car," the kid answered. The man told him to go get his horse and take me to his Aunt's house and tell her to let me use the phone. Soon I was behind the kid on an old mare who eyed me suspiciously riding through the woods. He had brothers in the Navy, it turned out. I was seriously wondering how all this was going to work out. I really did need to be on my way to Boston—bad!

The events that had set me up for these trying moments had their beginnings a year earlier, in Savannah, Georgia. My Navy ship had visited the port in Georgia taking a load of Navy Reservists on a training excursion. I witnessed a crime while there—a deed that bought me a subpoena to court many months later. The Navy encouraged me to "honor" this by giving me some "free" leave time. Making the best of a bad deal, I bartered enough time from them to make a side trip from Savannah over to Stonewall, Oklahoma, my hometown and a

WAYNE BULLARD, PHARM. D.

place my "sweetie" a girl named Pat lived. I wanted to stay as long as I could.

I had been told by my captain to check in by phone, so I did—and he told me that we were "steaming" that Saturday morning. I was the only ET (Electronic Tech.) on the little Destroyer Escort and he needed me back. That was Wednesday—a day I should have just gotten in my Olds and started back. I didn't. A "hot date" with Pat that night in Ada caused me to linger and I didn't leave until the next morning—Thursday. And now here I was—broke down—riding a horse through the woods near Wetumka, nowhere near Boston. As is my practice when I get myself in a bind I prayed—for myself, my formerly fast car, this little boy and for his Aunt's phone.

Allen Chevrolet in Weleetka sent a truck and towed me in. This seemed to take a lot of time but later that afternoon they had replaced the rotor in the distributor and the Olds Rocket-88 was once again, a fast car. The uniform and prayers had helped me get the free ride to the free phone and now they had paid off again. The dealer in Weleetka would not accept one cent for towing and repairing my car.

In spite of my fast driving, Friday evening found me well short of Boston. I was worried and exhausted as I called in again. The Officer of the Deck told me to just hurry; they wouldn't leave until about noon Saturday and he didn't think they could leave without me or somebody to set up the radios and stuff. I flogged the poor car and myself all night drinking gallons of coffee and made it before noon. As it turned out my ships sailing had been postponed 'till Monday. The Captain's decision to spend a little extra time with his sweetie left me feeling sort of like I had just kissed my sister. I can't remember which country we headed out to Monday (Columbia or Venezuela) but I won't ever forget the kindness of strangers those 55 years ago from a little town called Weleetka and a little Wetumka boy with a horse and his patriotic old daddy. For sure I'll never forget the kind car dealer that towed me in, bought me a burger and saw to it that I got on my way—just because I was in the service. I drive the Wetumka/Weleetka highway often these days— taking this same little sweetie (we've been married for 54 years now) to the doctor up in Tulsa. I'll always have a warm place in my heart for those people.

Have a good weekend and be sure and go to church this Sunday. You might need a little help from prayer yourself someday.

Wayne Bullard, D.Ph.
waynebullard@sbcglobal.net

06-04-09
Riding Old Butt and Trains

It was Christmas 1945 and Morris Dean Ray was sick—very sick. The Rays lived on Muddy Boggy south of Allen and the doctor had been by again. Getting to the Rays was no small feat. Muddy Boggy Creek, still unfettered by the hundreds of flood control lakes that would eventually be built, was often a wild and raging creek. The last flood had left the large old wooden bridge partly washed out and unsafe. Uncle Matt had built a parking area out of native dirt on the north side of the bridge—a bridge the three families on the other side could still cross on foot. So when we went to visit, we had to walk across this shaky bridge.

Named after Dr. Morris of Allen, my youngest "twin cousin" Morris Dean Ray was what they called a "blue baby" in those days. His heart didn't work very well which resulted in a bluish tint to his face. Now-a-days, this would require a quick trip to Children's Memorial Hospital in Oklahoma City for a surgical fix and Morris Dean would have grown up with a little scar on his chest and playing sports in the Allen School system. But that was then and Dr. Morris was limited to the technology that existed then. There was little he could do for his little name-sake, Morris Dean.

I named Walker Ray (AKA Corky) and his siblings my twin cousins because our mothers were twin sisters. My brother Gerald reminded me sometimes that there was no such thing as a twin cousin, but that was just his opinion. Corky and his little brother, Chesley (AKA Tiny) were like brothers to me, even if we weren't together all that much. My mom spent several nights out there on Boggy helping her twin sister care for the sick little boy and I shared an upstairs bedroom with Corky and Tiny. Some nights we would lie awake watching the kerosene lamp flicker strange shadows in the room and listen to the weak and pitiful cries of the sick baby—cries that were weakening.

Corky, the oldest child, had to grow up fast. There was a lot of work to do on that muddy farm with its tight soils and free-ranging ticks and run-a-way weeds. I admired Corky's maturity and his abilities as we grew up. He did what he was told to do and much more—always looking after his little brother, Tiny. Corky missed a lot of school taking care of all those chores his dad laid on him—but life was hard on Boggy and you struggled to survive. He made shortcuts through the woods to the little one-room schools (Lucille West taught at one of them) and he marked their way with slashes on the trees through the wild "bottoms" so little brother Tiny wouldn't lose his way when he had to go to school alone.

It was after a visit by Dr. Morris that Uncle Mathis told Corky to saddle up "Old Butt" and get some prescriptions filled in Allen. The old red mare was a nervous wreck with a frightful fear of trains—and would run if she heard one. The road to Saffarran's Drug Store ran alongside the railroad tracks along the dirt road that passed for SH-48. Like I said, Corky was a brave little boy but he was about to be tested and he would need all the maturity and strength an 11 year old could muster in a few minutes if he was to get the medicine back to his baby brother by nightfall.

He rode up to SH-48 and rested Old Butt that cold afternoon in 1946 as he scouted the way ahead for trains. None seemed to be coming, so Corky headed Old Butt north. Of course, that's when he heard the whistle. The mare heard it too and she laid her ears back and took off—fast. More than once the terrified run-a-way got too close to the fence ripping Corky's right leg—tearing his overalls and giving him plenty of scratches. The train turned west, following the tracks west to Steedman but it was awhile before Corky was able to get the nervous mare stopped. Corky told me years later that he made real good time getting to the Drug Store that day. When he tied Old Butt to the light-pole in front of Roy Saffarran's Drug Store Corky was a mess. Clara Saffarran and another lady cleaned and dressed Corky's chewed up leg while Roy filled the prescriptions. Mr. Saffarran offered to take Corky home in his old Plymouth but Corky thought it best to ride the mare home and complete his delivery that cold afternoon in January, 1946.

In spite of Dr. Morris's best efforts and Corky's valiant ride little Morris Dean Ray died on the last day of that awful month in January on the 31st. He was 52 days old. I remember Uncle Matt holding the small white casket in his lap as he sat in the back seat of a 1941 Ford on its way to Lula Cemetery. Morris was gone but we found comfort in knowing he rested in the arms of Jesus.

My best friend and "twin cousin" Corky is also gone now, claimed by an accident on SH-1 a few years ago. He remained throughout his life on earth, steadfast and true to his purposes—serving his country as a Marine, his Lord and his church as a Deacon and his family as a father as faithfully as he had served his little brother one day in January, 1946 on an old red mare they called Old Butt. A small tombstone marks the baby's grave out at Lula and Corky is buried in Allen. May they both rest in peace.

I hope all of you have a good weekend and that you are able to go to church this Sunday.

William Armstrong Holding Mana Sue
in Centrahoma about 1940

10-01-09
Traveling with Grandpa

My grandfather (my mom's stepfather) was a real nice old guy. He talked a lot, chewed tobacco and told some of the same stories over and over. He enjoyed going to Colorado in the summer months to visit my Uncle John and Aunt Lula on their red bean farm near Cortez. He said the air was dry and he didn't "smother" so bad up there. So he would pack up his Digoxin and Nitro-Glycerin tablets and get on the bus there in Stonewall and eventually make it to Cortez. But he was forgetful and in 1947, while waiting on the 8 O'clock bus at Burnett's Drug for several hours (he was there at 4AM) he sat there talking and forgot to board. My Dad chased the bus down and got him on it anyway but the damage was done—it set my mom to thinking about next summer.

"We just can't let Dad go off that far on the bus anymore," Mom said," we will take him." I don't think my dad was real keen on the idea but resistance was futile—we were going to drive him out. Gerald stayed home as the 6 of us climbed into our '47 Nash with grandpa sitting in the right rear seat of the car. It was a nice car and dad was concerned about the tobacco—as well he should be. The little rear wing window would open about 4 inches and by the time we reached Cordell there was a thickening trail of tobacco spittle hardening on the shiny paint of our new car. Back then there were water hoses at gas stations and I took a hose and washed the tobacco off—best I could. There was no small amount on the inside of the glass but those of us who know snuff-dippers and tobacco users are keenly aware of how nonchalant these people are about their aim: Grandpa showed no apparent concern.

Dad kept his mouth shut and fired up a Roi Tan Cigar as he started hurrying the trip a little—a trip that was to take 3 days. The tobacco juice started accumulating and drying on the right rear of the car before the cops got us. We were just over in Texas on US-66 just east of Shamrock when it happened. Dad had been passing a long line of cars that was dawdling along about 35 MPH. We finally got around the last one (we thought) a semi plugging along but there was a patrol car hidden in front of it. He took dad into town where an old blacksmith was pounding iron. The bearded man was Justice of the Peace and as he pulled his sooty apron off he spat (he chewed tobacco too as his beard would attest) and he listened to the charges. He found Dad guilty and fined him ten bucks, plus a nine dollar court cost.

Mom sat out in the car with the rest of the family in the hot Texas sun as Grandpa and I saw the show. Dad was already furious at the way the officer had caused such a traffic tie up and operated such an obvious speed-trap and he spared no words. "Nineteen bucks or you go to jail," the nasty-bearded blacksmith intoned. Grandpa and I were alarmed at the prospect of our driver being cast into prison. My mother had a license but couldn't drive worth a flip, grandpa had never driven and I was 13. But dad paid and left after giving the authorities a look that could have gotten him arrested, again.

Everything went well until the next day. We stopped atop Wolf Creek Pass in Colorado. Grandpa turned blue and couldn't breathe very well. He ate up most of his Nitroglycerin tablets but I didn't notice my dad hurrying up to get down the mountain. In the years following that pioneering trip it became a ritual taking grandpa out to Cortez. And no matter how blue he turned, we always stopped atop Wolf Creek Pass to throw snowballs and to enjoy cool air in the midst of summer. But we never went through Shamrock again. There are other routes.

I hope all of you are enjoying the nice cool fall mornings and that the flu bug doesn't make you blue. Be sure and go to church this Sunday.

Wayne Bullard, Pharm. D.
waynebullard@sbcglobal.net

10-15-09
Happiness In A Bottle

My old Navy buddy, Harry Sheldon of Hoosick Falls, New York, keeps me up to date on all kinds of "stuff." For instance Harry tells me why our grandparents were happier than us and then told me why. I am always eager to hear what Harry says and was surprised to learn that it was the medicines they took back then. Let's have a look at just what Harry is talking about.

Singers, teachers and preachers had a lot of help from a product called Gragee's Antiseptique's which proclaimed on its label to provide "for a maximum performance" and was great to "smooth" the voice. Dragee's contained generous amounts of cocaine and may be why preachers preached so long in the 1800s and if your own preacher is "running over" you may need to check his cough syrup too. Another miracle drug, Mariani Wine, hit its peak in 1875 as the most famous Coca wine of its time. Pope Leo XIII used to carry a bottle of Mariani with him all the time and awarded Angelo Mariani (the producer) with a Vatican gold medal. If the Pope says it's good, it must be good—however, that may have been back before they declared him "infallible." There were many other Coca Wines but one brand marketed by The Metcalf Drug Company was a real "stand out" advertising that it not only had medicinal properties, it would flat out make you happier—a condition which America's most cheerful generation was not hesitant to drink to.

Between 1890 and 1910 Bayer sold over-the-counter (OTC) heroin." It was labeled as a non-addictive substitute for morphine. It was also used to treat children with strongcough. I'm not sure what strongcough is but might know it if I heard it. I've had some customers who would develop a strong cough for the privilege of sipping heroin.

Thank goodness those addictive medications have been withdrawn from the market. When I sold my pharmacy in 1996 I had a full bottle of Laudanum which still had its seal intact when I sent it to the DEA for destruction. But many other drugs were in full bloom in the 1960s. After I had been in Allen a few days I asked a lady patient why she was taking Eskatrol* (Amphetamine) every morning. "Well," she replied, "I started taking it to help me lose weight but I gained instead, but it makes me feel better about myself." "Doesn't it interfere with your sleep at night?" I asked. "Not actually, you see I take a big old blue pill at night called Eskabarb* (phenobarbital) and I can't hardly wake up in the mornings, so I needed my Eskatrol to get going." She was just thankful that the drugs were not habit forming.

People rubbed Tincture of Opium (paregoric) on their teething (but happy) babies' gums and cheerfully drank it for diarrhea. It wasn't just the drug stores selling happiness those days. Vanilla extract was available to bring some early morning smiles and those who were poor could buy Lavacol* a rubbing alcohol that was actually ethanol for 49 cents. One customer drank so much vanilla extract that the local grocer speculated that his flatulence's smelled like vanilla wafers.

Pharmacist Otto Strickland (who operated a pharmacy in Allen a few months before moving on) claimed that he had hooked up a 50 gallon barrel of "Ginger" (Jamaica Gin) to the center spigot at his fountain allowing him to spruce up any drink and giving new meaning to 10, 2 and 4. Main street merchants had never been happier.

Nowadays when I look at the drug "problems" we have in America I say that the more things change, the more they stay the same. Have a good weekend and don't forget to go to church this weekend. You don't need a bottle to have happiness.

12-03-09
Pearl Harbor & The News

"Pearl Harbor Day" on December 7, 1941, was a pretty big news event in my life. After all I was in the news business myself at the time—a paperboy for The Daily Oklahoman. I took good care of my six paying customers in Centrahoma and sometimes I contemplated how rich I would be if all of them ever paid their bills. My dad—an early-day Roosevelt Democrat—often loaned me enough incentive money to pay my Daily Oklahoma bills and I repaid him by listening to the news with him every chance we got.

The biggest news story of that time was, of course, the bombing of Pearl Harbor by the Japs. That day was a Sunday and as usual we got stuck with feeding the visiting preacher and his ravenous family. Dad was always pleased when the preacher got finished before noon so that he could walk across highway 3 to where we lived and switch on his big Zenith radio for the 12:00 o'clock news. This was how we learned about the bombing of this place called Pearl Harbor. There was no doubt that this would change everything. Our Pacific fleet had just been wiped out and according to my Grandpa Armstrong we would soon see Jap tanks rolling down highway 3. It was a worrisome time.

Another effect of this new war meant the end of Centrahoma as a viable town. Almost anyone of its poor residents could migrate to places like Richmond, California or even Oklahoma City and go to work in the shipyards or airplane factories that were sprouting up like weeds. And migrate they did. To me, it seemed like that the only purpose of our grocery store in Centrahoma was to save cardboard boxes for our customers who were planning to move away. Most of these families never returned and hundreds of ghost towns were being created across the plains of America.

A few weeks ago I was reminded of another big news event of those terrible days. I was inside the Smithsonian Air and Space Museum out by Dulles Airport (Washington, D.C.) just walking around looking at the exhibits and I saw a beautiful B-29 Super fortress on view. Catwalks allowed for close-up inspection and interior lights showed off the interior of the craft. "Enola Gay" was painted on its nose, the name of the pilot's mother. The pilot's name was Paul Tibbits and he had piloted the 4-engine craft to a place called Hiroshima, Japan to drop a super-bomb called "Little Boy" on the unsuspecting city. Hiroshima, untouched up to now was virtually obliterated.

I still remember how I first heard of the strike. David Ray Alexander stopped me in front of the Main Café in Stonewall and told me about the bombing. I had been to Goat ridge all weekend prior to August 6, 1945 and hadn't heard anything about the mission. 'It was a bomb no bigger that a soft ball' and it killed 100,000 people instantly'the radio says the war is over.' David had it right as far as the news went but it turned out the bomb weighed 8,900 lbs and had been delivered to Tibbits by the cruiser Indianapolis. The Indianapolis was sunk a few days later by a Japanese torpedo as it returned to the United States-dumping more than a thousand sailors into shark infested waters. About 300 survived.

At the time I thought all my kin-folk would come home from the war and their jobs and things would be back like they had been. But the people stayed marking the end to a way of life in America.

I hope all of you have a great weekend and that you attend the church of your choice this Sunday. Remember, Next Sunday night at 5PM the "Hanging of the Green" program is held at First Baptist Church. Everyone is welcome.

12-10-09
Taking Care of Your Wife

The empty juice glasses just sit there on the breakfast table. It was hard for a dedicated-loving-husband such as me not to jump up, grab the juice out of the fridge and fill the two glasses—but that's not what the smart-dedicated-loving-husband does if he knows what's good for his marriage. I just waited, looking at my empty glass with a humble look. Pretty soon she noticed her error, apologized profusely while jumping up and filling up the little glasses—me first of course. We both had a good laugh over it.

I have written before about how important it is for a man to create ways for his wife to feel useful and needed by serving him better—but how do you handle it when she gets sick? That depends on just how sick she is. My wife hasn't been feeling well lately but rather than inducing feelings of inadequacy on her by trying to horn in on her housework-duties by doing them myself—as a majority of ill-advised modern-day husbands would do—I just try to be more patient. She needs to be given time to perform her labors and not feel rushed. Now is a good time to give her an "ata-girl" for keeping up with her work.

It is alright for a man to do housework when his mate is actually hospitalized, so feel free to do so. Exercise caution that you don't get the house too organized or clean while she's gone. That could induce feelings of inadequacy on your mate and we know you don't want that. Right before she comes home from some minor thing such as childbirth she needs to know she was missed. Place out a few dirty dishes and string a few pieces of dirty laundry around the house. She'll love you for it. Exercise gained from doing housework is the best treatment for post-partum depression. We all know that a busy woman is a happy woman.

A woman who breaks a limb can be a challenge to a loving husband. If it's a leg and she can get around on one crutch there is no problem.

She may need an extra Lortab now and then but with dishwashers and other gee-whiz gadgets in today's home, there should be no problems although it is wise to let her know that you are as close as your easy chair in the rare cases she would need any help.

Wheelchair-bound-wives present other problems. How much she can do in a wheelchair may be directly proportional to the amount of wheelchair access your home affords. I keep my hallways and doors open and wheelchair ready, just in case. Do not put a wheelchair ramp out front as she should not be wasting her energy outside her work areas. This will help her to stay up with her work thus keeping her spirits high. A broken arm may be a problem from a pain standpoint (remember the Lortabs) but it too will heal faster if she stays busy.

There are times when you can actually help her with her work. For instance, when she's vacuuming, you can follow her around and point out the spots she missed. This saves her the heartache of discovering (albeit later) that she has missed some spots. Pointing out dust on a table or handing her a spray bottle of Windex and watching cheerfully as she brings the glass to a shine builds memories and tightens the bonds of affection between the two of you. Keep track of when she last changed the furnace filters or polished the dining room light fixtures. She'll love you for it.

I would give you some more advice but I have to have the dishes washed and trash carried out before my wife gets back from her Christmas shopping. She was pretty firm about that. Meanwhile my hopes are for a blessed Christmas Season for each of you and don't forget to go to church this Sunday.

12-30-09
Good Days

Sometimes it's helpful to look at the past to understand the present. A new year brings such reflections anew and also gives us new appreciation for our family and friends. Christmas morning Pat and I slipped and slid our way down to the Nursing Home to visit my mom.—Still around after these 96 years. Walking around in a nursing home—especially on Christmas day can turn into a depressing adventure, or not. The blizzard of '09 closed most roads and some of the staff had chosen to stay overnight and take care of their patients. Having a hot cup of coffee with these health-care providers on a Christmas morning was pretty satisfying and served to remind me of just how very fortunate we are to have such people looking after our elderly family members.

Later that Christmas Day we drove to Tim and Leslie Costner's place out in the picture-postcard perfect countryside to enjoy Christmas dinner. We had a great meal of smoked brisket and all the trimmings before the kids went out to build their snowmen. Later we played dominoes and watched a movie. It was a good afternoon.

We came home and had e-mails from some friends of long ago. One e-mail was from William Willard, an old Centrahoma friend and classmate. As I sit here tonight I am reminded of those good times when William and I were in grade school—although I may not have realized how good they were at the time. Those were the 1940s when my family lived in the backend of an old grocery store and times were hard for us and hard for our customers—some of whom were cowboys.

I remember those mounted cowboys who appeared every morning out of the morning darkness. There were usually six or so of them, whose horses jingled with the paraphernalia the cowboys would need that day to do their work. The men tied their horses up on the East side of the Store to one of our two long hitching rails. Dad would open the side door of the store and he would pull on a light over the meat market and start building their sandwiches to order. Ordering a Subway sandwich is the closest thing I can think of with which to compare it. The men would tell dad what all they wanted on their sandwich and whether they wanted him to put in one of those little glass bottles of milk with the pasteboard cap or perhaps an apple or arrange—if he had any. The brown bag of goodies would cost between 15 cents and a quarter—an amount that was often charged to their account.

The main reason I would be there at all was the paper route. When dad opened up I would get up too because I had to go fetch my roll of Daily Oklahomans off the edge of Highway 3 and prepare them for delivery to my 6 customers. If it was winter I would help start a fire in the big iron stove. I liked to listen to the cowboys talk and plan their day. These guys wore cowboy hats, carried yellow oilskins for wet weather and they were the real deal—they were special. I liked to help my dad get the cowboys lunches fixed and be a little part of their day before they mounted up for a long day of riding and working their home on the range—The Cody Ranch. Afterwards, dad would pull the light off and go back to help mom with breakfast and I would go deliver my six papers.

Getting to start my days off with a bunch of real cowboys was both educational and fun. Starting off a day working with my dad— Priceless! My wish for you is that you will have many priceless days in 2010 and that you all get every day of the New Year started off right. One way to start your year out right is to take your family to church this Sunday.

02-04-10
Harry Truman

I can remember like yesterday a trip to Pauls Valley in 1948 with my family to hear a presidential candidate speak from the back end of a train. The man was Harry Truman and in my part of the world he had been viewed with skepticism. He had succeeded Franklin Roosevelt in 1945 and now he was asking voters to give him a 4 year term on his own merits. People held Roosevelt in high regard and many didn't feel that Truman could "cut the mustard." His opponent, Thomas E. Dewey, was a worthy man but had made the mistake of wearing a "Hitler-like" mustache. Exit polls and early voting gave the victory to Dewey and people over at Stonewall said Dewey looked too much like Hitler. But they weren't going to vote for a Republican anyway. Several morning papers went to press declaring Dewey the victor.

But Harry Truman squeaked in and the next morning he posed for the famous picture in which he is shown holding up the newspaper whose headlines declared Dewey as the new President. Believe it or not, back then there were several Republican newspapers in America. So Harry never did like reporters. Last week I got an email from a friend in upstate New York by the name of Harry Sheldon extolling Harry Truman and I thought I would share it this week.

"Harry Truman was a different kind of President. He probably made as many or more important decisions regarding our nation's history as any of the other 32 presidents preceding him. However, a measure of his greatness may rest on what he did after he left the White House.

The only asset he had when he died was the house he lived in, which was in Independence, Missouri. His wife had inherited the house from her mother and father and other than their years in the White House, they lived their entire lives there.

When he retired from office in 1952, his income was a U.S. Army pension reported to have been $13,507.72 a year. Congress, noting that he was paying for his stamps (and personally licking them) granted him an 'allowance' and later a retroactive pension of $25,000.00 per year.

After President Eisenhower was inaugurated, it is said that Harry and Bess drove home to Missouri alone. There was no Secret Service following them. When offered corporate positions at large salaries, he declined stating, 'you don't want me. You want the office of the President and that doesn't belong to me. It belongs to the American people and it's not for sale.' Even later, on May 6, 1971, when Congress was preparing to award him the Medal of Honor on his 87th birthday he refused to accept it writing, 'I don't consider that I have done anything which should be the reason for any award, Congressional or otherwise.'

As President he paid for all of his own travel expenses and food. Modern politicians have found a new level of success in cashing in on the Presidency, resulting in untold wealth. Today, many in congress also have found a way to become quite wealthy while enjoying the fruits of their offices. Political offices are now for sale. (Sic. Illinois)

Good old Harry Truman was correct when he observed: 'My choices in life were either to be a piano player in a house of ill repute or a politician. And to tell the truth, there's hardly any difference.' I say let's dig him and clone him!"

I wonder what Harry Truman would think of Nancy Pelosi and her $2,100,000.00/per-year travel expense (which included a liquor list as long as your arm) last year she hung on the taxpayers. I think I know what Harry would say about the whole mess—not something you would hear in church. I hope all of you did OK in last week's ice storm, that your power is back on and the sun is shining! Harry went to church every Sunday—another good habit to pick up. Wayne Bullard, Pharm D

Wayne, Gerald and Mana Sue

53

03-18-10
Spring and Fix Up Time

I've been waiting for global warming to start, or as we call it here in Allen, spring—for several weeks. The first nice day recently I wanted to have a look at my garden. It was still there. I decided to rotor-till it and went out to my little metal building to get my rotor tiller out. Everything looked real nasty out there so I decided to clean up and service all my yard and garden stuff first. The building needed sweeping out too. I have two old riding lawnmowers in there and both would have to be pulled out but as I climbed upon the one nearest the door I saw it had a flat. Sadly, the tire was malformed and I couldn't get it to air up and even worse, I had let my little bottle jack go. It didn't matter that much however, as I decided to take the rest of the day off . . .

The next day I am in Wal-Mart. My wife is at the other end of the building shopping and I see a jack. Just like the one I had. I quickly put it in my cart but I can see they have the next size jack on sale and it was about as cheap as the "little" bottle jack so I take the big one. You never know when you might need to jack up something heavy, like a 2-story house or something. Since I didn't much want to explain to my nosey wife why I was buying a 12,000 pound jack I went ahead and checked out alone—paid cash and put the jack way back in the trunk of the car. Perfect.

Later as we drove home she asked; "what on earth will you need that enormous jack for?" I replied, wondering how she knew, "Uh, I have a flat on the mower and can't get the wheel off without a jack." "Where is the jack you've had for 35 years?" she asked in not such a sweet voice. "It went with the motor home we just sold," I replied. "Can't you use that trolley-jack?" she asked, staring into my right ear. "Can't find it," I replied truthfully. "It's there," she said. Later, after not being able to get the 12,000 pound jack under the mower (an inch or two too tall) I found the trolley jack and fixed the flat. I'm pretty sure the bottle jack will come in handy sometime—for something. Decided to take the rest of the day off—my building was still dirty and my garden still unplowed.

Eventually, I went back out and the mower wouldn't start—bad battery. I had to jump the mower to get it out. I climbed on the other mower. The right front tire was flat and I had to take it off and down to Bob Plunk's car wash to air it up—using my new jack on it. It worked—lifted that big lawnmower right off the floor. But it wouldn't start. I went in the house for a nap.

The next day I added some gas and charged the battery which required running a 100 foot extension cord to the little building. I decided to go to town and take the rest of the day off. The next day I got the green mower running and out of the still dirty building before calling it a day. By Saturday, Meegan was helping me carry stuff back and forth from the little building to my garage (as long as I would let her drive my golf cart). This was before I got run over.

I was about finished out there as Meegan sat backwards in the golf cart watching me—with her foot on the pedal. I was putting in the new battery Melvin had sold me for my yellow mower. My building was swept, the implements cleaned and oiled. I was pretty pleased with myself until she accidentally let her foot press the pedal down. Here it come—bowled me right over (those things are sure quiet) but I wasn't hurt real bad. I should be back to normal in a few weeks—as soon as my ribs heal up. Everything looks real nice in the little building but I still haven't tilled my garden—I'm taking some more time off. I'm a little sore. Meanwhile I hope all of you have better luck with this long awaited spring than I am having and be sure and go to church this Sunday.

Wayne Bullard, Pharm D.

07-01-10
Driving in the South Without a Toothbrush

We slipped out early on the empty freeways and turnpikes that feed traffic in and out of Miami and were getting well along our way north before my first phone call interrupted my complacency. I was pretty pleased with myself—getting up and getting out early on a Sunday morning and having the broad Superhighways to myself. My caller asked, "Is this your black shaving kit here on the kitchen table?" Of course it was. There aren't many feelings that compare with leaving something way behind, like 140 miles behind. "Got all my medicine in it," I replied feeling like somebody had just run over my dog. I mentally started to count up all the other "stuff" like my toothbrush, my comb, my—oh good grief—I need all that stuff" Pat and I were parked at the Fort Drum Plaza on the Florida Turnpike when I told her she had forgotten my shaving kit. "Me!" she exclaimed. As usual, she was unwilling to assume the blame.

We had been down to celebrate the birthday of my grandson, Colton. On the way we had stopped in Alabama to check on Pat's ailing brother, Don Ellis. Don was fine and after 3 nights there we had driven on down to Weston, Florida for a visit and to attend the birthday party. But that happy event was not history as we pondered the courses we had available for us. Perky Pat told me she had put my pills in a different bag, strongly implying that she halfway expected some act of stupidity on my part—however, being the gentleman I am I let the "slap in the face" pass and it was only a few moments later that we told my son to just mail the thing to Allen. I had stuck some of my "beauty aids—a comb" down in my cargo pants and we were in good enough shape to go on.

That afternoon, somewhat subdued from the unmerited early-morning enthusiasm and exuberance that had so affected me that morning; we drove into the gauzy-green country-side that makes up the old Confederacy. Later in a Troy, Alabama Walmart I bought a new toothbrush, mouthwash and throwaway razor and things of that sort. Cost me $27 bucks and my wife pipes up (on our way out) and says "you should have gone to a dollar store—you could have gotten all that for six bucks or less." "There isn't one around," I said defensively (lying of course)—"I looked." "Well," she replied, "what's that?" There was both a dollar store and a Dollar Tree in the shopping center right next to the Walmart. I thanked her profusely for all her help and moral support during my time of suffering and grief and proceeded to once more, drive north—north toward Branson—and she continued to stare at my ear.

Tomorrow, with any luck at all I will drive into Branson hoping that I don't string out or lose any more "stuff" in Hotel rooms before I make my way back to Allen—and my plans for the rest of this busy summer include getting the mail, hoeing my garden and taking a few long naps as I give my heart-felt thanks to whoever invented air conditioning. If you notice me hanging around the post office a lot more than usual it's because I'm hoping my shaving kit will be in my mail box. Have a good weekend and if you get to go on vacation remember to keep track and get home with all your stuff—your shaving kit and perhaps your wife.

09-23-10
Westward Ho

This trip I am on is a result of what happens when you get old. At my age one gets to thinking of what else they want to do before they "kick the bucket." I wanted to go West and see some things I had always planned on seeing either for the first time or seeing again. So this will be a report on my most recent "Bucket" trip. This trip would include visiting a bunch of National Parks, Santa Fe and riding the train to Silverton, Colorado from Durango, Colorado. Also a must was to pay a visit to my old school chum from Stonewall, David Alexander and his wife, Donna. It was important to me to see my Uncle Jack and Aunt Bobbie in Los Angeles again. I was sitting in my comfortable den at home making plans with my maps and brochures spread out all around me. My game, but somewhat apprehensive wife said she was "ready to go."

We left out of Allen Monday, September 13 being careful to unplug the iron and not leave any of our "must have" items behind. My car was groaning under the weight of my cargo as we drove up onto HW-1 out of Allen. When I hit a bump the car had all the sound effects of a chuck-wagon and a junk dealer. We stopped at Groom, Texas—the place where the giant cross is. I never had time before and it was a good refreshing stop. We drove on down I-40, took the Santa Fe turnoff and stopped at Glorieta for about an hour. I was feeling pretty spiritual by the time we rolled into Santa Fe just up the road. It was cool there and we visited the points of interest in the 400+ year old town—the oldest in America. No problems so far.

Day two we drove into Durango, Colorado. The scenery on the way up was beautiful and we had to look around for a room. Finally found the last one at a Super-8. After Santa Fe, the room looked cheap and dingy but we were glad to get it. That night I made reservations for the train ride to Silverton. This same train has been making the run up through the most scenic places you can imagine since 1882. Its old steam engines are still powered by shoveled coal. The next morning's temperature was 44 degrees and it wasn't long before the train (there were 3 of the long trains leaving 30 minutes apart) chugged out and through the length of Durango. It was doing 10 MPH and frequently the old rail coaches would catch a load of smoke and cinders. It took 3.5 hours to climb the mountains to Silverton, about 52 miles away. The only casualties thus far were my lips which were badly chapped. My wife had forgotten my chap stick, of course.

The scenery out the window was a photographer's paradise. You could raise the windows and you could walk around on the train. Way back there was luxury class (a tad expensive) and people were being served food in the diner but I had to settle for a Diet Coke from the concession car. Everyone had a good time on the ride which took up the entire day with 2 hours in Silverton getting something to eat and shopping around. That night we had a good meal at Applebee's, got a few winks and the next morning headed for Mesa Verde which is about 50 miles west and near Cortez. We enjoyed the hours we spent exploring the ruins and pueblos before once more, heading west.

A few hours later, after driving through more very scenic mountains and high deserts we arrived in Blanding, Utah. Blanding is a nice and pretty little town with a shortage of hotel rooms. After 2 false starts I found an empty looking Motel-8, again. There was no one inside it appeared. The large and impressive lobby was empty. A note on the front desk said "dial 300" for service. After dialing, the door labeled "Office" sprung open and a terrorist came out. Well, that was just my first impression. I asked the Arab if he had a room—with all the authority a man can muster that's been married 52 years. He said "yes but no discounts—no AARP—and no free breakfast" as I eyed him closely to see if he had any explosives tied to his torso. He didn't and since I was desperate we took the room. I was to find out, as I went west on my westward bucket trip that getting a room was not an easy thing and my trip was hardly started. More next week.

I hope all of you are enjoying the last days of summer and are going to church next Sunday.

10-07-10
Vacation To Bryce Canyon and Beyond

A two week driving vacation reminds me of what Donny Johnson said about marriage: "Marriage is like a hot bath, after you've been in it awhile, it ain't so hot." We were kind of weary as we took a 16 mile detour in order to sleep in a bed at Bicknell, Utah. The next day we did a drive through Burger King for an egg sandwich and were soon revived by the drive down one of Utah's most scenic highways— HW-12. Going on down the good roads through Dixie National Forrest, the Boulder Mountains and Escalante Canyons we made it into Bryce National Park. David Rowe remarked to me that Bryce Canyon was the prettiest part of that country and he may be right. The park is full of Hoodoos, beautiful rock formations resembling people (according to the Indians.) The views were breathtaking and interesting, yet easy to access as side trails make the place very special and refreshing.

That afternoon we drove on toward Zion National Park, our eyes darting this way and that searching for a room. Pat was doing her 800 numbers and was told the closest room was in St. George, Utah—at least 50 miles out of our way—so we went on. A nice lady at a sumptuous Best Western in Mt. Carmel Junction tried to find us a room but again, it was Pat who found one. This time down in Kanab, Utah—again out of my way but it sounded good. Its name was "Four Seasons" and I told Pat with a name like that it has to be good. It wasn't, but I took it anyway, paying more that I had paid for any room the whole trip. While I stood there trying to convince Pat that it wasn't so bad, the complete light assembly fell from the ceiling to the floor. Moments later she discovered that the lavatory drain was broken and she couldn't drain the hard desert water out. The mechanism was sealed in early '50s plywood so I couldn't fix it but we stuck a plastic fork in its edge making it drain. After making our customary check for bedbugs we re-made the bed and slept fitfully much like the rangers did that night in the movie, "Lonesome Dove—Streets of Laredo" as

Mox Mox prowled the unknown outdoors.

A Sunday morning trip through a Kanab McDonalds and we left the defunct motel in Kanab behind as we made the short drive to Zion. At Zion we were able to spend time at the visitor's center before going in search of more Hoodoos. Zion Park doesn't allow auto traffic beyond certain points but provides ample and free shuttles up the canyon with lots of stops. It is a very convenient and easy way to see these awesome sights. The ride was well worth our while.

The shuttle ride ended at the "top" of the canyon and we had the option of hiking on up in the canyon. An easy trail goes 2 miles and provides some real special scenery and experiences along the way. We made the walk and were glad we did. It was a warm day, in the 80s, but cool dripping springs and ample shade made for cool and pleasant walking most of the way. I have posted pictures of this and other parts of the trip on my Facebook if you want to take a look. A real good pair of char-broiled hamburgers and fries on the way down took care of the appetite we had created on our long morning.

As soon as we got back to our car later that afternoon Pat whipped out her pink cell phone and wasted no time in finding us a nice room—in Vegas. From Vegas we drove on to my old Stonewall buddy (Class of 1952) David and Donna Alexander's beautiful house in LaHabra and had a great visit. Thanks David and Donna! Next day I went over to Fullerton and spent two nights with my Uncle and Aunt, Jack and Bobbie Bullard. We drove up to Semi Valley and did the Ronald Reagan Library—a must see which I have pictured on Facebook—and had a great visit before driving East on I-10 to Mesa, Arizona. Believe it or not, my wife (she's learning fast) had me another great room to rest up in before heading for the Salt River Canyon, Petrified Forrest and Painted Desert. You may notice that Pat has assumed command of lodging by now and the next two nights, one in Gallup and one in Shamrock; we finally drifted back to Allen. We were a little tired but glad to be home again. I noticed her glancing at a road map yesterday. I don't know where she will want to go next, but I think I'm ready.

Have a great weekend and don't forget to go to church this Sunday.

10-31-10
Happy is the Man

"Happy is he who doth not become a college football fan" should have been our memory verse in church last Sunday. The men who gathered around the long table of the Men's Class (also known as the Cemetery Class) down at the Baptist Church were pretty glum last Sunday Morning. They looked like they had just buried their mothers. Yes, their mighty Sooners and Cowboys both lost the evening before and the next morning the sun had failed to rise. The men gathered sipping their coffee, handling their Sunday school literature like so many worry beads. Dreams of winter vacations to a BCS bowl game had been dashed in the wet gloom of the morning and now their prospects were limited to the vision of a long cold winter; a winter without a bowl game in Arizona. The lesson was about Christian maturity and happiness.

We can't win every football game but I enjoy watching sports. Especially high school sports. Our local teams have already provided a lot of entertainment this school term. Whether it's a girl's softball team or men's football, our athletes have competed well and in the process have become better people for it. We have a better football team this year (at least in my eyes) than we have had in years and they have been very exciting to follow. We had some highly ranked teams in our conference and while we were not able to win every contest, we won more than our share and a lot of respect. I think it's safe to say that most years this team would have won their conference. I congratulate Coach Kenny Deaton on his success and the hard work he does with these kids. Let's be sure and continue to support these youngsters as they finish up a great season the next two weeks and let's cheer them on. We play a very tough Dewar (Ranked #1) team for our last home game this Friday night and we travel to Canadian the next week to finish the regular season. Thanks guys.

Former Allen Booster and merchant, the late W.D. Blackburn once said nearly all publicity is good for business. Well, he said that back in the '70s, before we started throwing live turkeys from atop the Farmer's State Bank building in downtown Allen. Yes, it's true. The Chamber of Commerce aided and abetted by former banker Vernon Burright and Harve Butler, Jr. brought a truck load of fat and fairly untamed turkeys from western Oklahoma and on the last Saturday before Thanksgiving, held a "Turkey Toss"—tossing live turkeys off the top of the Bank.

This went over real big and the people (and the press) loved it. Channel 4 in Oklahoma City sent down a truck and of course KTEN-10 covered it each time we did it. The 3rd and last year we did it, the main perpetrator, Vernon Burright himself, made sure we had some very aggressive turkeys—even taking them out of their cages the evening before and stirring them up with exercise. That last "toss" was a good one, in the eyes of most of the crowd. The aggressive turkeys fought back that sunny Saturday afternoon with 2 or 3 escaping completely and leaving several would-be captors bloody and empty handed. It made for great video and the closed street was packed with would-be turkey catchers and potential customers. It reminded me of the running of the Bulls in Spain.

However, it was a sad and gloomy meeting when the Chamber next met. One lady (who shall go nameless) threatened a suit with the ACLU, PETA and SPCA backing her up if we ever did such a stupid thing again. Our lawyer would not offer us any hope of winning such a court battle (he thought it was stupid too) and so the bloody event became just another part of Allen's rich and colorful history as the Board of Directors voted to discontinue the wonderful event. Vernon and Harve were both great boosters of Allen and I don't think either of them ever got over this sad development. But I think I am about over it.

Sometimes, this time of year, when I am walking by the Farmer's State Bank I glance up at the roof. I think I see 2 guys who look a lot like Vernon and Harve with a turkey in each hand. But I guess it's just my imagination since both of these good friends have passed on. I hope you are having a good week and you won't have to use your imagination to know a better life when you make time to go to your church this Sunday.

11-18-10
Prisoners of War

It was 1941 and I was in the 2nd grade when America entered World War II. My grandfather lived across HW-3 there in Centrahoma and I was concerned after grandpa said he was afraid we couldn't lick Hitler and Japan both. But Roosevelt put me at ease a few weeks later when he said we would indeed beat them both. Roosevelt was important in our house. His picture hung on the wall right next to the picture of Jesus. When FDR came on the radio we listened.

A man came into my dad's grocery store and asked: "Did ya'll hear? They're building a big prisoner of war camp down the road a piece." And they did too. Locals grumbled when they heard it and griped some more when they saw how nice it was. Before it was finished they had hired several Centrahoma residents to work down there and care for the dreaded Huns.

A lot of people didn't like the POW camp because it was so close. "We'll have escaped Nazi's all over the place" one woman said. The Germans and especially the Japanese were not known to take care of their many U.S. prisoners. But Roosevelt seemed to have a plan: We would treat them well—very well indeed. The Geneva Convention Accords called for POWs to be housed in as good a barracks as those provided their own troops and FDR probably exceeded that requirement.

Just how nice things were for the prisoners is told in a book called "Aliceville." It is the story of one POW camp in Aliceville, Alabama. A much larger camp than Stringtown and I won't go into all the details here about what they did for those Germans, but for years now, former POWs come back to the Aliceville (and other camps) seeking out the guards, the farmers which they worked for and the ladies who cooked and cared for them like they were long lost relatives. The Germans never forgot the natural kindness and Christian spirit of their "captors," those Americans.

Prisoners were transported on regular passenger trains—not cattle cars and were provided opportunities to attend classes and work for wages. Writing home was encouraged and tended to. All this was well documented and the Red Cross representatives were ushered about to see all this and make sure the German Government was aware of the good treatment we afforded their captured soldiers.

The care was so good that some folks around Centrahoma complained when they saw the POWs receive food and other items that were rationed or unavailable to them. Some of the more senior German officers were convinced the good care was a trick of some sort. But it wasn't. Our people knew the bombing raids and future battles would most likely result in massive numbers of additional prisoners in Germany—and it did. But no one is very sure it worked very well. It probably helped in a few instances but it seems that it mostly went unnoticed by the German government.

After the war, German officials said their prisoners ate as well as they did but all you have to do is look at the skin and bones pictures of prisoners and then at the well-fed German guards to know they were lying. No great efforts were made to provide any sort of medical care nor did they trouble themselves to give over the abundant Red Cross packages America sent over for their men. Lists of prisoners taken by the Germans were sparse leaving families not knowing of their kin were alive or dead. The sorry inhumane treatment of our Thomas Milne by his captors after the Battle of the Bulge was late in the war. He was denied medical treatment and nearly starved to death in a shameless camp called Stalag 9B.

So, did we waste our time lavishing good treatment on the thousands of POWs we brought to America? Was it just naïve to expect reciprocity from Germany? No. I think what happened is just what used to be called 'American goodness.' It is just our way-practicing the Golden Rule. As I look back on what actually took place it makes me proud of my government and the way its citizens conducted themselves. Doing what is right has its own rewards.

I hope all of you have a good weekend and get to go to church this Sunday. And if you enjoy your freedom to do so, thank a veteran.

03-31-11
Relaxation at the Paradise Club and Inn

I got an email from an old shipmate last week about the good old days in the Navy. Of course, like me, he remembers those times through rose colored glasses. One thing I remember from those days was the "Locker Clubs." These were sometimes a part of the Ship's watering hole—a dive. These clubs had dues of about $3.00 a month and provided lockers, showers and other amenities where you could change into your "civvies." All in all it was a very handy service to have in San Diego where uniformed sailors were about as welcome as a hair in a biscuit.

Later on I was assigned to a small ship on the East Coast—the USS Johnnie Hutchins, DE-360. We officially home ported in Boston but spent many months getting repairs from the Brooklyn Shipyard. It wasn't too long before one of my shipmates said: "Our new place is the Paradise Club and Inn in Brooklyn." Only a block from the gate, the Paradise had a nice lock club with all the usual amenities. Unfortunately, the toilets in the Paradise were 10 cent pay toilets but were clean and pleasant.

Our toilets aboard our old ship were just toilet seats attached to a long metal trough with a large 6" pipe on each end providing a continuous flush. When the ship pitched or yawed you could get wet and sitting in there was often an adventure. Frequent jokes such as lighting up a wad of paper and allowing the flames to make the trip down the trough with the resulting mayhem were not unheard of. It was no wonder I always made certain that I always had an extra dime at hand whenever we tied up at Brooklyn. The pay toilet to sailors from the "Hutchins" was a dime well spent. Then there was Grover. A tightwad.

Grover never had a dime. He would stand around and wait for someone to come out and catch the door before it closed—thus saving a dime. One evening I was making a stop in there with my newspaper and was very relaxed—just relaxing there wondering how life could get any better when old Grover yells, "that you in there Bullard?" "Yeah." "Well, hold that door when you go out, I gotta go too." I told him I'd be awhile and go get some change." "I'll just wait on you," he replied. I decided to just ignore him and see if I could read the entire New York Times. "Bout done Bullard?" Grover asked for the 3rd time. "No I ain't," I answered, by this time I was getting kinda sore. He had taken the joy out of my 10 cent visit and I couldn't concentrate on my reading as he pecked on the door with his fingernails. I finally finished the comics and the editorials and waited as he paced back and forth, all the time groaning and whispering. I waited 'till he was forth and quickly slid out and locked the pay toilet door behind me.

Grover gave me a look like he was seeing the Devil's own Angel and jumped. His hand caught the top of the door and his foot hung on the doorknob as he started climbing over the top. He never saw the ceiling fan. Ever see anyone get their head in the path of a ceiling fan? Whop Whop Whop it went before he turned loose and smashed onto the concrete floor. Grover got up slowly, pitifully and my normal caring self kicked back in. I reached in my pocket, extracted a dime and inserted it in the slot, opened the door and said, go on in Grover. I heard him whimper, "too late" as he pulled the locking door shut.

Grover put in for a transfer the next Monday morning and in 2 or 3 weeks was gone to Pensacola or someplace. He never was the same. Not too long afterward, the state of New York outlawed pay toilets. I don't know if they did it because of me or what. I hope you have a good weekend and are enjoying the first week of spring. Don't forget to go to church this Sunday.

04-14-11
Eula Goes to Church

There was a time long ago when there was a café on Easton Street right behind where the Allen Food Center now sits ran by a lady named Eula Pence. By the time I moved to Allen in 1964 the café was gone and the building had been refitted to be a residence for none other than Ms. Pence herself. My drug store was just across the alley and she would sometimes call and ask if we could bring her something such as her prescription or something out of the drug store. "I would like you to bring it yourself as I have something to talk to you about," she would sometimes say. So it was that sometimes I would go in her back door and drink a cup of coffee and share a little "quiet time" with Eula.

Sometimes we would talk about my dad. Before moving up to Allen from Lula in the early 30s dad painted and sold landscapes to whoever would buy them. He would sell them cheap too. Money was a scarce commodity and Mrs. Pence liked the large and colorful scenic landscapes he painted eventually buying several to hang in her café. Dad had just sold her a painting one Saturday when Taylor Bullard (no kin) invited my dad to go to work in his grocery store. Since my family had been living mostly on black-eyed peas and hope out at Lula he quickly accepted and he, mom and my brother Gerald moved to Cleveland Street in Allen. That was back in 1933.

"What did you do yesterday?" Eula asked one day as we were enjoying a visit. "I went to church," I replied and we talked a little about that when she said "I wish I could go to church but I don't have a way." "Where do you go when you do?" I asked. "Oh, I go the same church you do," she replied. "Well I could swing by next Sunday and pick you up and take you—you wouldn't be any trouble at all," I said. Since I am forgetful I made myself a note and told my wife to remind me.

The next Sunday I remembered and I left my Sunday school class a few minutes early and drove down the back alley and sure enough, Eula was dressed up and ready. I helped her out to my car and we drove slowly away. I parked as close as I could get to the church and went around getting her out and headed toward the steps of the church. As we advanced toward the building I could tell she was looking around a lot finally drawing me to a stop. "What church is this anyway?" she asked. "This is the First Baptist Church" I answered. "Well I don't go to the Baptist Church; I go to the Church of Christ."

I reversed course and loaded her up once more in the car and we drove slowly east for a block and again I parked my car. "I think this one is it" she said. No one paid us any mind until we got to the main entrance. Services were about to start and as we hobbled in Richard Norman (an usher) hurried over to help. Eula wanted to sit close to the front so she could hear so the 3 of us made our way down the main aisle. I don't know whenever I had so many people watching we walk her down that aisle. My good friend Neville Reeves walked me out after inviting me to stay and worship with them. I graciously declined but he did promise to see that she got home OK.

I never heard anymore about this visit except from Richard Norman and of course, my friend Neville Reeves who thought the whole story was hilarious. He said he didn't know which was the funniest: me trying to drag Mrs. Pence into the Baptist Church or my visit to The Church of Christ. Whichever it was, I never forgot it and strangely enough, she never asked me to take her to church again.

I hope all of you are enjoying this nice spring weather and the little rain we got. Be sure and go to church this Sunday and it helps if you know which one you go to.

Wolf Creek Pass US-50 June 1947

DORA   MANA SUE   WAYNE   GERALD BULLARD

**Dora, Sue, Wayne, Gerald
at Wolf Creek Pass, Colorado**

05-07-11
Vacation Time 1947

"Cecil, your car will overheat and you'll rue the day you try to drive across that desert at high noon in July! What you have to do is leave about suppertime this evening and drive across at night." It was my Uncle Bill Hampton in Indio giving some good advice to my dad but my dad wasn't having any part of it. "No," he replied, "we'll leave real early in the morning. I have a new car and it ain't going to overheat and I want to see a little bit of Old Mexico since I'm out this way." Dad had planned this trip for years and now the war was over and he had a brand-new 1947 Nash Ambassador with overdrive. We were in week three of his life-long dream—Just him, mom and the four of us. I was discouraged.

It had started in Stonewall on a real nice morning. In high spirits (I had never seen my dad so happy) we drove west all day to spend three nights with Uncle Marcus and Aunt Blanche. They had about nine children—all girls except for one son, Clytee, who was lucky enough to be grown and gone. The ten of them lived in a two bedroom-company house in a little place called Phillips, Texas. To this day I don't know how or where the 16 of us slept.

We must have really cheered them up for they were almost euphoric when we finally went on west to a red bean farm 18 miles from Cortez, Colorado to visit Uncle John and Aunt Lula and 12 year old Charley. Water had to be hauled from a few miles away in uncovered barrels. Charley drove a red pickup to do this chore and our complete access to an arsenal of weapons to use as we hauled this water made my mom pretty nervous. None-the-less, we received a great deal of comfort and joy running around the desert for a few days terrorizing the wildlife (and not a few Hopi Indians). My kin lived on a very red dirt road and the last night we were there, a rain of biblical proportions fell. There was no gravel. It didn't seem we would be able to leave, but Uncle John made Charley get a big old horse and a rope and he dragged us six miles to the highway—whether we were ready to leave or not.

Driving on to California we spent nights in cabins with kitchens so mom could cook for us and enabling dad to avoid the costs of cafes. I presumed mom was having a real good time but then again, I'm not so sure. I had grown tired of the whole adventure. I sat on a water can a lot and to this day I attribute some of my medical problems to that particular seating arrangement.

We paid visits to Uncle Ezra and Aunt Paralee in Sebastopol and Uncle Orland in San Francisco before going to L.A. and falling in on Uncle Tracy, Uncle Jack and Uncle Ernest and their families. We made a few tourist stops there but eventually we got to a place that my brother called Hell. Indio, California. It was 125F every day in Indio and Uncle Bill said it was even hotter where we were headed. He was right. Later the next day dad wisely aborted his trip to Mexico but had not forgotten it. Later as we arrived in El-Paso he said, "We're going to Mexico tonight," and we did.

The border guards told us we couldn't bring back any fruit and while strolling around the streets of Juarez we bought snacks from vendors and as we finally loaded up in the Nash to go back to our Cabin, my four year old sister Linda Kay pitched a fit for a bag of pretty oranges. Boy, did she love oranges. Dad bought a sack and sure enough at the border the agent ordered Linda Kay to turn them over and she said no. Dad tried to twist around and help the Mexican, who by this time was in the car and Linda Kay had a death grip and was emitting a scream that could be heard for miles. The cops made Gerald and I get out so they could fight her better. Finally the two policemen backed off, saying "Let her have them." They were not smiling and I wouldn't have been surprised to see them fire at the car as dad sped away.

We were tired and burned up with the heat when we finally drove back into Stonewall. Yes it had been three weeks and I hope the fact that we never ever took a three week vacation again—ever—doesn't dampen your summer vacation plans any. I never again saw my dad as happy as he had been in Juarez and I guess our visit cheered up a lot of our kin. Every one of them seemed to have been overcome with joy as we left. Have a great summer and be sure and go to church this Mother's Day Sunday.

Wayne Bullard, Pharm D.

06-01-11
Jerome Jay Ersland

The elderly widow had been brought into the police station for questioning after she had shot and killed an intruder who had tried to rape her in the middle of the night. "Madam," the D.A. said as he continued his questioning, "is it true you pulled the gun out from under the bed and then you shot him?" "Yes," she answered, "I did that." "Is it also true that he then attempted to flee?" "Yes," she replied," that's what he did." "And is it true you caught him where he lay wounded by the front door—no longer any threat to you and you chose to shoot him five more times?" "Yes," she answered. "Lady please help me understand why you would shoot this helpless-bleeding young man, prone on the floor, no longer any danger to you or anyone else—five more times?" "That's all the bullets I had," was her honest reply. The story makes me think of the Jerome Ersland case.

Pharmacist Ersland had been robbed before so he had a permit to carry a gun. Soon enough there was another robbery featuring two young black gang members who entered waving guns and wearing masks as they shouted obscenities at the three pharmacy employees. Terrified, the two women, a woman and her daughter ran to the back as Ersland drew his gun and fired knocking one down and running the other one off. When the smoke cleared that fateful day in his pharmacy, "Speedy Parker" lay dead on the floor of the pharmacy—his mask still on his face and an empty sack in his hand. Some say that would have been the end of it if Jerome had kept his mouth shut. In the excitement Ersland said things that cast suspicion upon him concerning the circumstances in which he killed Parker. Unlike the woman in my story, he had no glib replies and some of his stories were exaggerations. It was a story just made for the news and probably a book or two.

This same afternoon members of the black community gathered and set up a demonstration in front of the pharmacy demanding justice

WAYNE BULLARD, PHARM. D.

for Speedy Parker who they said had been murdered in cold blood. It still seems inappropriate for people to agitate in behalf of a felon who has just tried to rob their neighborhood pharmacy but they did. It gets crazier. Prater quickly charged Ersland with murder and won a conviction using racial guilt, class envy and character-assassination. Oklahomans had never seen such gross misuse of office and are now clamoring for the Governor to step in and pardon Mr. Ersland. Ersland's attorney Irwin Box, who charged Jerome $5,000 a day, should give his client a refund and an apology while Prater ought to send Box a thank you note. Thanks to these two, Jerome Ersland has now lost his job, his license, all his money and faces the rest of his life in a cell.

I could easily say that I don't know how I would react to similar circumstances—specifically those that involve the last 5 shots that Ersland pumped into Parker's chest but I'd like to think that I would have spared young Parker's life. But having stared down a gun barrel myself on more than one occasion; I wouldn't want the legal blame had I panicked and kept on shooting. It reminded me of the young man that came into my store some years ago wearing a ski-mask and toting a shotgun. I had the drop on him and I chose not to shoot when he took off running, but if I had it should have been legal (in my eyes). He gave up his legal rights when he chose to arm himself and put on a mask, then entering my pharmacy. What price should Ersland have to pay for poor judgment—for his panic? Must Ersland serve a life sentence for false bragging about his wartime experiences? People get mad when veterans exaggerate their military exploits as Jerome did but a life sentence? Prater and the people who voted for him should be ashamed. Have a good weekend and be sure to attend church this Sunday.

74

06-02-11 Building in Allen

The Town of Allen may not be in an actual boom but it is certainly holding its own in these times of recession. There are still some old empty stores downtown but surviving businesses have been remodeling and are looking good. A bright new Dollar Store shines in the spot that once housed the old J. I. Jones Dry Goods Store and the Farmer's State Bank is completing the most comprehensive enlargement and remodeling in its history. The bank expanded to the East into what had been Allen Hardware incorporating the buildings next door into their main bank building. It gives them a lot of new space for lobbies and offices. New facades on the exterior plus the opening of a very nice looking drive-in gives downtown a whole new look.

There is an annoying commercial on TV of a woman trying to get her dog to sing: "We love our bank." The irony of this is not that the dog can sort of sing it, but that anyone would love their bank. Well, I think people in this trade area like their bank too although not enough that they will be training their dogs to sing it. This bank and its directors and staff are to be commended for their dedication to continue bringing state of the art banking services to their Allen customers. And well, just let me say thanks to each of you.

I notice that 5 new brick homes have been built and look to be completed since late last winter. It would be nice if this pace could be maintained as Allen has a lot of houses that have just worn out or served their purpose. Some of these are currently being torn down but one house really caught my eye. That's the late Ruby (Kidwell) Yount house in the 800 block of East Lee Street. One of the older homes in Allen, the house has been in the Kidwell family for about 100 years and I understand it still is. The old house has been remodeled, upgraded and looks like a million dollars. You have to drive by and see it to fully appreciate what they have done. Meanwhile, "Brother" Cooley has built and or remodeled several older homes here in Allen. Just West of his former best work at the NE corner of Broadway and

Baltimore is the old Saffarran's home. It too is nearing completion and is finishing out very pretty.

I live in a very old place myself, although not as old as Ruby's house, so I have an appreciation of keeping that which is old and good. Sometimes when you go to ripping into these old houses you can confront both pride and despair—pride when you see how well they are built and realize some of the historical value of the structure and despair when you run into restoration surprises. I have found that living in an old house can save a lot of money. They often can be had worth the money and depending on how much and how you do them they can provide you with a lot of "living." Our old 1929 home has served us faithfully since 1966 and I'm pretty sure it's going to outlast me.

Nevertheless, Allen remains plagued by numerous trashy and unsightly yards and while the city works hard at this too—they can't do it all. We all need to work with our city council to abate these problems. These properties and junk yards steal money from the property owner's pockets as they continue to drive property values down.

I hope all of you are having a great summer and that you are considerate of your neighbors by keeping your property clean, neat and mowed. As always, be sure and go to church this Sunday. I have it on good authority that every church in this town has been carefully inspected and the roof is not likely to crash down if you walk in.

Wayne Bullard, Pharm. D.

waynebullard@sbcglobal.net

Picnic on Leader 1943, Wayne, Mana Sue & Gerald

06-09-11
Selling Ice in Centrahoma

"Can I get some ice?" the man with the big camera asked us as we ambled across SH-3 in Centrahoma that pretty Sunday morning in 1941. "Sure," my entrepreneur brother Gerald answered. But first, he posed Gerald and snapped his picture up there on that old ice dock. Even more surprising he actually sent us a copy of it which is with this story. We both went on to church that morning—across the highway at the new First Baptist Church. If you wanted to be a well dressed boy cutting a figure like Gerald that morning you needed to be dressed in a slack suit made by your own mama. Mom had made both of us new "slack suits," probably out of flour sacks. Shoes were optional summer attire in 1941 Centrahoma.

Dad had been real "helpful" that summer letting Gerald be in charge of the ice business at Bullard's Grocery Store there in downtown Centrahoma. Gerald did most of the work and I think our continued room and board was part and parcel of our pay package. Dad had built us a duel-wheeled homemade wagon capable of carrying more ice than we could pull around. Gerald walked the town out giving each potential customer a window card—about 14" X 14" which they could put in their front window facing the street. The number on top was your order. Not many people in Centrahoma had refrigerators but everyone had an old "icebox" in which you put a chunk of ice (preferably a 25 lb chunk) in its top compartment which would keep the contents—uh, cool. You could take your ice pick and knock off a little piece for your ice-tea or pop.

Once the system was in place all we had to do was walk the dusty streets of Centrahoma where Gerald would note in his little book how much, if any, ice a person would need that day. He often sent me to ask or make sure about an order. Many customers were C.O.D. When he completed his master plan he and his able assistant (me) would walk back to the icehouse where he would decide how to run the route, how many trips it would take and how much the two of us could tug and drag up and down the hot rutted streets. A heavy quilt gave the ice a measure of protection against the blazing sun and meant we could get the ice into the iceboxes pretty much as advertised, collect our dime and get along. One lady always felt we owed her a penny when she handed us a dime. "Too much melt" she would say. Mrs. Soffit was careful with her money but then, so was my dad. If she wanted a penny off for melt she would have to get it from God or Franklin D. Roosevelt—both of whom shared equal respect those days in Centrahoma.

Child labor laws were lax in Coal County then on about how much a child could lift or push or pull as it was about child pay (zero in our case). it wasn't unusual for us to "allow" Letha Mae Moore (my favorite squeeze at the time) to serve as a pusher on those sandy roads. We had one customer that lived east around the curve and down the hill from Bessie Lee Sorrel's house and fortunately there was not enough traffic on the highway to keep us from piling into the delivery wagon and coasting down that hill. Like I said, it was a tough wagon and we were never able to break it down. My brother had some girlfriends there in Centrahoma too, so he claimed, but I don't remember ever seeing Mary V. Downard or Dotty Faye Howell pushing the ice wagon. But that may just be my memory being faulty. It was a long time ago you know.

The Baptist Church is still in business over there on old SH-3 but little else that I recognize is left. The ice wagon pushers, the customers and even the entrepreneur of the old icehouse have moved away but sometimes when I stand very still out on that old aging blacktop, I think I can hear a familiar sound: The sound of a squeaky wagon wheel and the happy sounds of pushers riding around the curve in front of Bessie Lee's rock house.   I hear the" pushers" in Centrahoma still sell "ice" but it ain't the kind of ice we sold in 1941. And don't neglect going to church this Sunday.

Wayne Bullard, Pharm. D.
waynebullard@sbcglobal.net

07-21-11
Ersland and Anthony

I thought it would never get over—the Casey Anthony trial in Florida. The Florida court system ground out a form of justice in a waste of money that is unique to that state. Or was it? It looked pretty obvious to me that she was guilty. The death penalty seemed around the corner for this partying woman who had allegedly killed her little girl because the 3 year old was in the way of her wild life style. But the Florida jury said innocent.

Meanwhile up here in "sensible" Oklahoma Pharmacist Ersland was charged with first degree murder after he shot and killed a youth who was robbing his pharmacy. Ersland shot one of the robbers—knocking him down, and then chased the other fleeing felon emptying his pistol at him. He returned, then took another gun and finished off the first one. Some people, including me, think of this action as regrettable. In the tradition of Tex Ritter he should have backed off and given the guy a chance—not polish him off—but that may just be me. I figured Ersland would get off anyway—that no jury would be caught dead convicting a pharmacist who shot and killed a robber who was robbing his pharmacy and terrorizing his two female employees. But I was wrong. Within an hour an angry mob had formed on the street against Ersland and he was arrested and charged with 1st degree murder.

The two cases show the worse sides of trial by jury. In the case of Casey she was (apparently) wrongly freed. Double jeopardy laws mean that there are no further legal actions. Ersland's lawyer is appealing the strange trial which seemed to have racial overtones. The judge made the trial difficult for Ersland not allowing his lawyer to call six witnesses. I would be surprised if the appeals court doesn't kick the whole thing out if they aren't worried about the racial harmony in NE Oklahoma City.

A lot of things have changed in America. I was reading a blog the other day in which the "blogger" was complaining about the price of gas and how the government needed to take over the oil industry and set prices—low of course. In fact, he like a lot of others think everything needs to be changed over to a socialist society. I have to agree that capitalism isn't perfect but it's still the best system ever devised. You could say something like that about trial by jury too. Not perfect, but the best.

Those of us who enjoy our freedoms and sometimes have to serve on a jury need to consider what writer Michael Connelly* once said about trials: "Everybody lies. Cops lie. Lawyers lie. Witnesses lie. The victims lie." But Jerome Ersland's lies were the only ones that counted. We now know that Ersland exaggerated his military service and his broken back. The District Attorney, The press and others have focused on his faults to the point that the facts in the actual case itself have become lost. "Lock him up and throw away the keys—he's a big liar" has been their cry. That he exaggerated his military service (not the first to ever do so) lied about his health conditions and they made people believe he's a white racist who probably wouldn't have shot that boy if he had been white. "They" wanted to throw the book at him and that's just what they did. Jerome Ersland is now in prison where he may remain for whatever is left of his life. I hope he gets a new and proper trial—one in which justice is done. I think he should be cleared and put back to work in his pharmacy although I don't know how a man can safely operate a pharmacy in Oklahoma City without a loaded pistol under the counter. You sure can't in Allen, Oklahoma.

Have a good week and enjoy the summer. Don't forget to attend your church!

Wayne Bullard, Pharm. D.
waynebullard@sbcglobal.net

Michael Connelly is the author of the bestselling Harry Bosch series of novels and best seller "The Lincoln Lawyer."

07-28-11
Wayne's Vacation

I have to ask myself: "If I am retired do I still need a vacation and from what?" So here I sit in this splendid camper trailer with A/C nearing the end of this 14 day vacation. My "vacation" plans were put on track during the icy days of last winter as I plotted to set up a nice camp on Lake Texhoma where we would have fun eating, playing dominoes with Chock and Eula and running about in our boat which would no doubt make a cooling spray as we sliced through the waters pulling a happy and contented grandchild in a large tube. At nights we could drive our boat under the Roosevelt Bridge and fish the deep cold waters for Texhoma Strippers—repeating the feat of two years ago—coming home with pictures and stories of large fish. Such visions are what dreams are made of.

Things don't always work out like we planned. First, the VA called and told me I had a dental appointment and one with my dermatologist on day 3 of my vacation. I told my family, "I'll drive up there from the lake—no big deal."

Day one (boy was it hot!) we launch the boat and go for a cooling swim out in the deep part of the lake. The water was nice. "Why does that bilge pump just keep on pumping?" I was asked as we paddled happily in the clear water. "Oh, I replied reassuringly, the boat has a little leak and the pump takes care of it real good." The leak got worse and by the end of the day the boat was in the shop. "Be two weeks before I can even get to it," the mechanic said. I stayed in Allen that night.

I drove up the next morning to the VA with my trusty wife and it was a bigger deal than I thought— I had six stitches in my mouth and pain meds in hand before I limped up to the 5th floor to dermatology. I was greeted by a kid who said she was my doctor and soon she told me she had decided to do surgery on a mole. "I'm going to just cut that off" and she and her 13 year old 3rd year medical student did just that.

"Don't swim for 2 weeks" she said as I staggered out the door thinking of my vacation going down the drain.

I stayed home in Allen until the next Monday before I went back. Boy was it hot! I had used my delicate condition as a reason to stay home and I wondered at the wisdom of going back at all to the family camp. There was no boat, nothing to do but go shopping at Durant, play dominoes, read and thanks to a little black box I can get online down here. Bought a new book at Dollar General in Durant (my second) so I would have something to read. Skimming through it I found out why it was only $3.00. It was too hot to cook. We ate a lot of Corn Flakes.

I enjoyed riding my bike around the little blacktopped roads but soon after I got back it had a flat. Boy was it hot! When you get my age you develop a special kinship to your bed and your bathroom more so than when you were 40. We have a nice little bathroom in this camper. Good shower too. Unfortunately we are on holding tanks causing me to use the public facilities. It's a dank place and smells funny. It has mysterious bugs and did someone mention snakes? But I'm a big boy. Just as I got my clothes off and was stepping into this dank-darkish--forbidding shower stall a big black bug about the size of a Blue Jay jumped on me landing in the area of my belly button. Could have been worse I guess. I will be eternally grateful there wasn't anyone else in there as I'm not particularly proud of how I deported myself in that helacous place. No way for a veteran to act. Spit bath anyone?

I told my wife that night that I had remembered several things I had forgotten to do at home and we would have to go home early. "I really need to be back in church this Sunday" I said. I was sincere in that as I thought of having to make more trips up to the restroom. Boy was it hot.

I wonder if next winter I'll look back on this and remember it as a good time or will I just continue to wonder how it is those yellow jackets and wasps got inside the camper? I hope all of you have a good summer. They have some nice travel packages up to Alaska I hear. Don't forget to go to church Sunday. You think it's hot here.

Wayne Bullard, Pharm. D.
waynebullard@sbcglobal.net

08-01-11
Uncle Jack

One thing about old memories is that over the years we choose to remember what we want and tend to forget the hard days and bad times—and that's good. I can remember some hard times in 1942—those war years when most of my Uncles went away to the big war and my brother and I were "shipped" down to a place called Goat Ridge—near Wister—to "help" out on the farm. I'd like to forget those days of digging potatoes, cutting sprouts and working under conditions that (I'm pretty sure) violated the Geneva Conventions pertaining to the treatment of POWs. Sometimes we likened our labors to those in the movie "Bridge over the River Kwai." Instead I like to think about the good parts of our visits with my grandparents and kin. I had cousins sprinkled freely throughout the area and my favorite recreation area was the Bluff Hole. The Hole was a deep clear and cool swimming area with bluffs to jump from on one side and a gentle sandy slope on the other for those that weren't such good swimmers.

That's all in the past now. My grandparents are long dead, the farm gone and all but one of my cousins moved away to the cities. The Bluff Hole on Little Caston Creek is "gone" too. Pollution from chicken and turkey farms turned the creek into a cesspool making it unfit to swim in and killing all the beautiful sun perch and goggle-eyes that made for good fly fishing. The few living creatures in it now are snakes and funny looking carp.

I still have my Uncle Jack. Sometimes when I think of him I like to think of my Grandparents front porch on a summer night in 1943. There was no electricity on Goat Ridge in 1943; instead the scene was illuminated by an oversized moon and jillions of fireflies moving as if they were part of some Broadway musical production. Grandma and Grandpa would sit on the East end of the south-facing porch, gently rocking n their porch rockers. The soft night air is still and has the welcome cool of the evening in it. Music floats out through the flower beds around the long porch from the guitar Jack quietly strums. We sing songs we've heard on the radio and at the Ridge's Panola Church. I was fairly sure that Uncle Jack was the most gifted guitarist to ever pick up a $7.00 Sears and Roebuck guitar. But that may have just been me and the lightning bugs.

My Aunt Inez, Uncle Tracey's wife was there for a few months with her baby girl, Gail while my Uncle Tracy was off serving someplace in the war—WWII. She sat in a chair in the center, holding her baby daughter as she quietly orchestrates and directs the evening's "entertainment." The music would stop at time and someone would tell a story. We would all listen even though we had probably heard that story before. Sometimes we would just be quiet as we sat transfixed— watching the fireflies—and thinking or not. Then there would be more music and another song—or perhaps another period of listening to the woods awhile. The whole world may have been at war that night but we were at peace on Goat Ridge—a perfect peace—a rare condition indeed in today's world. It was a condition that I was used to up on Goat Ridge, in Oklahoma in 1943.

The next summer my teen-aged Uncle Jack was gone. Grandpa had hauled him to Poteau in his Studebaker Wagon where there was a train waiting to haul him away to that war—a place which a lot of America's youth never got to come home from. I know Memorial Day is past but anytime is a good time to thank our veterans for their service and sacrifices made and still make for us and our great country. I hope you are enjoying your summer and that you go to church this Sunday.

Wayne Bullard, DPh

08-18-11
Going to Church in Alabama

As a seasoned member and ambassador of the Older Men's Sunday School Class (AKA the Cemetery Class) in the Baptist Church of Allen I like to visit other churches when I go traveling. A fellow can learn a lot doing that. Last week after attending a funeral in Alabama I got to attend the First Baptist Church of Glendale in Birmingham. It was a wonderful worship experience, but it was from the church I ran across later down in Southern Alabama that I learned more than just a few things about church management and how to handle staff matters.

Here's the situation; Senior Pastor of the Church in Elmo, Alabama (suburban Mobile) had decided to fire his song leader (Minister of Music) of 8 years. After the morning services, Pastor Brother Riley brought his Chairman of the Deacons, Harvey Hunt, into the office with him to meet with Brother Moore the Song Leader. Moore, smelling a rat, brought his mama, Sister Angelia in too and when Deacon Hunt handed Moore a $300.00 check and told him this was his last Sunday. Moore, before he could even think or pray about the matter, used a taser on him. Twice. At some point about this time, the meeting became more public and there was some pushing and hitting and that's when Sister Angelia, the song leader's mama pulled out her 18" knife and started doing a little cutting. The police finally arrived and several people were taken to the ER where several yards of surgical catgut and other suturing material were used.

Minister of Music Moore's head was badly bashed from Senior Pastor Riley (who was said to get in some good licks himself during this after church business meeting) was heavily stitched—all over. Moore said, "It's a good thing I took my mama in there with me—I don't know what would have happened to me if I hadn't." Mother Angelia said from her cell that "That weren't my knife."

Church leaders across the south and other areas as well are studying the developments in Elmo. One seminary said it was rushing into print some training materials so pastors will be able to read and learn how to handle such problems in the future. One popular brochure "Don't Tase Me Bro." is in for its 2nd printing. "To tase or not to tase during business meetings" is getting more than just a few reads. "How to fire your Music Man without getting tased" hit the presses yesterday and not ignoring the needs of song leaders, a new pamphlet called: "Moving On. And how to tell when your music ministry is finished" may soon be compulsory reading by song leaders. Meanwhile, several senior pastors are reportedly taking self defense courses in States such as Oklahoma and Texas.

Senior pastor Riley said that from now on when he fires a song leader he was just going to mail him a letter and the check—and then leave town a week or two. Moore is at home now recovering from his Tase and also the head injuries he suffered from Riley's whacking him in the head several times with the church's money box. As for Sister Angelia Moore-- she is now on the receiving end of the church's jail ministry but hopes to be back in church next Sunday if she can get them to lift the restraining order. Moore thinks he will look around for another church—after they take the stitches out and after he gets out of jail. I wonder who has Sister Angelia's knife and if she'll move her letter eventually.

I hope your summer is going great and be sure to go to church this Sunday but don't take your taser to church or you may have to move your letter too.

Wayne Bullard, DPh

08-29-11
Little Boy Gone

I had just come home from church and my afternoon was pretty well planned out as Sunday was the only day in the week I had off. The phone was ringing. "Mr. Bullard, my little boy died last night. Can you come over?" "Where is he now?" I asked. "He's here," she replied softly. I told Pat I was going to Conway Twitty Dr—a nickname I had given to Conway Street on the North side of Allen—and I told her why. I drove the city ambulance down to the old trailer. My wife and some other women were soon there seeing what they could do to help—like Allen people normally do.

The pretty and young Indian woman had dressed her little dead boy in his best clothes. Her husband stood nearby. He was an overweight drunk. I had seen the little boy riding his tricycle the day before and he looked pretty healthy to me and after asking a few questions I suspected that the large fat father had rolled over on the child and killed him. I called the Sheriff's Office and he was unable to send anyone, telling me not to move the body as it was an unattended death—and after a few more calls I knew that no one was coming and Dr. Oglesbee and the City Marshall were out of town. Eventually I loaded the tiny body into the ambulance and drove it over to Valley View.

I pushed my way to the head of the line at the ER in the old Valley View where I showed what I had wrapped up in my little blanket and the nurse said: "Put it in here." She and an Ada doctor did a quick exam and then asked me what I thought had happened. I told them what I thought and requested an investigation which I got. They sent the body on to Oklahoma City.

I drove the ambulance back to city hall and didn't hear anymore for a few days until I received a call from the medical examiner's office in Oklahoma City and was told the baby smothered and probably did so as a result of his daddy rolling over on him. He said he didn't know if they would do anything about it or whether it was actually criminal or not but he would send his report to the local District Attorney. "Oh, by the way," he went on, "the daddy will be going to prison anyway. He deserted the U. S. Army 10 years ago and may already be under arrest"—but he wasn't.

The next day the quiet spoken mother came in and told me they would have a graveside service that afternoon and she said she would be very pleased if I could come. I took a Polaroid camera for pictures of the service and of the mourners and the two well-dressed FBI agents. I gave the pictures to the mother and never saw those folks again. The agents took the dad away.

It was over a year later and on another afternoon that police Chief Welton Priest and a County Deputy rang my doorbell. "Wayne could you come with us down to the cemetery and help us find that grave we put the little boy in a year ago?" "His mama wants to move him to the family plot." The little metal marker was gone and there was seemingly no sign of the little casket but they finally found it. I went on home. The next day Welton was on my porch again. "You should have stayed yesterday." "Yeah," I replied, wondering what on earth he could want this time. "Well we found that casket OK but there was nothing in it. "Whoa—what happened?" "Its side was rotted out and the body was gone. The undertaker didn't know what to think." "Uh yeah," I muttered, as my mind whirled with all kinds of unsettling theories. "What did they do?" "They took the casket and left," he said.

Sometimes when I drive down Conway on my golf cart I remember the squeaky wheels of a little tricycle ridden by a smiling little Indian boy who always knew me and then I literally wonder where he went. Have a good week and don't forget to go to church this Sunday.

Wayne Bullard, DPh

89

09-01-11
Walking around up at the VA

As most of my readers already know, I get my medical care up at the VA in Oklahoma City. Not only is it cost effective (costs me nothing) but I have found it to be pretty comprehensive and in most ways superior to the way I received health care in the private sector. I think part of that is not that the doctors are any better or worse up there but that responsibility and management is placed on those health care providers that "force" them to do certain things that in general, health providers seem to avoid. The most important of these is follow up. If a doctor orders tests on a patient and says, "I'll let you know in a day or two" it ought to mean something: Like they are going to actually do it. The doctors I've experienced often avoided that call. If you wanted to know something it was you who had to call their chronically annoyed office nurse who would most likely say: "If there was anything the doctor wanted you to know he would have called and told you."

In a lot of HMOs (Health Maintenance Organizations) the rules of follow up are forced on doctors who as it turns out, do need management and supervision in order to do their jobs and I appreciate the VA for providing this management. However, this dedication does not cover events out in the parking lots. Last week as I trekked up to Oklahoma City, seeking relief from a painful neck I found myself under attack. No, not from some criminal sort or even another veteran, it was the wooden arm barrier that raises up and down to admit cars into certain lots. With my neck screwed down real tight and my sunglasses failing in the mid-day sun I didn't see the arm—but it saw me. The thing came down pretty fast, whacking me on my already sore left shoulder, near my sore neck and my now sore collar-bone leaving me with a nice dark bruise. Of course, it's like falling on the ice, one looks around real fast to see who saw you do this dumb thing and of course, everyone did. The faithful smokers on the East end of the building saw it all and were quite amused at my whacking.

They doctored and x-rayed my defective neck before giving me some pills to take. My neck still hurts but now I have the painful left shoulder to help get my mind off of it. The inside of the VA building is a little bit like a mall. There are all kinds of little shops and eating places along the main concourse on floor one. One of those is a pizza place and it was after noon as we went in to have a pizza. The solitary soul operating the joint was way behind but making a gallant effort to keep up in the tiny area behind the counter. It didn't take too long for us to figure out what was wrong: She had new help. The new guy was a youngster who must have been over 450lbs and besides all that he was short. He literally couldn't go back there. It would have been like putting an elephant in a shoe box. So the boss-lady just had him sit out there and watch her cook and keep the tables clean. You can learn a lot by just sitting around and listening. She would glare at him once in a while and he would get up and very painfully (with grunts and moans) wipe off 2 or 3 tabletops and then resume his sitting position. If looks could kill he would have been a dead fat boy.

All of which brings me to our next topic: OU Football. So what does OU football have to do with Pizza? Well it has to do with fat behinds. I've noticed that now all fans stand nearly all the time at the ball games. Why? Is it all that exciting, all the time? Well, uh, no. I noticed last year during a particularly slow part of a game (besides the halftime) that everyone tried to sit down—all at the same time. Well, that no longer works. The numbers on the benches are still the same distance apart but the fans are now about 25% wider than they used to be. So what we have to do now when we grow real tired is to take turns sitting down. If by chance the stadium were to reposition the numbers so everyone could now have a seat we would lose about 18,000 seats which would be a financial blow to the University. Somehow I don't look for them to do it. Nor do I expect the Tulsa game Saturday night to be a nail biter so I wonder where we're all going to sit?

Churches are more forgiving. Pews are unnumbered and roomy assuring all of us, fat or lean, a place to sit in comfort when we go to church Sunday—something I hope all of you do.

Wayne Bullard, DPh

09-08-11
The Devil Comes to Allen

Did you ever wonder what you would do if you saw the devil walking down Main Street? Several people found out last Thursday... At least two people dialed 911 which I don't think is biblical—something I would never have thought of had I been there and saw that old serpent sauntering down the street. The Devil wore signs stating: "I hate them and they hate me "referring to a local church. The responding police were very curious to see what the devil looked like and the purpose of his walk. They soon found out but since he had violated no laws (even the devil has his rights you know) they unleashed the demon right there on the street. The Devil made himself at home and Main Street soon returned to normal.

Some main street watchers felt that the devil was an impersonator put on the street by a local church to promote their own agenda—but until now I never knew of a church unleashing the devil on a town. Another man, hearing of the sighting feared it was his ex-wife coming after him—or perhaps her lawyer. And as Forrest Gump would say: "that's all I have to say about that."

Several people have called inquiring about my wife. She took a spill early Saturday morning down on the Mustang Walking Trail spraining her right ankle and banging up her left arm. I took her to the ER over at Valley View Sunday afternoon. "Why did you wait so long?" the nosey doctor asked. "I didn't know she had hurt herself until later in the day Saturday and by then it was too late," I replied. "Too late?" he asked. "Yeah doc, by the time I realized she might need some medical attention it was time for us to go to the OU Football game." "You mean you made it to the OU game banged up like that?" the nosey doctor asked my wife. "Oh no, she couldn't go so I got my daughter to go with me," I replied. "Why didn't you bring her over this morning?" "Well, I wanted to go to church and after church I had a dinner invite, "I replied with some indignation.

She didn't have any broken bones so the doctor told her to just lie around and for me to re-wrap the thing in Ace Bandages every 3 hours and so forth (like I don't have anything else to do). I told him I would do what I could. Personally I feel that it's good for a woman to be up and around on a sprain. It keeps the ankle from getting so stiff. But I must say it has slowed her down. I didn't think she would ever get back up the steps after she put the trash out Monday morning and it broke my heart to have to tell her it was Labor Day as I told her: "You'll have to put those garbage cans back where you found them." She was really grunting by the time she came back inside the second time and I told her not to worry about the breakfast dishes: "I've already put all 4 items in the dishwasher." It makes a man feel better about himself when he can help out his crippled up wife.

This Labor Day finds everything pretty quiet in Allen. I just finished reading my Daily Oklahoman and my 4th cup of coffee. I'm going out now and mow the yard. I hate to be inside on a pretty morning like this and I can't stand to hear the sounds of the vacuum cleaner—something my wife just dragged out to clean her floors. Women can be so insensitive some times.

I hope all of you are enjoying this end-of-summer cool weather as much I do. Be sure and go to church this Sunday and maybe you'll know what to do next time you run into the devil walking down Main Street.

Wayne Bullard, Pharm. D.
waynebullard@sbcglobal.net

09-15-11
Sunday School Time

"What are you doing now?" I asked my crippled up wife as she dialed the phone. "I'm getting someone to teach my Sunday school class this morning." Being something of an expert on Sunday school myself I told her, "Look no further. I'm your man." Should be easy, I thought to myself. I've been teaching off and on for years—even adult classes such as the learned cemetery class." "Well, I don't know," she went on. "What class is it anyway?" I asked. "Second graders, about 7 of them," she responded. Pretty soon she had dragged out her teacher's book and had given me an in-depth review of the lesson. It was real simple—the story of Samuel who lived in the temple with Eli and the time that God spoke to Samuel as he was going to sleep (Samuel not God).

Pat seemed more worried about me teaching the 7 year olds than she did about her damaged arm and ankle but I had no fear as I walked into the small classroom. Two boys and two girls showed up and I gave them their snacks and we visited a bit. After reading the story of how God called Samuel from his sleep and how that Samuel thought Eli was calling him I had the kids act it out. Naturally, all the kids wanted to participate so they took turns being Samuel and Eli. "Did you call me Eli?" the Samuel actors would ask and 2 times Eli said no. The 3rd time Eli (apparently a little slow himself) figured it out. After all he was the head preacher and they were living in a Temple sort of place. "It ain't me, it must be God," Eli told Samuel and he told him next time to go ahead and have God speak to him.

This reenactment didn't go all that well. One actor, playing Eli, was very irate to be awakened and chewed Samuel out pretty good. One actor playing Samuel, upon hearing the voice of God sprang up and bounded into the nearest wall and landing back in the floor hard enough to break the bones of a grown up. "Why did you do that?" I asked. "Well, when God spoke to me it was so dark that I didn't see that wall." I had the boy do it again and "do it right this time" I said. He lay down and the voice of God (played by me of course) called his name and this time the boy jumped up and hit another wall. "Still dark in here," the boy said. I reassured the concerned teacher from next door that all was OK. Again.

One little girl asked why Samuel lived in the church house. I told the story of Hannah and how she couldn't have children so she promised God that if He would let her have a son she would give him away to God. When he was 3 or 4 years old, sure enough, she took Samuel by the hand and took him to the Temple and left him there with old Eli. "Did he cry a long time?" she asked. "Well, I er, ah, uh, the Bible doesn't really record just how that part went but I think Samuel understood the moment and accepted it like a big boy. "I don't think I would like it if my momma took me to church and gave me away," she replied. I told them I wouldn't either but we needed to be moving along.

The next phase of the lesson pushed the story line a little further. We were in the process of learning our memory verse when a "farting" contest broke out between the two males in the class. We had to adjourn and open the door while the air cleared. We finally learned our memory verse, sort of, and I heard a wonderful sound: The bell. From now on I'll stay where I belong—down in the cemetery class—where we couldn't learn a memory verse if they paid us a hundred dollars a word but we do know not to indulge in contests of deliberate flatulence while seated in a tiny room and in Sunday School.

This Sunday I am in a place in Virginia called Virginia Beach attending a reunion of the USS Johnnie Hutchins DE-360. I hope this convergence doesn't bring about any more unseemly contests—especially concerning—well you know. Stay tuned. Be sure and attend your church this Sunday.

Wayne Bullard, DPh

09-22-11
Number Please

One thing we lost in the past is the local telephone operator. Last week someone sent me a story about telephone operators—about how they knew what time it was, how one operator told a kid how to do his homework. The relationship between operators and telephone customers was often just that—a relationship. That story reminded me of when my family moved to Stonewall in 1944—of a lady named Myrtle Morris who was the "number please" lady there. I was fascinated with the voice on the phone and when I learned where she was I paid her a visit there at Broadway and 5th street.

Myrtle soon showed me how the little switchboard worked and in fact let me run it a little bit. Her office was on my way to town so I would often park my bike and go in and give her a bathroom break or perhaps let her run over to Earl Cradduck's Grocery. Myrtle and her mom ran the switchboard 24 hours a day with their daughter Mary Nell's help. Myrtle knew "stuff" like where everybody was and what they were doing, who the kids were dating and who was seeing who. I never mastered all the "rings' out on the country party lines. Sometimes there were 15 to 20 homes hooked to one wire so the combinations of shorts and longs had to be learned like a code.

Many years later I was in San Francisco in the Navy and tried to call home. There was a pay phone at the end of a fog enshrouded pier and it was sort of cold. I walked out there and told the operator I wanted to call 17 in Stonewall, Oklahoma. "Oh, she says, are you from Stonewall?" "Uh, yes," I replied and then she told me who she was it was a last name like Reeves that I had heard of and they had lived there at one time.

We chatted for a long time before she told me it would take a few minutes to put the call through—get the routing and so forth. Long distance was a lot different in those days. When the Ada operator finally answered she and the San Francisco operator struck up a long conversation. They knew each other of course. Boy was it cool out on that pier. I finally cleared my throat and joined in as I enjoyed the company that dreary evening. She finally went ahead and rang Stonewall. When Myrtle picked up, another new conversation started up all over again.

I finally reminded Myrtle I wanted to talk with my folks and said, "Wayne, I can ring 17 but it won't do any good—they are all out at the Winton's and Brooks eating ice-cream. Want me to ring 'em out there? So we did. All of us. And, yes, I finally got to talk to my mom and, yes, all 43 operators pitched in and once more contributed to the happy phone call.

I eventually finished the call and had forgotten my reasons for calling home except I was perhaps, homesick. Walking back up the pier I remembered my handful of quarters—still intact—it had been a free call. I went back to my base on Treasure Island that night full of information on everybody I could think of in the Stonewall/Ada area and some pretty warm feelings about some telephone operators—feelings I still have about Stonewall and about how things used to be and perhaps should still be. Be sure and go to church this Sunday. You'll find all the important stuff in church is unchanged.

Wayne Bullard, DPh

09-29-11
Virginia Beach

"I still think we should have just driven out there," I said to my wife as we turned north out of Atwood toward Tulsa on 48. "Well, we have our tickets now so I guess we'll just fly," she replied. Late that night we were on the ground in Norfolk, Virginia picking up our rental car. After a 10 minute delay on the shoulder of I-64 I finally figured out how to turn on the headlamps of the little Dodge Challenger. That's why they call it a Challenger.—it's hard to drive. It was a dark night but we eventually muddled our way about 15 more miles over to our hotel, The Sandcastle.

The old hotel had some "sleaze" to it which I told my wife gave it a lot of character. I don't think she was buying the "character" part as we made our way to our room that night on the 5th floor. The next morning we got our little car out and drove back up I-64 to a 13 mile long bridge and tunnel system that took us across the Chesapeake to Northampton. This little piece of Virginia is a peninsula containing beaches, parks and camping—old plantations and beautiful old houses. On our return trip across the bridge we stopped at a restaurant over the harbor entrance and ate the best seafood we had been served in years.

The next day I told my wife I had my heart set on doing the Mariner's Museum up in Newport News—about 2 inches away on the map. It turned out to be over 40 miles of urban driving, an hour of which was spent waiting on an aircraft carrier to pass under a drawbridge. Later, I remarked that there was plenty of parking as we hiked over to the main entrance sporting a sign which stated it was closed on Mondays. Saddened, I drove us back through the heavy traffic to Virginia Beach and that night met with the reunion crowd from the USS Johnnie Hutchins. Our crowd was pretty small this year—altogether we numbered about 18. The next morning we went on a cruise of Norfolk Harbor. This was very interesting and included a sumptuous meal. Everyone had a good time.

Being stubborn, if nothing else, on Wednesday we drove back to see the Mariner's Museum and it was well worth the drive. It has the shipwreck Monitor and some of Merrimac inside. If you are into naval history this is indeed the place to go. That night was our big banquet and I suppose our final gathering. No plans exist at this time for us to meet again. The next morning we said our goodbyes and parted. I'm sad to say I'm pretty sure I'll never see those guys again.

I know Bill Robinson enjoys my trips—the parts where everything goes wrong. Well, Bill, sorry. This year the hotel failed to catch afire and we had no naked Japs out in the hallway. In fact, everything went like clockwork until we started home—and a cloud came up. We were sitting there in the back end of the MD-80 wedged tightly between the loud engines and the odiferous toilet when my wife said:"That engine sounds funny." "Yeah, I replied," it sounds like it needs a squirt of WD-40." Then the lightning and thunder rolled across the airport. The ground crews were ordered inside as our pilot announced that because of the severe weather we not only couldn't take off, we were abandoned with all the baggage doors open. This was apparently good for the safety of the ground crews, but what about us? Finally the crews came back and eventually we were able to take off. I guess someone must have squirted that WD-40 in the starboard engine as it quieted down. It was the next afternoon before we got home—about the same time it would have been had we drove—when I said: "We should have driven."

Be sure and go to church this Sunday. You can drive your car.

Wayne Bullard, Pharm. D.
waynebullard@sbcglobal.net

10-06-11
Hunger in Oklahoma

I always (nearly always) enjoy hearing from my readers and my mailbag has been pretty full this week. For those of you who wrote concerned about my wife's injuries you might want to know she took yet another tumble last week breaking her glasses and cutting her leg open. She was taking out the trash—something some of my loyal critics say I should have been doing all along. Being the tender hearted person that I actually am I want you to know that I do take out the trash—sometimes. She is healing rapidly and I expect her to be back up and able to do her chores again soon. I asked her Sunday morning if she wanted me to teach her Sunday school class again and she said no.

As for my disgruntled readers who are tired of me writing about "fat" or "obese" please be assured that I have no malice toward fat people. In fact, I'm a little bit fat myself and some of my best friends are fat people. So today I'm going to write a few words about hunger in America—a problem that seems to be everywhere. "Thousands of children go to bed hungry every night," goes the refrain from press releases. Here in Oklahoma, many schools now crank out breakfast for those kids because we all know a hungry child can't study and learn. These free breakfasts are followed by (what else?) a free lunch and now there is after school care where the still hungry kids are snacked again. And yes, I have it on good authority that fat kids get hungry too. In fact, I'm a little hungry right now.

So what can we do here in Oklahoma about parents that make kids get up and get themselves to school each morning without any breakfast? You just can't go out and arrest people for their poor parenting skills any more than you can arrest people for having poor life styles. Educators will say education is the answer, politicians say we need more federal spending and churches say we need more compassion. Everybody knows kids need to eat to grow and thrive including the parents in question. In fact we already know better on a lot of things—mostly about things we ignore. Most everyone knows unhealthy foods from healthy, know we need exercise and that it's stupid to smoke cigarettes but we ignore it.

It's not that we haven't done anything about these problems but the net result has been so far is to make it easier to be an irresponsible citizen by feeding their hungry children for them. I suppose that is as it should be. No one wants to see little kids go hungry in a land of plenty. Before we get too hard on ourselves as a people remember that all Americans, including the millions of "poor" are very fortunate. Even the 50 million Americans drawing food stamps on average own more than one car, have cell phones, own their own homes and have flat screen TVs. In short, our "in poverty" people are better off than the majority of the people in the rest of the world. So you can't really say that America has forgotten its poor people. They have been well provided for.

With the economy and our tax base continuing to shrink "change" may indeed be on the way to America but it may not be the change we wish for. We may find out what happens when some of this welfare dries up—when the well goes dry. As Forrest Gump says, "that's all I have to say about that." I promised not to get off on obesity this week but will say one more thing here: The biggest health problem facing our poor remains you-know-what and smoking.

Have a good and healthy week, be sure to go to your church Sunday and go easy on the covered dish luncheon afterwards.

Wayne Bullard, DPh

10-13-11
Texas and OU

For those interested parties who wonder how my better half is doing just let me say this: "My wife continues to improve somewhat and is hobbling around in the kitchen fixing me a bite to eat, even as I write." We just drove in from the Texas/OU game where I attended the game without her. Attending a game without her is not all that much fun and I missed her and her purse a lot. Besides carrying a lot of change for the concession stands she packs into each and every game just about every kind of pharmaceutical nostrum that one might need. She makes sure I have my game day radio and correct ticket as well as special medicines and balms for nausea, diarrhea, itching skin, smarting eyes, ringing ears, dizziness and headaches. Nitroglycerin 0.4 for surprise angina, band aids for wounds, Hall's Cough Drops and comprehensive lists of prescription medications we take in case a sudden trip to the ER is needed. But like her, the nostrums stayed home too.

Saturday's OU/Texas game was probably the most important game so far this year. My readers will be happy to learn (as was I) that I didn't come down with any maladies during the game and in fact, as the Sooners ran up the score on a hapless Texas team I became totally oblivious of any and all medical concerns. There was another blessing: I was able to palm off her ticket for face value (no small amount of money in itself) to a preacher from the OKC metro so all in all I came out pretty good. The preacher, a good old boy named Mike Kebone was good company and between the two of us we enjoyed the game very much—even if I did call him "Tim" most of the time.

When the carnage ended that OU visited upon the football program of UT it was easy to see that head coach, Mac Brown hadn't stopped his whining. One Texas sports writer wrote that Bob Stoops and his Sooners accomplished something that David Boren and the entire

Big-12 had failed to do: The complete humbling of Mac Brown's Texas Football program and their Big-12 busting Bevo-Vision stuff. One other news item tells of the giddy victory dance performed by Joe Castiglione after being awarded a game ball by Bob Stoops—but it wasn't for his play, it was his birthday.

We did the fair a little bit after the game, partly to view the sad remnants of Horn fans as they roamed the grounds forlornly in grumpy remorse. I don't know why they didn't just all go home. It was not a pretty picture but we went ahead and ate an abundance of unhealthy fried things—skipping the fried candy bars and other ridiculous heart-stoppers. Later, we walked back over to a part of Dallas that looks a lot like Haiti and rescued my car which I had left guarded by a native of the area. The next morning Pat and I (after making sure our OU decals and flags were still in place) drove home in a welcome and refreshing rain.

I hope all of you are enjoying the nice weather this fall as much as I am. It's always a good Sunday morning in the Allen's Older Men's Class (AKA Cemetery Class) when OU, OSU and The Allen Mustangs win their football games. Be sure and go to church this Sunday.

Wayne Bullard, DPh

10-27-11
Goodbye Omar Gaddafi

Another dictator has been killed. Muammar Gaddafi, dictator of Libya since nearly forever was discovered leaving his rat hole in a large convey from the town of Sirte The vehicles were attacked by a US drone(under the command of NATO) wounding Gaddafi. A bloody Gaddafi then sought shelter in a "tin-horn" under the highway. Later he and his bodyguards were dragged out and Gaddafi was arrested and placed in custody. Video at the scene showed he was then shot and killed and placed on the hood of a pickup before being driven into a town called Misrata where his body was put in a deep freeze at a local market. Press reports are that Muammar's body is still there, a special market attraction for the curious Libyans wishing to have their pictures made with him. Those Libyans sure know how to class something up. Western news sources said: "It is a pretty disgusting sight."

So, how is the world reacting to this latest "killing" of a Head of State—albeit a hated one? In Libya there was uncontained rejoicing. Fawaz Gerges a guy who thinks he is in charge of the country now said the killing was wonderful although some may have wished to try Gaddafi in a court of law. Ya think? President Obama took it pretty well too, detailing his death as just another in a series of dictators getting what they had coming to them. One Allenite flagged me down this week and asked if I had heard about Muammar's death? I told him I had. The happy man told me that "Obama has killed 3 of 'em now. That's more than Bush or any of his Republican buddies has ever killed." "Old Bush killed Sadam but heck, Sadam wasn't so bad and Bush lied about him so he could kill him and get even with him." "Want to know why?" I told him no and drove away. I failed to tell him I too was sort of glad Gaddafi was dead but somehow I felt a little uneasiness when I watched it on the news.

But our man in Allen was not alone. A lot of people felt like he did and gave Obama the credit and praise. Although not an Allen person, Sergei Lavrov, Russian Foreign Minister was upset about the killing. "They violated the Geneva Convention" and he said Gaddafi was in custody and as such was a prisoner of war protected by international law. "And what about our treaties and deals we had with Libya?" speaking of the fat contracts to do things for Libya such as building a railroad from Gaddafi's home town of Sirte to Tripoli. That may be why Russia opposed NATO interference by trying to protect Libyan civilians from Gaddafi's Air Force—a job they did pretty well. It's good to see Russia finally getting worked up about the Geneva Convention though.

Needless to say, China opposed the United Nations and NATO in this adventure for the same reasons I would suppose Russia did. Jaing Yu, China's Foreign Minister was pretty worked up over it as was the "Dear Leader" in North Korea. Another follower of the communist's party line is the terminally ill Hugo Chavez of Venezuela. Hugo went a step further calling Gaddafi a Martyr who will never be forgotten—but he will. I guess I should have stopped in St. Louis last week and asked the pro-communist demonstrators in the banking district how they felt about it but I forgot about it as I drove by.

Thus ends the story of Muammar—a man whose very name we could never spell. I tried looking it up and found Gadhafi, Qaddafi, Gaddafi and Qadhafi. I sort of like the ones with 'h" in it but my "Word" program likes "Qaddafi." And really, how are Allenites taking this? Most just ask each other, "Did you hear about Qaddafi?" And I guess everyone had. A special thanks to the readers who drop me an email once in a while. I enjoy hearing from you and knowing where you live and what you're doing now. I also hope your weekend is nice and that you find time to attend your church this Sunday.

Wayne Bullard, DPh

**1944 Centrahoma, back Cecil, Linda Kay and Dora,
front Gerald, Wayne and Mana Sue**

11-17-11
Linda Kay

My beloved youngest sister, Linda Kay went home to be with the Lord a week ago last Sunday. The doctors did what they could but were no match for the cancer that had attacked her stomach. Kay will be remembered in my family for her sweet personality and for talents that set her apart from the rest of us. She loved animals and as she grew up she especially enjoyed working with horses. She was good at it and won more than a few rodeo events involving barrel racing and the sort. Our good neighbor, the late Everett Shaw, himself a world champion calf roper taught her much of what she knew about the sport. Everett saw to it that Kay got to ride some good horses and participate in the many rodeos in the area.

Linda Kay was an award winning and outstanding basketball player in Stonewall who later played professionally and was even

106

invited to compete in the Olympics. Linda married and chose to be a mom, raising 3 children, 2 girls and 1 boy. Linda Kay was a working mom and after retiring she embarked on a 2nd career—working at the Ardmore Vet Clinic over in Ardmore—where she lived. The job was very fulfilling to this little lady who loved animals so much.

Kay was a pretty girl who contributed to the worship services at First Baptist Church in Stonewall with her participation in music. Kay is remembered for her ability to see the best in people. She avoided judging people and when the conversation turned that direction her voice was notably absent—often offering a positive word or two about the one getting talked about. Kay could always see the good in people and this was one of the things that made her so very special.

We will all miss this good person and fine lady, Linda Kay. Thanks to each of you for your prayers, cards, food and kind words to us during this time. It is appreciated.

Be sure and attend your church this Sunday.

Wayne Bullard, DPh

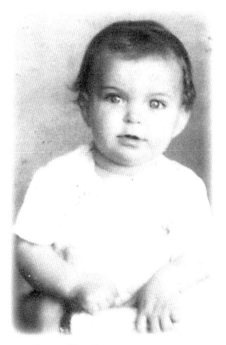

Beautiful Baby, Linda Kay

11-29-12
All I know I learned from the movies

As some of you know I have been laid up for about 2 weeks post-surgery and have watched a lot of movies—mostly old ones. A few years ago I wrote about how that I wasn't a very good student over at Stonewall (1944-1952) and you could say that much of what I learned about life over there came from watching movies. You see, my dad owned and operated the Main Theater and I worked there as I grew up. I saw all the movies and I learned a lot.

I learned early on that if you had to shoot someone, you should shoot them in the hand. Contrary to what you may think, when you shoot a bad guy in the hand it only stings a little while, causing him to drop his gun and want to be a better person. I learned to be honest and always to do right, returning stolen money to the oppressed and being nice and to sing to girls. I learned to wear a white hat and to keep it on when in a fight with your fists or drag a bad guy off his horse. There was a lot to learn but there were a lot of movies.

Frank Capra, the socialist, made a movie called "It's a Wonderful Life" starring James Stewart as George Bailey (1946). I learned from this movie that you don't always get what you want from life. George was a "good guy" who mainly wanted to flee Bedford Falls and travel the world. But George was doomed by circumstances to run the poorly performing family savings and loan business where George worked for years helping poor working people afford decent homes and improve their banking habits. The bad guy (Lionel Barrymore playing Henry Potter) plotted always to enslave the hapless residents of Bedford Falls with his slum houses and high interest bank. George falls into very hard times when his incompetent (but somewhat lovable) Uncle Billy looses the bank deposit and throws the firm into instant bankruptcy driving the ever-frustrated George to contemplate suicide. George, by now a very unhappy man, wishes he had never been born.

This movie also teaches the value of prayer. George's friends and family started praying for him. Consequently, a somewhat defunct angel named Clarence (Henry Travers) is assigned to rescue George and decides to grant his wish (that he had never been born). Clarence escorts George on a trip through town where he finds that Bedford Falls is now named Potterville and is an awful place of slums, alcoholics, prostitutes, saloons, casinos, pawnshops and flop houses. No one remembers George as it is revealed to him the impact he had indeed made in his life. The movie shows that good prevails and everything we do has an impact—one way or another.

In the movie Groundhog Day TV Weatherman Phil Connors (Bill Murray) is sent to Punxsutawney, Pa.— every groundhog day every year to do a show. He hates it and in general hates his life and everyone else except Rita, his pretty co-worker. In Punxsutawney he finds time frozen: Every morning he wakes up and it's still February 2. He tries everything to escape this "eternal curse" doing all sort of bazaar and entertaining things such as suicide and finally even kidnaps the groundhog, steals a pickup and drives himself over a cliff but as usual wakes up in bed—and it's February 2, again.

Phil finally learns in this movie to make use of the specialness of this day and turn it into positive gain—even though his motives aren't pure. He still wants Rita. To modify her feelings toward him he learns to be an accomplished sculpturer, piano player and develops a feeling for the downtrodden. He totally changed himself into what appears to be an ideal man which enables him to finally win over Rita. At this point Phil wakes up and it's February 3. His long nightmare is over—and he still has Rita. Our lesson from this movie is that we are given a new day every 24 hours to improve ourselves and minimize our negative features. I learned that we, as did Phil, have to confront our fears and realities if we really want to be better people. Phil got Rita. What do you want?

Have a great weekend and be sure and go to church this Sunday.

Wayne Bullard, DPh

12-08-11
Remember Pearl Harbor

"It was his Pearl Harbor day" or "They had a Pearl Harbor" is another way of saying it was a real bad day or a time of disaster for someone. Yesterday was the 70th anniversary of the real event in history—Pearl Harbor. December 7, 1941 was a disaster in which our Pacific Fleet was almost completely destroyed. It was a day that galvanized the attention and efforts of the American people toward defeating the Japs—the ones who mounted the sneak attack. It was the start of a great war.

The attack triggered off a number of negative events for rank and file Oklahomans that dismal Sunday in 1941. For one thing it didn't do much for the Christmas spirit over at Centrahoma and   rationing started almost immediately. But before it could be enforced there was a run on new cars, tires, coffee and appliances as the government shuttered all automobile factories—turning them over to produce such items as ships and tanks. Tires were made of natural rubber—the synthetic stuff hadn't come along just yet—and all of our rubber came in from Asia and the Japs had just taken all of that over. We were cut off. The German U-boats kept the rubber and coffee shipments out. One farmer went over to Wards in Ada and bought all the tires he could for his car, pickup, hay truck and tractor but government "agents" came and picked them up a few days later.

That scary Sunday the churches in Centrahoma (and probably all over the nation) went into an emergency praying mode. At the First Baptist Church there weren't regular services that night. In fact, there were people already at church—praying— as fearful residents prayed both for America and for our own deliverance. Rumors had swept the nation about invasions and when I asked my own grandfather (who knew everything) about it he assured me that we would see Germans coming from the East and Japs coming from the West—right down highway 3 in tanks and trucks. Centrahoma would fall, according to him. The prayers that night were not in the abstract.

As it turned out not one enemy tank ventured into Coal County and Centrahoma was safe. The only Germans we ever saw were the German POWs who were hauled around to work on the highways and do other labor around the county. But the irritations of not having enough Folgers's coffee, Lucky Strike cigarettes and sugar were real. Gasoline rationing was swift and cut to the bone for many. But we had "drip tanks" (condensate from natural gas wells) around Centrahoma which would make your car run if you didn't mind the pinging.

Many rural counties in Oklahoma emptied out pretty fast after the war started. First it was the military draft and then it was the promise of good jobs in the cities assembling airplanes in Oklahoma City, building ships in California or making bombs in McAlester. Wages were fairly good and many people left and never looked back at the hardscrabble farms they had left behind. Not a Christmas season goes by that I don't think about this mass exodus—especially of my kin. Many of those who left have passed on, leaving family that doesn't know my part of the family and while that in itself may be sad, it is just life.

Finally I have this Christmas reminder: Be thankful for the gifts of God—your family and the greatest gift of all: Jesus. Be sure and attend church this Sunday.

Wayne Bullard, DPh

12-15-11
Bringing home the butter in Centrahoma

It was said that back in the 1930s and '40s Saturday was butter and egg day in rural America. Those days are past now but back then the sale of butter, cream and eggs was an important and vital part of the economy around here. The day was also a good time to take your fiddle or guitar to town and perhaps make some music after you raised some cash from the sale of eggs and stuff. Such social activities made going to town quite an event.

You would sell your stuff at a placed called a "Cream Station" which was outfitted with state certified scales, propane fired Bunsen burners and centrifuges. How to buy, how to know the quality of products such as eggs, butter and cream was well described by the State of Oklahoma handbook and you didn't have to be a chemical engineer or brain surgeon to determine the price of farm products. You did need the patience of Job, the stamina of Moses and the Wisdom of Solomon to deal with the 10% who loved to haggle about how their stuff was worth more than other people's stuff. The produce man out of Coalgate bought our stuff and would phone us when any prices changed. Sometimes it was my job to walk over to Smith's or Moore's store to tell them the new prices. We had the only working phone in town for a long time: A pay phone in the back end of the store served our needs after the Centrahoma Telephone Company had gone broke back in the mid 30s.

One nice Saturday morning Mrs. Shoffet brought in her little bucket of cream her old skinny cow had produced. It wasn't much and I believe cream was around 10 cents a pound at that time. My Uncle Ezra worked our cream station at that time and after he measured the specific gravity with his handy centrifuge and weighed it out and handed her some money—less than 20 cents as I recall. She replied, "I can beat this in Coalgate, so if you want it you had better up your offer." Uncle Ezra held firm so she walked over into the store and confronted my dad about Ezra's unfair prices. My dad told her that the prices came from Coalgate and that was the best he could do. Mrs. Shoffet took her pail of cream and walked out saying that she was on her way to Coalgate.

I knew dad had to go the bank over in Coalgate and I was watching so I could ride over with him. Mom said, "Cecil, I thought you were going to the bank." "Uh, I am, he replied, but I'm waiting on Mrs. Shoffet to get a ride. I don't want to have to take her to town." But car after car went by and after the lady didn't get a ride dad decided he had to go on. Dad made me get in the back seat and we drove over to Mrs. Shoffet's on the highway. Dad acted surprised to see her and asked her if she wanted a ride. "You know I do, she replied and put out that cigar—you know I can't tolerate tobacco smoke of any kind much less cigars."

As the old 1935 Ford rumbled out of town on four well-booted tires the lady passenger reminded dad (who had put his cigar out) that the national World War II speed limit was 35MPH and he'd better not get over it if he didn't want to be reported to the government. He drove 35. In Coalgate he drove her to the produce house over there and as she painfully got out, she told dad to be back as soon as possible to pick her back up because she didn't feel like walking all the way out to the edge of town to hitchhike home. Later I asked her what she got for her cream and she looked at me a while and said she had gotten what she wanted for it. I was sorry I asked.

I wish each of you a Merry Christmas and hope you can attend your church this Sunday. You'll not be sorry you did.

WayneBullard, Pharm. D.

wayne bullard@sbcglobal.net

12-22-11
Christmas in Centrahoma

Living in Centrahoma at Christmastime was a little bit like living the classic "Dickens's" Christmas—except we weren't that prosperous. In fact we didn't even have our own Scrooge—instead we had a lot of Crachet's and Tiny Tim's back in those days. Times were tough in Centrahoma but we would still hang up our stockings hoping for a little bit of Christmas candy in our stockings. Firecrackers, a standard gift back then, were cheap and since my dad like to set them off we could count on a few of them.

Of course we had the school programs up at the Centrahoma School. Our teachers, Ms Ina Klinglesmith, Ms. Pearl Downard and Ms. Williams worked hard on the costumes we wore for the Annual Christmas musical/play. After the programs we were sent home and (someone) made sure each child got a bag with an orange, an apple and hard candy. For many that was as good and perhaps all they got.

In those days we had movies up at the schoolhouse every Friday night. Cost a dime for a kid to get in. War movies and westerns were my favorites but the thing many of us noticed was how well American's seemed to live in places other than in Centrahoma. These "movie" American's all had jobs and had a maid to help out in their pretty 2-storied homes. Modern kitchens and telephones were standard equipment in these nice movie homes and there was no evidence of an outdoor toilet—such as was needed in Centrahoma. Of course, there was always a beautiful late model car parked in the garage. I remember a movie featuring kids at Christmas back in 1943 really captured my imagination when a boy in the family got this fancy electric train. Talk about envy and greed—I wanted that train—bad.

I consulted my personal advisor and older brother Gerald. "I was planning on a train this year—from Santa," I said on my approach to the important subject. "I went on, I know there's a war on and I don't think they are making any toy trains—besides dad said he couldn't afford one if they did. Santa's my only hope." I went on: "Letha Mae Moore (my very best friend and classmate at the time who lived across the road from us) said she thought Santa was her daddy." Somehow I couldn't think of Santa looking like Billy Moore. I maintained my belief since it was my only hope anyway. I told Gerald that I thought Letha was wrong. Gerald said something like, "I don't think Billy is Santa either but I'm not sure Santa even comes to Centrahoma." "Well he better," I went on. "He's my last chance for a train."

Christmas Eve night rolled around—finally. "Let's go over to the Moore's and see what they got," Gerald said. "Can't," I answered. I'm staying up all night if I have to—I need to know about this Santa business." Gerald insisted it would be OK to go and that old Santa would not be coming 'till late that night. So we went. I remember that the cynic Letha Mae already had a new doll but as I recall nothing from Santa. About that time Gerald used his remarkable hearing and reported that he thought he heard reindeer on the roof across the street. Sure enough, I had been had again! Old Santa had sneaked in and paid a call on us without me getting as much as a peek. The good thing was this: There, fully assembled and working was my perfect made in USA train. And yes, I let my dad and brother play with it all they wanted to that pretty Christmas Eve night. And yes Letha, there really is a Santa Claus. And yes Gerald, he still comes to Centrahoma.

I hope your Santa comes to your house this year and all your Christmas wishes come true. Be sure and go to Church this wonderful season. Jesus is the reason for the season!

Wayne Bullard, Pharm. D.
waynebullard@sbcglobal.net

12-29-11
Happy New Year

It's been an eventful year for folks here in Allen. The oil patch continues to provide new jobs and prosperity to quite a few people and of course we are glad to see it providing additional revenues to operate our schools and build highways. Construction of new homes in Allen, although still slow is steady and rejuvenation of older homes have really brightened up the looks of several homes on Broadway. The latest house undergoing rebuilding is the old Miles house on the corner of Cleveland and Broadway. The old Saffarrans place just down the road is about finished and never looked this good before. If we could just keep Reverend Cooley busy buying and fixing up we'd eventually get the whole town upgraded.

The major improvement this year is Farmer's State Bank. This bank has served customers in a wide area around here since 1922. Area residents have depended on this bank for the cash needed to buy, improve and operate their home-grown businesses and farms for over 90 years. Some would say this bank has been the glue that's held Allen together through some rough times. I know they were helpful over the many years I operated a Pharmacy here in Allen and I couldn't have made it without 'em. This year the bank completed their remodel (I think) enlarging their building—taking in the building next door which gave them space for new offices they have needed for so long. A new up to date drive-through was constructed at the bank and altogether giving downtown Allen a bright new look.

Allen's new "Dollar" store is open, looking good and is a busy place. This was another case of an older building being gutted out and completely rebuilt. It looks great and was a much needed addition to retail in Allen. The entire downtown has been cleaned up and looks great. Beverly Wilmoth, Joy Anderson and several "newcomers-old-timers" and just plain helpers did a lot of hard work hanging up old and new Christmas decorations on the main streets of town. The school has erected a large Marquee information sign downtown keeping the community up to date on school events as well as time and temperature. Again, thanks for this attractive addition on Broadway— it looks great.

I like it that our school campus is located right in the middle of Allen. Many schools have moved their campus out to the "boondocks" but I enjoy having our school right where it is. One of the things I enjoy this time of year is going to school events. This year school patrons were treated to the best Elementary Christmas programs ever. Our kids are exceptionally good singers (what me biased?) and the hard work was appreciated. Patrons showed their interest and participation in their kid's lives by packing out the big auditorium. I finally found a seat in the back and thanks to a good sound system I could hear just fine. Special thanks to the music teacher, Mr. Coty, for his hard work.

We continue to have good community support of our winning basketball teams (girls 8-0, boys 7-1) which is also demonstrated by the large crowds attending the games. The "new" gym we built back in 1985 serves its purpose with a lot of capacity and a great playing floor but falls well short of the mark when it comes to lobby space and concessions. Perhaps next time the school works up a building program it can include an enlargement of our lobbies and amenities at the gym. I'm very proud of our school and I especially appreciate what our school board, administration and teachers are trying to accomplish here in Allen. Our school campus has never looked better.

I wish to thank my readers for the emails. I do enjoy hearing from old friends and I wish each of you a healthy-happy new year and that you attend your church. It's a good way to start a New Year.

Wayne Bullard, DPh

01-19-12
On Being Perfect

I am a man who enjoys a very good relationship with his wife—and why not? I cater to her every whim and need while sparing no efforts to make her happy. So it was a little more than surprising when local reporter professional photographer and newspaper editor Dianna Brannan chose to question me about my role as a good husband last Wednesday. You see, several noticed that my wife Pat got to feeling bad during the Allen-Stonewall boy's game. During the 3rd quarter she got real pale (my wife, not Dianna) and I, being the compassionate male, asked her if she was alright. No, she replied, I don't feel very well. I gave her my best practical pharmacist look and told her that she was going to be OK and reminded her that it was two minutes into the 3rd quarter of a very exciting basketball game with the score tied. Yet, in spite of all that she thought she should go home.

I took her out to the parking lot and drove her home letting her out at the back gate. When I got back to the gym there was only two minutes left in the 3rd quarter but Allen was ahead a little bit. The next day Brannan said, in less than a real nice tone, "Boy, you weren't gone long." "Did you take her home or did you just walk her out to the car?" "I took her home, all the way home," I replied—hurt. "In fact, after she got out of the car she fell down in that hole in the yard (a hole she had failed to fill in for over a week) so I got out, helped her up and walked her to the back gate. It was the least I could do." She did indicate that it might be nice if I would help her up the back steps and even stay with her, but when I reminded her of the close ballgame with Stonewall she quickly relented and encouraged me to hurry back to the gym. I did it for her—I knew she would want to know the final score as much as I did and of course we all know how women get carried away sometimes about the least little health problem.

There's a lot more to being a loving, considerate and successful husband than just taking your wife to Branson, movies and ballgames.

After 53 years of caring marriage to my wife I know how important it is to see that your wife stays in good health. That means as she grows older, more trips to the doctor—to nip those sick spells in the bud, so to speak, Along with a proper diet (something she's not likely to get eating out) exercise is very important in maintaining a woman's health. This morning, for example, after she made the beds, washed the dishes and ironed a few of my shirts, my wife started up her vacuum. It wouldn't work. Even though I was very engaged watching an important WWII episode on the Military Channel (featuring some never-before seen film of Hitler) I put it on record, dropped all I was doing, grabbed my screwdrivers and went to work. You see, it wasn't so important to me that the floors be vacuumed every day but her health was. She needed to be pushing that machine around and pretty soon, after I applied some of my male expertise, she was happily back at work—again. I shut the door to the den (It's hard to hear over that noisy thing) and soon found myself enjoying the new pictures of Hitler. Thank goodness for that little black DVR box.

Like life itself, marriage can be a real challenge to the less experienced and the young, but when you rise to meet that challenge, your married life can be very self-fulfilling as well as satisfying. I take my wife to another doctor this week. I don't think there is anything wrong with her but you can't imagine the peace of mind it gives me to know she is healthy and able to continue with her "exercises."

Have a good week and remember if you're married, take good care of your spouse—and for this advice just let me say one more thing: You're welcome. And don't forget to go to church this weekend.

Wayne Bullard, DPh.

**Letha Mae Moore holding neighbor boy (Albert) and
aviator and Nazi killer in goggles is Wayne Bullard 1942**

04-12-12
Going to Church at Centrahoma

Going to church on Easter and watching a group of children line
the stage and sing "Jesus Loves Me" was a treat and a good way to
start an Easter Sunday Service. Participation in the music was not
equal—some of the kids just moved their lips while the others carried
the song along but it sounded good enough to the large group of people
that filled the pews last Sunday at First Baptist Church in Allen.

Believe it or not, it reminded me of another place and another time:

Going to church back in 1941 at Centrahoma. There were 3 main churches open for business those days and we attended all 3 of them. There was also the Holiness but its preacher, Clyde Nickell of Allen couldn't make it over very often. He didn't drive a car plus the old church building was falling down.

My family belonged to the Baptist Church, but the pastor of the Nazarene Church worked in my Dad's grocery store and sometimes we had prayer meetings on Wednesday nights up there. The Baptist preacher only came on Sundays we would go up and listen to Brother Craig (as did some Methodists) as he would conduct and preach. We were pretty liberal about stuff like that in those days with frequent revivals at all 3 churches attended by congregations from all 3 churches. It was the neighborly thing to do and besides, there wasn't all that much to do in Centrahoma anyway.

We had BTU (Baptist Training Union) every Sunday night at the Baptist Church and many from the other churches attended it too. My grandpa called it the BUT. It was at the "BTU" that I had a chance to win a nice looking ribbon—all I had to do was memorize some bible verses, stand up on the stage and recite and identify each. A piece of cake, I figured. My main competition was a pretty little girl and my best friend, Letha Mae Moore. The big night arrived and Letha got up and ran off an impressive amount of verses as did some of the other kids; but really, it was between Letha and me. I got up and did my recitations and sure enough, I had just a little bit more than she did. I won. At least I thought I did.

Letha and I were competitive. Her hand shot up and the moderator asked her what she wanted. "I forgot to say one of my verses" and he proceeded to let her come back and do the forgotten verse. She said, "This is John 3:16 and here it is—For God so loved the world that he went home and forgot his only son." Although she said it wrong, she got the little ribbon. I was a perfect gentleman, of course— after my brother kicked me and told me to calm down and shut up—as she walked up on the stage and took possession of the coveted prize.

Gerald was a worry, too. He had gone up to one of the Methodist Church's revival meetings and gotten himself "saved." Since the Methodist's weren't as fiery as the Baptist and Nazarenes, I worried about his eventual destination but he did stick with us and didn't join the Methodist, instead joining the Baptist. The Methodist guy was smart enough to not stir that pot too much. Sadly, after becoming an adult, he went over to the Methodist after all. But I figured it is probably OK now since I have learned that most of my ancestors down in Alabama were active Methodist (several preachers) and it appears they mostly turned out OK and possibly went to heaven.

Well, anyway, getting back on subject, I hope all of you went to church on Easter and can find your way back there next Sunday. Who knows? You might win a ribbon or something.

Wayne Bullard, Pharm. D.

waynebullard@sbcglobal.net

04-19-12
The 120 MPG Carburetor

I get all my health care up at the VA in Oklahoma City but it's when I am standing in a line or sitting in a waiting room that I find out a lot of stuff. Last week in a slow line I noticed this red-haired guy in front of me, turning around and eyeing the crowd preparing to make a speech. I see this up there quite often and as he started to speak I cleverly attempted to avoid eye contact with him by studying the ceiling tiles. It worked fairly well as he diverted his attention to the two hapless victim's right in front of and behind him. Both were trying to be polite veterans.

"You know it's time they start giving the little guy a break. This gasoline is way too high." About 4 or 5 guys turned around and murmured their approval of the subject and the guy was off and running. "They need to make a decision soon," he went on, "to either up the gas mileage on the cars they sell or mark down their gasoline — it's way too high and they know it." "You know, they can make those cars get whatever gas mileage they want and that's why they cranked it up to 35MPG but now gas is so high they need to set the mileage up to about 50." The guy in front of me looked a little suspicious as he asked him how they could do that.

"It's very simple", the self-proclaimed expert replied. "I served in the Army with a soldier who invented a carburetor that got 120 MPG and that was on a big Ford pickup truck with a V-8." Nobody said anything and 2 or 3 guys turned their backs to him and grinned at each other. "Yeah," the guy went on, "Ford Motor Company heard about it and gave him $150,000 dollars for it and killed it. You know that all those car companies and the oil companies are in this together and they get together and set up the price of oil and gas and decide what mileage they are going to let us have. Yessiree, they are afraid of that carburetor."

The dude in front of me said, "You do know that they quit using carburetor's several years ago, don't you? It's all fuel injectors." "Oh yeah," the guy responded, "but it's all the same." "You think they can just crank up the mileage?" The skeptical listener asked. The guy looked around for some support but everyone got real busy looking at their paper work and I continued my work staring at the ceiling tiles. His audience was gone and besides he was getting close to the head of the line himself. But he knew his work was done and he did review his main points: A "They" committee did indeed exist and they did decide the price of oil and gasoline and more importantly they decided how much gas mileage your car gets.

This must be a true story as I have had this carburetor story explained (with varying details) many times in my life. I have had the "They Committee" explained many times before but I wasn't aware that there was a "They Committee" in charge of gas mileages who also set gas prices. Thank goodness for the VA Hospital.

I hope all of you are enjoying this nice weather and that you aren't worried about the gas mileage you get on your way to church. I have it on good authority that it's being looked after.

Wayne Bullard, Pharm. D.

waynebullard@sbcglobal.net

04-26-12
Take care of those trophies

About 20 years ago I watched as the "Governor's Trophy" (a big gold looking cowboy hat) was awarded to the winner—Oklahoma. Well, as so often happens, OU won that year and much to my surprise one of the OU players put it on and went gallivanting around showing off his spoils. This was the first time I had seen such a relaxed attitude toward such an expensive showpiece, especially a traveling trophy. I wondered what would happen if such an important artifact would get damaged or even lost.

I thought of all that one night while checking to make sure our coveted 1983 Class 2-A State Golden Ball Championship trophy was still in its proper place—in the trophy case in the Allen Gym. It is and I'm always glad no one has stolen it or anything of that sort. It's good that the trophy is properly secured or some kid would (like the OU player in Texas) get it out and start trying to dribble with it.

Getting my thoughts back to OU, they possess seven National Champion football trophies which they keep under better security than which the Government places around the U. S. Constitution on display in Washington, D. C. Then there is Jenni Carlson writing about the carelessness at The University of Alabama. They won one of those beautiful crystal National Championship trophies last year. I don't know how many they have (but I'm sure someone will tell me next week) but they didn't take very good care of this one. Some brainless idiot put the thing on a flimsy pedestal where the first time a clumsy viewer came through, it would get knocked over and broken. Sure enough it wasn't long before an "unnamed" player tripped on the carpet and knocked it off. Broke it to smithereens.

Now you all know me, I'm not all that critical of people but if that old boy is that clumsy he shouldn't be playing football anywhere except maybe at the University of Texas. If you let clumsy people suit up you can wind up like Oklahoma that time in Nebraska. Billy

Sims fumbled the ball away on the 2 yard line and we lost the game. Clumsy! Alabama isn't alone in their ability to make poor choices. Florida State had two trophies stolen in 2004. Then in 2008 a poorly coordinated boy named Orsen Charles somehow fumbled the crystal trophy away breaking it into a million shards. Sounds like a bad joke or something. Perhaps schools like Florida State and Alabama should be made to attend a special school called: "How to care for and protect your new Championship trophy."

Anyway, I'm proud and pleased that so far no one has busted into the Switzer Center or anywhere else in the Gaylord Family Football Stadium and stolen any of our precious trophies nor have they been placed in such a manner to get knocked over, played with or otherwise endangered. You know how free Oklahoma is with that death penalty—not to mention having Bob Stoops mad at you.

All this causes me to wonder: When are we (Allen) going to go after a State Basketball Championship again? It's been a long time since 1983 and while I saw some very good basketball players playing championship level ball most of the season, I didn't see but one who had actually won it and he was the coach.

Before closing I want to say this: The class of 2012 is said to be the best academic class in recent history. They also provided a lot of good leadership for our school and community not to mention the fun and entertainment many of them provided in sports competition. Thanks. We all appreciate you.

Don't forget to go to church next Sunday. And try not to break anything.

Wayne Bullard, Pharm. D.
waynebullard@sbcglobal.net

**Cecil Bullard holding Linda Kay,
Gerald and Wayne**

05-03-12
Fort Holmes

I was driving grandpa to Wister to see some of our kin. It was 1952 and as was his habit, he was talking—talking about old times. "There weren't any good roads then just a few wagon trails he was saying. The meadows were endless and the tall grass everywhere. I

remember being a part of a group of Deputy U. S. Marshalls preparing
to cross a wide valley and they asked me to climb up a pretty good
sized tree to look for smoke. The day was windy and the grass was
dry. If it caught fire while we were out in the middle, we might not be
able to outrun the flames for the grass was up to our horse's bellies."
I tried to visualize how the grasses and trees must have looked as I
drove.

Will Armstrong was born in 1871 and lived a long colorful life as
a peace officer, merchant and farmer. Like many peace officers of
that era, grandpa was often employed as a deputy U. S. Marshall for
the Federal Court in Fort Smith—a famous fellow and judge named
Parker. There are pictures in old copies of the newspaper in Wister
of grandpa escorting a hapless criminal to the hanging tree there in
Wister and another picture of the man dangling at the end of a rope.
Grandpa explained to me the man was arrested by a posse at a fairly
well-known place called "Horse Thief Springs" located on an old army
road now called the Talimena Drive.

Our state is full of history and a lot of it is right here. Out by
Holdenville Lake is the Fort Holmes historical marker—right on
the highway.   Fort Holmes was named for its builder Lieutenant
Theophilus Hunter Holmes, an officer in the First U. S. Dragoons
under Col Henry Dodge.

The Fort was built at the confluences of the Little River and the
South Canadian on the north side. In addition to the Fort, a man
named Edwards built a large impressive store on this site. Edwards
was married to Jesse Chisholm's daughter—the man the famed trail
was named after.

Edwards Store was a good place to lay in supplies as it was the last
store on the old army road which so many traveled on their way to
western lands and the gold fields. By 1850 business was booming as
travelers found the plentiful water and grass in the immediate area to
be a great place to layover and rest. Some liked it so well they settled
in and made a settlement on this side of the Canadian near the area of
the artesian wells that are just south of the Francis turnoff—a place
called Cold Springs.

It's impossible to speak of Fort Holmes without talking about the
Dragoons. These units were special army units wearing extra-dressy
wool uniforms staffed by men who knew how to ride and to strut at
parade. Each unit was outfitted with special and expensive horses—

all the same color. Each company would all be the same color of horses, such as black, whites and one of bays, sorrels and so forth. The Dragoons were a special organized group of companies formed to impress the plains Indians and the "Civilized" tribes who were here from their forced deportation from back east. As the soldiers rode along they were said to be a beautiful site. I'll have more on the fate of the dragoons next week.

In 1834 the Dragoons made a special journey from Fort Gibson to the Kiowa and Wichita country 200 miles to the west—passing through the Allen (Cold Springs) area as they did. This area was already a favorite camp site of buffalo-hunting Indians such as the Osage. The Historical Marker out west of Allen takes note of their passage and next week I'll be writing about this famous group of Army officers and their 400 best-dressed soldiers camping in what we now call Allen. Stay tuned. A lot of things have changed over the past 175 years but some haven't. Be sure and go to church this Sunday.

Wayne Bullard, Pharm. D.
waynebullard@sbcglobal.net

J. T. and Ruby Smith Bullard - Wedding Day - Jan 1, 1900

05-17-12
Have Dogs Will Travel

My Great-Grandfather, Jimmy Bullard (yes there is a long line of Jims in my family) came to Oklahoma back before statehood by wagons. Two of his sons (and families) besides my grandfather, James T. Bullard came with him. It was the first of 3 trips. While the men seemed to get on pretty well in Leflore County the women (bless 'em) didn't. They said the country was too wild for them and my G. Grandmother Sarah Ramsey feared that after she died that the Lord wouldn't be able to find her if she was buried in this wilderness called Oklahoma. She demanded to be taken back to Alabama even if the men folk thought it to be a land of milk and honey.

This was about 1909 after the cotton crop had been ginned that these decisions had to be made. All but my grandpa J. T. and grandma Ruby would return to Alabama and live. J. T. and family wanted to stay. He really liked Oklahoma but the family was more than a little afraid to go alone so J. T. and his entire family loaded up and went with them.

A recurring argument in the days before leaving was: "Are we taking the dogs?" The two dogs were blood hounds and the men weren't about to give them up so grandpa (who seems at this point to be sort of in charge) says they can follow us by foot. And they did. It may have been considered cruel by today's standards (PETA) which would have demanded the dogs be given a ride. I suppose Mitt Romney would have made the dogs ride on top of the wagons while Mr. Obama would have eaten them as he says he did in his book—"Dreams of my Father." But the dogs walked the 750 miles and enjoyed every step of the way.

This trip (as were the others) was eventful and well remembered in family lore. Grandma Ramsey, the worrying Christian for whom the trip back was made, said there was no way she was riding in a wagon 750 miles and announced she would be driving her personal buggy. It was said she had an attitude. The numerous kids in the party walked most of the way too and fussing at times over who would get to ride in grandma's buggy and for how far. She just allowed one rider at a time. A favored milk-cow made the walk too and trudged along without complaint tied to a wagon. The three-wagon train and buggy camped by creeks and rivers and my grandmother Ruby said they crossed the Mississippi on a ferry. "Scared our little old mules to death to get on that ferry," Grandma said.

It was cool weather as they left Oklahoma and they would close the wagons up snug at night to stay warm in their beds. A campfire would be maintained as the men took turns keeping watch over the camp and you can be sure they were armed to the teeth. It snowed in Mississippi and they were allowed to stay in an empty farmhouse a night or two, although my grandparents slept in their bed out in the wagon. Grandma said: "It was a lot warmer in that wagon than it was in that old house."

As you might expect, the two valuable hunting dogs made the trip just fine. "Sometimes they would scout way off wanting someone to come and see what they had but usually we just kept pressing on and the dogs would find their way back to us." Grandma reported that the dogs had a good time over the 90 days it took to get back to Lookout Mountain—brought a lot of pleasure as well as fresh meat to the trip. They were hunters you know." That spring Grandpa and Grandma came back—this time they got rid of their "stuff" and rode a train to Poteau. I still have a recording made by my Uncle back in the 50s on which my Grandma recounts the events of this last epic journey to Alabama—and back.

Have a good weekend and be nice to your dogs. And yes, be sure and go to church this Sunday.

Wayne Bullard, Pharm. D.

05-23-12
The Class of 2012

Marilyn Olivo Coulson was keynote speaker at the Academic Banquet and Awards Ceremony last Thursday night. Marilyn was raised in Allen and is a 1970 graduate of Allen High School. Ms. Coulson is the daughter of Don and Mary Olivo. Marilyn took her bachelor's degree from East Central then went to Oklahoma Christian University in Edmond where she earned a Masters' in Business Administration. Marilyn then won her Juries' Doctorate degree. Marilyn serves as a Vice President of the Home Savings and Loan Company in Oklahoma City as well as an Oklahoma City Municipal Judge.

Judge Coulson pointed out in her keynote speech that Allen Schools have produced doctors, lawyers, teachers, university presidents, judges, politicians and even movie stars over the years making the point that those that want an education here at our school, can certainly get one. I appreciate this lady taking time to remind us that we can be just about whatever we want to be if we work hard for it. Sadly, a few of our kids choose to give up their own futures for reasons that sometimes escape me. Their lives just evolve into an existence that may include failure to launch. Not the class of 2012.

The Mustangs graduated 38 this year. A good number with fewer dropouts than one might expect. The grade point average is way up this year too as this bunch of ambitious youngsters produced six valedictorians and 30 received academic awards. Twenty three were named as Oklahoma Honor Society members. Three (Brook Kidwell, Steve Nelson and James Moss) chose military service to fund their college educations and over $600,000 dollars worth of scholarships were passed out to the seniors on Thursday night. I am very proud of this class of 2012 and congratulate each of them for their achievements.

One more thing: Good classes don't just happen. It takes a lot of encouragement, hard work and dedication on the part of parents to bring these people up through the grades and on to college. A good school staffed by good teachers puts the icing on the cake. I thank each of you.

Have a good weekend and be sure and go to church this Sunday.

Wayne Bullard, Pharm. D.
waynebullard@sbcglobal.net

05-24-12
George Hill Visits the Navy

Everybody knew George Hill. George put out the Coalgate Register for many years and people in Coalgate and Coal County knew everything that happened at a school board meeting or a City Council or the County Commissioner's get together –and more. A few readers probably didn't appreciate George's journalistic efforts. In fact I know that one night one of those disgruntled readers decided to become a newsmaker himself by tossing some dynamite over into Hill's front yard. George told me years later during a football game between Coalgate and Allen "I know who did it" but as far as I know no one was arrested. It blew a hole in the yard and took out George's big picture window.

In 1955 I was serving on board the aircraft carrier Lexington when word came we would soon be hosting a group of 75 weekly Newspaper editors from all over the USA. The captain soon had lists sent around with the names and hometowns of these editors and a plea for any crewmembers from those towns to volunteer to host these people. Within 24 hours every editor had a host and some cases, two. I found it remarkable that out of the 2,500 crew we were able to get that many matchups with the home towns. There was one, however, who was without a host—you guessed it—George. Since I knew who George was you would think I would get on the phone and volunteer but I didn't. I was covered up with work and just didn't want to mess with it. Besides, if you've been in the service more than 6 months you try to keep your mouth shut and keep a low profile. You volunteer for nothing if you know what's good for you.

The ship's newspaper, The Minuteman, had a story the next day thanking everyone for their cooperation and mentioning in passing, that the Coalgate newspaper guy didn't have a host just yet. "Anyone who happened to live anywhere near Coalgate was urged to step forward." I kept quiet. My division officer, a Nazarene preacher (passing himself off as my division officer) named McCluskey called me in and asked if I wasn't from Oklahoma? "Uh yes," I answered, "from Stonewall." "Where is that in relation to this Coalgate place?" He asked. "Well, how far is it?" "Oh, I don't know," looking as dumb as I could. "I guess we could get a map." When Mr. McCluskey questioned me some more I failed to remember living for several years in Centrahoma. The Captain was getting a little worried and had a list of every crewmember from Oklahoma and their hometowns printed out. They got out their maps and I was nailed—and by now had royally miffed Mr. McCluskey, my division officer. I was it whether I wanted it or not and I'm pretty sure it cost me a promotion to ET-2 after he failed to recommend me for promotion the next time I was up. Go figure. I was told that the skipper was more than a little puzzled by my lack of help.

We were steaming off the big Island of Hawaii when the choppers came in. Turned out George and I had a great time that day. Old timers in Coalgate will no doubt remember that time as his visit used up a lot of space in the Register for 2 or 3 weeks. George was kind enough to go to Stonewall and make sure my parents had copies of the paper and some glossy prints of the many pictures he made aboard the Lexington that sunny day so very long ago out in the Pacific. A time that I wish I had gone ahead and volunteered for something.

I would imagine that they who knew him still miss George Hill. He was a good newspaper man—even if he did sometimes "stir things up." I hope all of you have a good week and are sure to go to Church this Sunday. And if you're in the newspaper business you may want to be careful what you write. Somebody might dynamite your front lawn.

Wayne Bullard, Pharm. D.
waynebullard@sbcglobal.net

05-10-12
Osage Village

There is a sign on highway 1 about 3.5 miles SW of Allen which is inscribed "Osage Village." The question I had after the first time I stopped to read it was "Where?" So I've been checking around. The Osage's in question were said to number 600 people. The visiting group was the Dragoons crossing the area on a 200 mile discovery ride across Oklahoma. They had historians, artists and fancy horses. The solders were unique and wore fancy dress uniforms made of wool—impressive but not too bright when you think of how hot it gets here. Each company of soldiers was mounted on matching horses and they were quite a sight in the wilderness of Oklahoma in the 1830s.

Those Dragoons spotted a large group of Osage Indians cleaning buffalo at the edge of present day Allen. It was 1834. The Indian's leader was a one-eyed guy named Black Dog—a big old boy that was seven feet tall. I don't know who was the most impressed with who but it is written that the Osages mainly ignored the soldiers and went on about their work. So much for getting all dressed up and riding matched horses.

Although the Osages lived mostly in NE Oklahoma and the adjoining areas of Kansas and Missouri, they roamed wherever they wished. The dragoons in general were pretty impressed at the sight of the Osages although their guy who wrote the journal wasn't. He didn't much like Black Dog and his group. He described the band as a shiftless people and they reminded him of wandering Gypsies. He also noted that they sometimes went around naked in hot weather further lowering their status in his eyes. Somehow I don't think the one-eyed Black Dog could have cared less. He may have thought them foolish to be dressed so warmly.

The expedition of dragoons led to many treaties with some Indians and provided a lot of information about them to the U. S. Government. The survey also provided a lot of useful information about places for future roads and railroad building. In the end, this march of the Dragoons was a disaster. As the soldiers left the Allen area the weather turned exceptionally hot and the soldiers, wilted in their special dress wool uniforms. Of the approximately 400 soldiers on the expedition, 150 died from heat and typhus but not one from an Indian attack. I have no idea what all those officers along on the trip were doing to see about their soldiers. Perhaps too many of these officers just went along to do their own jobs of exploring, surveying (and resume building).

Those who survived straggled back to Fort Gibson. They were nearly naked, emaciated, sick and exhausted. Some of the several officers along with the dragoons included names like Jefferson Davis, George Cooke, and Henry Leavenworth (buried near Kingston). The army's artist on the trip was the famous George Catlin. I wonder if the tall Indian Chief, Black Dog saw the Dragoon's return. I would guess that he was not surprised at the outcome of this march. I think I know how the solders must have felt—at least the ones that got back. I remember taking a long 3 week Bullard-family-vacation out west one July in 1947 in an un-air-conditioned Nash. We looked pretty bad too when we finally got home. Luckily no one died.

Have a good weekend and if you decide to ride a horse across Oklahoma this summer you may want to wear something besides a hot wool army dress uniform. Be sure and go to church this Sunday.

Wayne Bullard, Pharm. D.
waynebullard@sbcglobal.net

Old Allen Water Tower

06-07-12
Summer time in Allen

"Why do you put your email address on your articles?" It's an oft-asked question by people who worry about things like that. It's very simple—I enjoy hearing from my readers. I get very few "crank" letters and heck, those that I get are interesting. Most of it is friendly, welcome and interesting. Some mail comes from those that I've lost contact with and others are written so I can get "straightened" out about the facts of my stories and I welcome those letters too. All of us need to be "straightened out" once in a while—especially if we're wrong. Some of the letters are concerned about my lack of intelligence or wonder about my level of education.

One persistent writer speculated that I was not only an idiot conservative but also a racist. He wanted to know in another letter if I had ever traveled anywhere outside of Allen. I assured him (in a huff) that I had tripped both to Ada and Holdenville and had even lived among the savages of Coal County. So let it be said I generally enjoy hearing from my readers and your emails are welcome. It helps if you will mark something on the subject line saying something like "re-article."

Summer is now in full swing—the pool is open and little kids are seen walking and riding bikes up and down the mostly quiet streets of Allen to go swimming. The parks look well trimmed and ready for play and they are well utilized. The city is doing a great job keeping everything mowed and cleaned up and everyone is looking forward to the upcoming annual alumni gathering. In spite of my enjoying our idyllic life in this little small-town-paradise, my wife and I are consulting our highway maps trying to plan some trips while this summer hangs on. Stay tuned.

The Memorial Day program down at the cemetery was well attended and Aaron Finney did a great job honoring our hero's in his speech. Doug Stinson was Master of Ceremonies at the well-attended ceremony. Afterwards the veterans were honored by the Allen Masonic Lodge members with a great hamburger and hotdog lunch. Thanks guys!

I have had some emails asking about Pat's health. Most of you may remember that she carelessly fell down a few times last year and now has developed some problems to her right leg and knee. Being a thoughtful and loving husband, I kept a close eye on her swollen knee and her bad limp. After a few months I took her to the doctor even though I felt it was healing up—however slowly. But you all know how women are with their pain so just to be on the safe side I took her to a right knee doctor. He sided with her and is putting on a big brace. I, being the compassionate and free-spending husband am going ahead with this on an ASAP basis. My friends and family, especially my sister in Ardmore (who always sides with her) think it's the thing to do and so do I since I found out it's covered by her insurance.

The steady march of old age caught up with me last week too. A painful hip and a nosy wife drove me to go to the VA. I had them check me over real good to see if anyone had missed any bullet wounds from the war but they found no signs of wounds or the war on me. The young female doctor who took charge of me gave me some shots and sent me home with medications. Contrary to what my former friend Donny Johnson said at Church Sunday night, it was not a Midol Dose Pak. It was a Medrol Dose Pak. And yes, I am feeling better.

Thanks to each for your phone calls and inquiries—in case any come—and I hope all of you have a good weekend. Be sure and go to church this Sunday.

Wayne Bullard, Pharm. D.

06-14-12
The Moon, the Train
and Sleeping out in the yard

The great depression of the 1930s was not kind to rural Oklahoma. In fact, long after a measure of prosperity had returned to America, one little town I happened to live in called Centrahoma had failed to get the word. The only ones that went on about their business unaffected by the bad economy were the kids. Three lingering grocery stores, a gas station and Ms. Vestal's Post Office fought a brave but losing battle in keeping up appearances. Oh, and did I mention the railroad?

The track through Centrahoma ran from Oklahoma City to Atoka. It was said to have gone broke during the first dust storm and served little purpose afterwards but to give Hobo's and traveling Okies a free ride out of town. The little train had tried to drop passenger service but the people in the Corporation Commission said no. They did, however, allow the train to replace its passenger train (just had one) with the little motorized trolley the locals quickly renamed "The Dinky." There was just one. It headed up in Oklahoma City and provided service to the occasional passengers to places like Ada, Stonewall, Tupelo and points East as far as Atoka.

After the big war started (WWII) President Roosevelt wouldn't let the defunct railroad line shut down, worrying that he might need it for the war effort. I'm not too sure how much time he personally spent worrying about our train service but the little line was paid to keep their steam engine and one dinky going. Sometimes they would just roll into town with a few empty box cars and park the train—leaving it at a slow idle—hissing and spewing and making some noises that defied description. Sometimes it would return and just sit there huffing and puffing on the north side of our back yard—just waiting for some business.

My brother Gerald was a great believer in fellowship and it wasn't long before we had gotten past the warnings from the caboose: "You kids can't come in here" to just being family. One cold winter week I remember us giving away some of Dad's stove-wood to make points with the crew that had holed up and had to stay with the train. I don't know how they survived in that little caboose on the rear of that old steamer. But those were good memories for Gerald and me. We had hoped for a short ride, perhaps with us driving the big steamer—just a little way up the track and then back. It never happened but my brother said, "Doesn't hurt to ask." I think we were the only ones in our family—maybe in Centrahoma that appreciated this little dysfunctional train.

The next summer it got really hot. It was so hot that mom decided to put our beds out in the back yard. There was no fence and so our move to the cooler outdoors was very public. It worked too except my mom worried that one or more of her kids might stray and fall into the well that was right in the middle of the yard. Mom worried a lot and mostly out loud so many nights my little sister and I felt we should be sleeping in a life jacket lest we drown in the well. But there wasn't that much sleeping going on. The train joined us every night—that and what seemed like the brightest full moon since Xerxes took over Persia.

One night mom asked dad, "Cecil, what on earth are you doing?" "Trying to pull off this light," he replied. He was dreaming and standing up in the bed trying to find a stringed light switch to the moon. The faithful train would sometimes interrupt its irregular hissing and noisily pull out in search of cargo about 3:30AM. Just in time too: Dad opened up at 4 AM. It was a strange train but then I suppose we were a little strange ourselves.

Those hot and wonderful days are gone but not forgotten. There were a lot of nice families with lots of good kids to occupy our play time those dreamy long-gone days in Centrahoma--the place with an old dysfunctional steam train that didn't have much business or anyplace to go —but neither did the sleep deprived residents of Centrahoma. Have a good weekend and don't find yourself without a place to go this Sunday—you're always welcome at your church.

Wayne Bullard, Pharm. D.

06-21-12
Special Town

The big alumni gathering has finally come and gone and a fine one it was—like a reunion ought to be. There was lots of visiting, music and fellowship. I especially enjoyed the time Friday night at the street dance—as a large crowd just lounged around looking pretty casual as they enjoyed the music and burgers while keeping a keen eye out for perhaps someone special they would like to see. It happened a lot and when it did you could hear the explosion of happy words and laughter between friends and old classmates. It was a fun time for me too.

Seeing some of the old teachers show up was great for all of us. I think the single biggest out of town VIP present was Allen's foremost and most famous band teacher, Tommy Allen. My wife and I were first introduced to Mr. Allen and his band the 2nd day of being in business in Allen, Dec 23, 1963. This particular Monday morning he stopped his band, right faced 'em and played a tune or two for us. It was the band's way of welcoming us to Allen and as we walked out of the store to listen to them giving us a welcome salute I knew I'd never heard a better band. Pat and I were greatly honored—and impressed.

The Allen High School Marching Band in those days defined Allen. They set a tone of excellence in their discipline, marching and playing in every way possible that may never be equaled here again. During Tommy Allen's tenure he won just about every band meet he entered. The biggest win was "Tri-State" in Enid. The band overcame a lot of obstacles and even opposition and had it not been for the "band mothers" and other boosters raising a lot of money and standing up for the band and its director it never would have happened. Excellence is hard to define sometimes but when I want an example, I think Tommy Allen.

As I mentioned earlier, when Mr. Allen "practiced" his band he often took them right down HW-48—in downtown Allen. And if he wanted to stop the band and do a concert, he did. I remember one time an 18-wheeler revved its engine at the band. I don't know if anything was said or not but it was an uneven standoff as Mr. Allen gave him "a look" and that was the end of that. The band finished and marched off and as usual, looking very sharp out in front of the little motorized procession.

Although I was born here, I'm not an Allen graduate. My family left here in 1938 when I was 3 but 23 years later I made it back and I'm glad I did. Allen is a special community with some very special people in it. I live here by choice. I hope in the years ahead we can take some of that same positive energy (spell that hard work) that made Mr. Allen's band will be used to make our school and community into something better— a better place to live and raise our children. Support your school officials as well as your hard working city employees. It's an easy thing to gripe and complain about problems rather than pitching in and helping out. Remember, a little hard work by all of us keeping our yards cleaned up, the litter picked up out of our streets and parks goes a lot further than griping about it. It's a great way to show respect for your neighbors and their property. Have another great weekend and be sure and go to church Sunday.

Wayne Bullard, Pharm. D.

waynebullard@sbcglobal.net

06-28-12
Manliest City Award

I was pleased to read in the paper this week that Oklahoma City has been voted "The Manliest City in America" award. A very manly guy named Bert Sperling ran the research study funded by Mars Chocolate North America and Combos snacks. Bert ranked 50 Metropolitan areas and as I noted above, Oklahoma City came in first.

What, you may be asking, constitutes a manly town? Well, Bert factored in the amount of stereotypical manliness and he found Oklahoma City leads the way per capita in the following categories: drivers of full-sized pickups and American-made cars, number of Western apparel stores and the number of people who like to work on automobiles, fish, hunt, wear cowboy boots, ride motorcycles and do woodwork.

I was surprised to read that Oklahoma City beat out such great bastions of manliness as Columbia, S. C. and Birmingham, Ala. Another well known expert on manliness, Brett McKay (the founder of the Art of Manliness) who runs an internet blog with 8 million hits a month and 40,000 twitter followers wasn't surprised that Oklahoma City won. McKay ticks off several reasons that the manliness of Oklahoma City has driven it to the top. These reasons include our land run history, the recent success of the Thunder and of course, James Harden's beard. Who knew?

One can hardly read such breath-catching stories without wondering how many other manly towns exist in Oklahoma. By using their own measuring stick I think I could safely and with confidence submit my own hometown, Allen, Oklahoma into this lofty company. It would need to be placed in the population category of one to 1,000 people. And don't worry—work is already underway.

A careful study by yours truly revealed several positive points of interest. We not only have a great showing on full-sized pickups we have large groups of the ¾ ton and larger variety—nearly all of which are diesels made right here in America. Very few of those foreign-made Nissans and Toyotas show up in front of the Quick-Pic in the early morning hours. I now park my little ½ ton sissy Chevy truck in the back—out of sight—embarrassed. The moment belongs to the big American made Diesels growling and clattering like high spirited stallions—anxious to tackle a manly day of work. Well, just as soon as their manly masters finish up that cup of very manly strong Coffee.

All we have to do now is decide where to put that trophy when we finally get to compete. And did anyone say something about a best beard contest? Have a great week and be sure and join me in Church Sunday. I'll be the manly looking guy on the 4th row.

Wayne Bullard, Pharm. D
waynebullard@sbcglobal.net

07-03-12
Manliest people II

Last week's article on "The Manliest City" caught the eye of many readers. One of the things brought to my attention—and I apologize to all of you who were offended by my omission—is the manly practice of eating "Lamb Fries." I can't think of any place outside this region that is as dedicated to a good plate of "cowboy caviar." Also called "calf fries" by some, this delicacy (spurned by the less manly) not only makes for a delicious plate but in itself helps to make a more manly man—at least that's what some of my more manly friends say.

I am sorry, too, about not mentioning what laypeople call "hand fishing." This ancient sport involves catching fish by hand, of course. It is commonly called "noodling" and is shown frequently on channels 240 (Dish) and other manly channels. A former Allen physician publicized the sport by writing a medical article which describes not only the malady of "noodler's thumb" but offered valuable insight into the sport itself. The main purpose of the published article was to show the cause and treatment of this sport injury. The writer, John Oglesbee, M.D., a manly physician indeed was a frequent visitor to the nearby South Canadian River where there is an abundance of shallow flowing water. This stream harbors deep holes that serve as home to catfish that may weight over 100 lbs. Diving down into these deep holes wearing only denim shorts with eyes wide open and placing one's hand in the mouth of one of these giant fish requires a lot of manliness indeed—or something.

Several other suggested activities include things that I don't consider being all that manly. There is, after all, a very fine line between being just plain stupid and being manly. Walking a tight-wire across Niagara Falls is a manly thing but trying to jump it with a four wheeler is not. Racing up and down low rivers-beds in a 4-wheeler drunk as a skunk falls into this category too. Not manly. Same way with tattoos—doesn't do any more for you than putting on an earring.

In fact, if you're plastered with body piercings and tattoos, you're going the wrong way. One nice thing about an earring though, you can take them off but those ugly tattoos stay with you—during job interviews and everything.

A reader in Utah wrote me that although he had never been to Allen, he felt that Rock Springs, Wyoming would have us all outdone. Rock Springs, he said, is populated by miners, ranchers and oilfield workers and has a "cathouse" (whatever that is) on every corner. A. R. True, and old veteran and former shipmate of mine would know a manly town if he saw one and I concede that to him, for the moment. Rock Springs may be a manly town but the last time I was in Wyoming I didn't see any cases of noodler's thumb.

It's the 4th of July. We usually call it a July the 4th weekend but it landed on a Wednesday this year—sort of messing everything up. Many will stay at home this year which gives the "manliest" guy in the house a chance to show off his cooking skills out on the grill. But aside from that, this year is kind of a downer. You can make an extra-long weekend if it falls on any day other than a Wednesday. I never did like Wednesdays anyway and that may be why. So this year, along with many others, I'll just stay at home. I can still remember pulling in home late in the evening, my boat all nasty, and my body sunburned and tired and having to get up in a few short hours and get back to my job.

So, as you enjoy the day with your family remember those who sacrificed so very much a very long time ago so we can live in freedom in this great land. And don't forget to go to church this Sunday—another thing manly men do.

Wayne Bullard, Pharm. D.
waynebullard@sbcglobal.net

07-12-12
Not So Manly After All

I really didn't intend to have another word about this manliness thing. But there has been a lot of comment. Trying to judge who might be the manliest is similar to what the judge said about porn: "I can't exactly define it but I know it when I see it." Some of my readers who equate eating "calf fries" with manliness but then admit they haven't really eaten any in several years—well, it's hard to say if they're just trying to help their image or what.

For the past few years the famous dish has been in short supply. People who buy this delicacy found that actually getting their hands on this commodity was more trouble than one would think. One restaurant, Giacomo's in McAlester, didn't have any of the fries for a long time. I know in the past that people either at my table or in earshot tried to order only to be informed that none were available and nor would there be any soon. It seems that the middlemen on the product, the guys who actually capture these delicious morsels from their unwilling victims had failed to make the product of their work available to the market. Too much trouble they said. But the increasing prices have caught their eye—so the snipping resumes.

Now all is well. It was just a few weeks ago when I learned that the famous "Cowboy Caviar" was again available. I was in Giacomo's and as it turned out I had already ordered their famous steak instead. Maybe next time—if I feel manlier I'll give it a try. Chesley Ray weighed in on the question after reading the columns and asked if I ever went to Minnie's down at Krebs anymore. I had to tell him (sadly) that Minnie's had been closed and gone for several years but that Pete's Place down the road was still going strong. Chesley, old timers may remember him by the name of "Tiny" is a kid brother of the late Walker (Corky) Ray and attended school here back in the ancient 40s. Next time "Tiny" comes back I'll try to take him down to McAlester (Krebs) and have him eat some fries—and I'm not talking

French fries. We'll send him back to California manlier—maybe they'll rename him "Big Boy".

On a more important topic, Brenda Capps has just about finished her new home on Broadway. It's my favorite kind of home—a rebuilt and redone old house—a home with personality. I hope she'll have an open house when she gets all finished and remembers to invite me over for a look-see. I imagine that house has a lot of history. Preserving an old house is a worthy challenge and I am always glad to see an old home saved from the wrecking ball. It's bad to just see them rot to the ground. Way to go, Brenda. I'll have some more "stuff" about things on my favorite street (Broadway) another time.

Gardens are about as good they get this year. After last year's big crop failure (at least in my fields) it's good to see a great variety of tasty tomatoes back on my cabinet with more where those came from. My okra and tiny corn patch didn't overdo however. My co-planter and agricultural adviser, Meegan Costner was in charge of planting, layout and engineering. Her "garden boy" was me. We both learned some new things about gardening. One thing: Always keep track of exactly what you are planting. It's discouraging to plant Watermelons and reap pumpkins. To plant squash and get gourds. To plant sweet bell peppers and get jalapenos. This comes when you sort out your seeds in the house, plant them in little cups and label them later. It does make things interesting though.

I hope all of you have an enjoyable weekend. Be sure and go to church next Sunday. It might help you with your manliness project.

Wayne Bullard, Pharm. D.

waynebullard@sbcglobal.net

07-19-12
Tuning In To The Preacher

Lots of stuff happens over on Broadway in Allen. One day a resident up there gave me a call and asked me if I would deliver her prescriptions up there myself as she needed to talk to me about some church matters. I told her I would and later that afternoon I gathered her medications up for delivery. Ollie Hall called and asked: "Are you taking medicine to Wilma Doyle?" I knew that Ollie Hall, Nora Weldon, Carrie Muse, Wilma Doyle and Ma Kytle kept in close communication about their Dr. visits, their medical conditions and just about everything else so before I left for Wilma's house I had orders from some of the other ladies in that "Broadway social" circuit.

I stopped at Wilma's first. The TV was on and tuned to the Trinity Channel. A preacher was going strong—preaching away. Wilma said, "I'm glad you're here right now—I want you to hear this young man preach for a moment." I told her OK but that I didn't have much time. After about 5 seconds she said, "I'll bet you're missing my tithe down at the Baptist Church." "Well," I answered, "uh no, what happened to it?" "Last winter I was sick in the night and when I got up this little guy here was on TV at two in the morning and he's preaching his little heart out. He comforted me." "I decided" she went on, "to send my offering to him instead of the church— none of you guys ever come up here and help me at night when I'm sick and if he's willing to get out of his bed and preach to an old lady at 2:A.M. I'm willing to give him my offering." I started to explain about video tape but heard myself say, "I don't blame you."

I asked her what's the deal on your tape machine. You have your phone on it and that sounds like our pastor talking. "It is, she replied. I'm making Ollie Hall listen to it." You know we have a tape ministry and her church does too. She plays her sermons to me and I play mine to her." "Of course, I don't really listen to her preacher—he's not any

150

good. I just lay the phone on the end table but don't you tell her." I assured her I wouldn't.

I left her house and went to Ollie Hall's. She let me in and we visited a bit. I said to her, "your phone is off the hook," sounding as innocent as I could. "Oh," she said, with that twinkle in her eye, "that's Wilma. She's making me listen to her pastor's sermon. I make her listen to my pastor and she makes me listen to hers. Of course, I don't actually listen to hers but it makes her happy." Those lady customers of mine around and about Allen were a constant source of amazement, amusement and inspiration to me over the years and I miss every one of them.

Beverly Burkett Wilmoth lives in the house that Ollie Hall lived in so long. She has fixed the little place up and now it is again, a pretty little home on Broadway. This house fell into a state of neglect for a few years after Mrs. Hall passed on and Beverly really did a nice job fixing it up and making it once more a pretty home. Wilma Doyle lived in the big blue-topped house on up East of Ollie about 2 blocks. We had a few laughs over the fact that I too lived in that house in 1936 with my dad, mom and big brother. It was a duplex then and cost us $5.00 a month rent for the east end. Sadly this fine old house burned last winter resulting in the tragic death of the late Wilma Doyle's daughter-in-law, Pat Doyle.

We continue to enjoy great summer weather here in Allen complete with timely rains which keep us all hopping to stay ahead of our lawn mowing chores. I hope all of you are enjoying the stuff out of the gardens this year as much as Pat and I are. Have a good summer and be sure and go to church this Sunday.

Wayne Bullard, Pharm. D.

07-26-12
Michael Hooper Dying

Good news! Michael Hooper, the guy on death row at McAlester who is suing the state over his impending execution can now relax. The State received 20 more doses of the "medication" they will use to put him to sleep. Hooper and his lawyer have been concerned and even sued the state over the pain he may feel when he's executed August 14. There're was only one dose of pentobarbital left (the drug that puts him to sleep before we kill him) and up to now the state had no extra doses. Hooper was fearful (so he said) that if the dose failed he could suffer pain and suffering as the killing drugs worked on him. Like I said—not to worry—we have plenty.

Actually I feel that those put to death by the state should be "killed" humanely but I can't help but recall that this monster/felon shot a 23 year old woman through the head twice and then shot each of her two young children also twice in the head. Perhaps if the state continues to have a problem executing people of this sort—convicted murderers— they should consider new laws allowing the state to hire veterinarians to put these people down. In fact as I think about it, it would be somehow appropriate. But we have more important things to worry about than how to kill this guy.

Those of us who worry more about expensive repairs to our lawn mowers due to ethanol-in-your gas damage may be less dismayed by Michael Hooper's impending death than our gas/ethanol problems. The government is soon to take away our ability to buy 100% gasoline. However, it seems that the 10% ethanol/gas mixture is hard on small engines and older cars. My car burns the mixture just fine (the millage is a bit lower) but it's pretty aggravating to be mowing and your mower conks out due to a government mandate that is wrong. To make things even worse the fuel mixture is going up to 15% ethanol soon. This may require people to buy new vehicles—another blow by a liberal government against poor people who may not be able to afford corn ethanol and its effects.

These laws were dreamed up when it was thought that most of the world's oil resources would soon be gone and we would be riding horses and drifting back to the stone ages. But sadly we now have more oil reserves than we can say grace over and there is no need to trouble the taxpayers with these expensive corn subsidies and foolish laws forcing an unwilling electorate to use this inferior and expensive fuel. Even more sadly, the corn/ethanol industry has become addicted to the ethanol subsidies while stockmen can't afford to feed out their livestock on corn that has to compete with a highly subsidized corn/ethanol market. The taxpayers get to pay twice: Once when their taxes go to subsidize this ethanol and 2nd when they have to pay higher prices for beef and pork. Oh, and need I remind you once more of the inferiority of ethanol in engines?

Enough of this complaining. I'm having a good week. My wife is home from her hospital stay in Tulsa and improving every day. Thanks for your prayers, cards and calls this week. We appreciate it. Have a good week and be sure and go to church this Sunday

Wayne Bullard, Pharm. D.

waynebullard@sbcglobal.net

08-2-12
Lamb Among Lions

One writer said, "Republicans don't go to NAACP conventions to win votes any more than Christians went to the Coliseum to convert the Lions." I think Romney went before the NAACP conventioneers so he could get booed—not convert the audience. This podium also gave him a place to attack teacher unions. Romney basically told the group that they couldn't have it both ways—talking up education reform, while promoting the same groups that are blocking reform. Romney said teacher unions are the biggest obstacle in our society to quality education. Romney invited and challenged the NAACP group to opt for real education reform as a way to achieve success for black society. But Romney was wasting his breath. Republicans lost the black vote back in the days of Hoover and they won't be back for Romney. Ditto for the Jewish and Hispanic vote as expectations for a Romney win continue to fade.

Why? Obama can count on the black, Hispanic and the Jewish vote to go for him no matter what he does or what he might say. Another ace for him is the main-stream press. I was amazed this morning watching the Today Show. If you pay attention to them you would think Obama is a cross between Abraham Lincoln, The Lord and George Washington—a savior of the common person while Romney is a cross between the devil and Adolph Hitler. The love of Obama on NBC was almost erotic.

Of course, some soothsayers think the democrats are digging themselves into a hole with their love of the unions—that it will backfire. Conservative democrats (such as me) become more and more detached as we wait for our party to return from the left back to center. There are a lot of defections here in Oklahoma as more and more Democrats switch to independent status or move over to the Republican Party. Upscale middleclass black voters and Hispanics are also drifting away from the party—but very few. Meanwhile, the

Carters, Clintons and of course the Obama's have shown a marked favoritism toward the PLO and other Arab political/terrorist groups whose main stated policy is to kill every Jew that is still alive. So how much longer do you suppose we democrats will be able to count on the Jewish vote? We've done everything in the world to run 'em off.

What about other "government dependent" citizens? Will there be enough of these "pocketbook" voters to cancel out the votes of taxpaying people? And as more black voters continue to move up the economic ladder into the middle class (and supposedly into the arms of the republicans) will it counter-balance the food-stamp crowd? And of course, the big question: What happens in years ahead if the government becomes unable to keep its many commitments to social security and welfare? It could get very ugly and the political dynamics from such a condition are unknown.

Meanwhile, my democratic registration card rests uneasy in my billfold as I still can't make myself go over to the Republicans. Perhaps it was that Hoover guy or maybe I'm just lazy. Whatever, I hope you enjoy the last few weeks of summer. School starts soon and that means football— a whole lot better game than politics. Be sure and go to church this Sunday.

Wayne Bullard, Pharm. D.
waynebullard@sbcglobal.net

08-15-12
Coming To America

The busy streets looked clean and prosperous as I stepped off the shuttle bus from Travis Air Force Base to the Federal Building in downtown San Francisco. I had been in America less than an hour after being gone over a year. The flight from Tokyo had been hectic with a hard landing on Midway grounding the plane and passengers — all 120 of us for several hours with a damaged strut — the plane, not the passengers. Finally another Super Connie flown by Capitol Airlines arrived from Honolulu and got us back to America. When the coast came into view the passengers (nearly all were pregnant military dependents) broke out into applause. I was sort of surprised and not sure if they were cheering for America or celebrating the fact we made it home alive.

I stood on the sidewalk for several moments taking in the scene — it was the fall of 1956 and there were new cars on the clean streets and everything looked real prosperous and good. Well dressed citizens going here and there — it was good to be home in America again. I climbed into a taxi and there was a new kind of music on the radio. I wasn't sure I liked it all that well but knew I could grow to like it. Something called rock and roll. I remembered the women applauding their sighting of America and with a lot of pride realized that there really is specialness about our United States of America. There was a lot to applaud indeed. My rock and roll playing taxi took me to some of my relatives out in South San Francisco and after some good food and visiting I was driven over to Oakland for a flight to Dallas.

In 1956 you could still grab a DC-3 commuter plane out of Dallas to Ada and the next day that was where I landed — headed to Stonewall. Stonewall looked pretty good too that sunny October day. More recent trips in and out of the country to Mexico or Canada or Europe didn't evoke the applause of that nice October day off the California coast but it has always been grand to come home to America and I guess it always will be.

There were a lot of things that made the United States extra great in those years following WW II. The USA was riding high having not only making it possible for us and our Allies to win the war but we were untouched by bombs and war damage—a very important consideration. It was then that America established its greatness and goodness in the mind of people throughout the world— something called "The Marshall Plan." The USA spent billions worldwide rebuilding and restoring a war-torn world to prosperity.

Decades have gone by and many people feel that America has lost some of its greatness and values. A lot of things have for sure changed and we are poorer in some respects because of them. America again, finds itself in a time of great change. Massive illegal immigration of people who differ a lot from the influx of Europeans over 100 years ago is having some strange effects on our overall culture.

Will America be able to assimilate these people the same way they assimilated the Europeans? If we don't can America continue to be the greatest place in the world? Or will we just slide backward taking on the look of a littered Haiti with sinking economies like those in Europe? There are some things we can do about all this. We can get more involved in school and civic affairs seeing that our kids get a good education and seeing that local schools are financially able to carry out their mission. Speaking of which school starts next week so let's be careful in the school zones.

Meanwhile, be sure and enjoy the nice fall weather which is bound to be just ahead and don't neglect going to church next Sunday.

Wayne Bullard, Pharm. D.

waynebullard@sbcglobal.net

08-23-12
Driving Charley Home

I never knew why Velma would trust me to drive her husband's car. For one thing, I didn't have a driver's license. I was 14 and this was over at Stonewall. The deal was this: You just kept off the highway and the local cops didn't bother. Some people (like Velma) were known to complain about kids driving—especially if they squeaked their tires, or ever showed out while driving past certain members of the opposite sex. There were some other complications too. Velma had a phone and she wasn't afraid to use it.

So how did I come to be a driver for Velma at age 14? Me not her. First of all, Charley and Velma lived 3 blocks from their business yet each would drive their own separate Chrysler to their pharmacy each morning. Secondly, sometimes Charley would, for whatever reason(s) take a drink or two too many as the day wore on and then wouldn't be able to drive home. There they were, stuck with 2 cars and only one driver. That's where I came in. I was asked one day to drive his car home and park it in the garage which I did. She offered me 50 cents for my services which I wouldn't take. Where else would a 14 year old car crazy kid get the opportunity to drive a brand new Chrysler that cost $15,000.00—a princely sum back when new Chevrolets were going for $895.00 a piece? Since my price was right and I was willing to walk back to town afterwards, I got that job every once in a while.

I had another motive. Remember Velma's phone? She had called my dad twice to let him know I was driving in a reckless manner. This got me in all sorts of trouble at home but I pretended whenever I was in the drug store she and Charley operated that I didn't know she had called and she pretended that she didn't know that I didn't know that she knew. So our strange little relationship thrived over the years until I went away to answer my call to the Nation's military draft in 1954. During that time I developed a good relationship with Charley who was the town pharmacist (and a man I admired) over at Stonewall and we spoke more than once about my own aspirations to become a pharmacist.

My plotting to be good buddies with Charley and Velma failed miserably in one respect, she continued to tell on me whenever she thought my driving was less than proper. Of course I was extremely careful with their Chrysler as she knew I would be. Thanks to Velma and her phone I did eventually develop better driving skills and habits. Meanwhile, Velma, Charley and I remained good friends.

Velma's work on me was to bear dividends sooner than later. A few short months after getting into the Navy I stood in front of a grizzled old Marine sergeant who had told a large crowd of about 150 of us waiting to start a new school that he was trying to fit us into some temporary jobs so we could be busy. The first job he announced was for 15 typists. Although Mrs. Nelms had taught me to type and type fast, I didn't raise my hand. I just didn't want to have to sit in an office and type all day. The next job skill was for someone who could operate the little speed-boats they said they used to patrol around the island we were on out in San Francisco Bay. Several hands went up and the jobs were gone. I had to admit that the job sounded pretty good and there weren't too many of us left.

The next call went out for 6 men to answer the office phones and run errands over at the Chief's Quarters. A few hands went up but not mine. I was not some Chief's errand boy. The last call for the tiny handful left was for staff car drivers for highly ranked officers. I remembered my days of driving Charley's new Chrysler home for Velma and knew this was the job for me. I was selected for this choice billet. A few minutes later I learned the whole exercise was a cruel trick by the old Sergeant with the microphone. All 150 of us had been had and were given a trash bag, a stick with a nail on the end and told to pick up trash. All day. Fortunately I was too "smart" for them and had no intention of picking up trash all day. I worked my way around behind the large Enlisted Men's Club where food and pinball machines was available and hid my despised trash bag and stick. There were already 150 bags and sticks out there and I was one of the last to join the rest for a day of goofing off and drinking coffee. My training as a professional driver was wasted. Sorry Velma.

Hope you are enjoying the nice fall weather and will be sure and go to church this Sunday.

Wayne Bullard, DPh

08-30-12
Take care of your wife first

A guy at the post office stopped me and with a look of concern asked: "How is your wife doing?" "Oh she's coming around OK, getting stronger every day." "Well, it takes time to get over surgery," he replied and we both nodded, looking as grim as we could. I went on down to the Advocate to see if Bill had brought the papers yet—and he had. "How's Pat?" Bill asked almost immediately. "Oh," I replied tiredly, "she's doing OK for the shape she's in." Bill then said, with the Wisdom of Solomon, "We should be asking how you are doing, shouldn't we?" "Yes, you should, Bill. No one knows but just a few of us just how tiring is can be to take care of a sick wife. You of all people know how wives can be when they are a little off their feed."

When my wife ails I try not to make matters worse by trying to wait on her myself. A woman gets her personal satisfaction from waiting on a man and if he is considerate and wise he will allow her to do just that. As painful as it can be I have tried to do just that—allow her to do what makes her feel so good—waiting on me—something that always makes her feel better about herself. Oh yes, I know; it's a lot easier to take care of a sick wife if she will just sit down and let us wait on them but most won't easily tolerate that notion. As a female, she knows (with her female intuition) that it's her duty to wait on the male and when that can't take place—even when she's sick, she feels bad about herself. And that is sad too because we both know she needs the rest during these times that are so trying for the both of us.

My heart went out to her and recently as I said, "Honey you don't feel good—you just got out of the hospital—go in there and sit down and let me fix you some good breakfast." Did she? No! I finally gave up and took a seat in the breakfast room and drummed my nails on the table. Waiting is not my strongest point but wait I did. It seemed like forever but she finally shuffled around and served me some eggs over easy, bacon, orange juice and toast. I had already taken coffee but it was tepid by the time I got the rest of my breakfast. I held back on any criticism (far be it for me to create any more guilt she must have been feeling about this breakfast) as I slowly poked around the flaccid eggs and strange microwave turkey bacon. The toast had a strange quality of ocean sponge in it, but not a word of criticism escaped my lips. I love my wife, sick or well, as I sat there—my heart nearly bursting with pride and admiration for her beautiful female resolve.

Pat's doing real well now and healing up as she gains even more strength to do the things she "feels" she needs to be doing for me. I'm hoping she will soon feel like cleaning up the house. I cleaned the bathrooms the other day just in case the health department or guests came by and I sure didn't want it to reflect on her. She tries so hard.

Several friends have sent over some delicious foods and my only complaint would be this: I could have used more desserts. I especially thank Donny Johnson for his apple turnovers. If you haven't had any of those I strongly recommend feigning an illness long enough to get him to bring some over. Several of my neighbors and fellow Baptists could take lessons off Donny. Anyway, thanks to all for what you brought over. All of it was delicious and was well worth getting sick over—at least as long as it's her.

I hope all of you have a good weekend and contrary to a rumor I have not tried to sell any of your corning ware stuff on e-bay. I will try to get the rest of it back to you soon. After all, she's not completely well yet and we might need some refills. Be sure and go to church Sunday.

Wayne Bullard, DPh

09-06-12
Building The Church in Centrahoma

Any type of new construction or repair work would catch our eye. "We" being Letha Mae Moore and myself. So far the biggest thing happening in downtown Centrahoma had been when my dad dragged up a second ice-house and set it up just east of the Store. But it was a very short-term job and just as we were really starting to enjoy watching them put the little ice-house in commission it was finished and the big truck drove away. We also paid close attention to highway repairs and trucks that unloaded stuff into the 3 local grocery stores. Sometimes other construction engineers such as Little Annie Smith and Bessie Lee Sorrells would make an appearance.

We were happily surprised one morning to see that someone had laid out a new building just across the highway on SH-3 from our stores. There were the little sticks and strings defining the limits of the new building. Some piles of sand and boards were on the site. We were soon on duty questioning the lone construction worker. He told us it was the start of construction of the new First Baptist Church of Centrahoma. Up to that moment I didn't know there was such a church and that was because that there hadn't been one up to now. It was a big enough deal that Annie and Bessie soon joined us in our interrogation and Q & A of the lone builder. A guy named Marvin Gaskin, a pastor from FBC Coalgate had chartered the church.

The lone worker didn't give us much information except to say he would soon build a very tall brick chimney. We knew we would not be missing out on any of that and we didn't. We watched every brick laid and every board nailed. We couldn't all be there every moment so we took turns and were there as much as we could be to assure what we would call "quality control" in today's world.

Building the little church was fairly simple as it turned out. The chimney serviced a wood burning stove for heat. There was no plumbing, so no restrooms but an outdoor privy took care of that need.

The building was mostly a one room affair with two rooms in the backend that were classrooms. The building was wired and had two or 3 drop-down lights with large bulbs that would make plenty of light for the night services. That light bill was the only bill the church had to struggle with except for a small insurance policy and the ten bucks a week they lavished on their preacher. There was some early-day tension in the little church when one lady harped on and on about the preacher's pay. "If he really loved "Jesus" he would do it for nothing," she complained. "Oh, we should buy him a tank of that 18 cent gas so he can get back to his Seminary down in Ft. Worth and of course we feed him anyhow," she said. As I recall, the preacher got to keep his ten dollars.

Privacy for the Sunday school rooms was insured by hand-sewn sheets which could be drawn making the auditorium into 4 smaller classrooms. I don't remember them being soundproof but I guess they did the job OK. No money for the baptistery and no running water to fill it anyway so new converts were rushed out to Government Lake out south of town for dunking. A time or two I remember them rushing over to Coalgate and using the baptistery at their Church for wintertime emergencies.

I still stay in touch with Letha Mae and Annie and Bessie Lee. Even though Annie was a good Methodist, I'll bet she still remembers the time we supervised the building of the First Baptist Church of Centrahoma. A church, I note, that still stands and serves the Centrahoma community to this day. So I guess we did a good job girls. Be sure and attend your church this Sunday—especially if you expect it to last a long time like FBC Centrahoma.

Wayne Bullard, Pharm. D.
waynebullard@sbcglobal.net

09-13-12
Jefferson and Friends

I was brought up and educated to believe America was always the greatest and most wonderful place in the world. Over in Centrahoma our room had a picture of George Washington high on the wall—you know— that one where his eyes follow you around. American history was laid out like Exodus and our founding fathers were portrayed like Moses—men of valor and of the highest moral fiber. Our heroes in the history books over at Centrahoma and Stonewall were men such as Henry Ford, John D. Rockefeller and Thomas Alva Edison. We revered soldiers of the Revolution and the struggles that followed. America, so we were taught was a very special place and we believed in our "specialness." We were taught that if we worked and studied hard we too would be successful—and that there was nothing at all wrong with work or success.

Of course, following the war years of the 40s, the liberal professors started rewriting American history—destroying reputation after reputation of men long dead---men no longer able to defend themselves against a political smear. Of particular note is Thomas Jefferson. His name and past were severely tarnished by revisionist historians who even had DNA to "prove" this founding father had babies with slave women. It was just a small part of their ongoing efforts to rewrite and shape American history to their own viewpoints—viewpoints that hold America's history in utter contempt.

Lone Beasley of the Ada News wondered in a recent (and excellent) editorial about headlines in 1998 stating that DNA testing had conclusively determined that Jefferson had fathered at least one of slave woman Sally Hemmings' children. Eight weeks later the shocking DNA news was retracted when further investigation of DNA evidence actually determined Thomas Jefferson was not the father of any of her children. In fact and in addition, Jefferson was 65 years old when her first child was born. I never saw the headlines of the retraction nor did it keep Hemmings' kin from claiming poor Jefferson as kin.

David Barton wrote a book about this Jefferson snafu called "The Jefferson Lies" which angered so many of these liberal historians that they finally forced the book off the seller's shelves. Barton's book is both an attack on these historians and a vindication of Jefferson and other heroes. Barton claims the story was cooked up to shore up President Bill Clinton's chances of surviving Congress' attempt to impeach him. The reasoning went thus: "If a man like Thomas Jefferson could do this, then why not Bill Clinton?" It was a very outlandish case of finger-pointing and oh yes, it worked well.

This type of text-book journalistic rewrites include ongoing vicious attacks on Abraham Lincoln and other highly respected leaders from our past who helped make America what it is today. The concept of "Manifest Destiny" a dreamy term coined to describe the very existence of America is now a dirty word. Manifest destiny now means (at least to these new history writers) imperialism, racism, colonialism and war mongering—the very things that Americans have fought and died to overcome in the world.

America is a place of greatness with a sense of fairness. The outside social problems that were dragged into America from abroad such as slavery, class envy and Royalty have and are being dealt with. In order to keep this country evolving into a better place we need to know who we are and what we came from. These revisions and slanderous rewrites of our heroes and history are treasonous with harm meant to America. They are certainly no help.

Have a good week and be sure and go to church this Sunday.
Wayne Bullard, D.Ph.

09-20-12
Progress in Allen

People poking around Allen note a lot of changes taking place. Another new business down on the highway provides food and refreshment for curious and hungry Allenites. It goes by the unlikely name of "Dive In" and the Skelton's are in firm control of the place. The landscaping and décor down there is outstanding and makes our town look proud. Try their Vanilla Cappuccino milk shake if you want a real treat. Another major business is currently in the early stages of construction. A new Dollar Store will make its appearance at the corner of HW-1 and N. Commerce in a few weeks. The city has been busy too. Some more old derelict homes have been flattened and hauled off. I have lost count of how many so far but am promised that more will fall to the wrecker soon.

A lot of work has already been done to make Allen a better place to look at and live in. The City Park and The Walking Trail look better than I can ever remember and with public help and cooperation we can have the best looking little town in the area. Our city workers work hard keeping up with the normal work that keeps our streets open, our garbage hauled off and laws enforced. They help make Allen a nice place to live and I appreciate their hard work.

Helping us get a "leg up" on the litter and trash problem in town the city has two cleanup dates on their calendar. The first is scheduled for October 6th. This cleanup will zero in on the parade route for the annual homecoming parade. The streets will be swept and spruced up. They'll probably repaint the crosswalks and parking lines and do what they can to make the downtown look more photogenic. Then on October 27 there will be the neighbor-helping neighbor project. This city-wide cleanup will give some special help to residents who need it with mowing, hauling off trash, limbs, couches and other "stuff" that seems to find its way onto lawns.

Volunteers with a pickup or trailer are needed to help out that day. The Allen FFA has offered "muscle" to help us haul away our junk. The city hopes you will call and let them know if you need help or want to help with any of these things. They say the phone numbers you should call will be published later and a "dump" site will be provided. One more thing: I know that the people who just toss their litter out the car windows or whatever don't read news articles so it really doesn't do much good to gripe them out in the paper. In fact they may be unable to read! But be reminded anyway to place your trash in the trash cans around town. Don't just throw it on the streets and sidewalks. Those of you owning kids and grandkids might put in a word about this as this costly and unsightly litter is just another form of vandalism and it is something that we can do something about.

Enjoy this great fall weather and be sure and go to church this Sunday.

Wayne Bullard, D.Ph

waynebullard@sbcglobal.net

Inside Bullard Hardware 1954, Cecil Bullard & Herman Wall

09-27-12
Charley Acker and Stonewall

If it hadn't been for Charley Acker the Bullard family would probably never have made it to Stonewall. My dad owned a little grocery down HW-3 in Centrahoma and he banked over at Stonewall. He had tried his hand in the movie business once over at Calvin and hadn't made it but he knew one thing—it was a lot easier and more fun than selling groceries. Mr. Acker was a banker who had operated the First National Bank in Stonewall until a guy named Pretty Boy Floyd walked in with a machinegun and robbed the place. Times were tough back in the 30's and the bank closed and joined forces with the First National Bank of Ada.

Some years later Charley Acker, an officer at the Ada bank, had papers on the old Main Theatre in Stonewall. The little movie house had been doing pretty good until its owner got the thing afire and burned up the projection room. The fire left a hole in the roof and Mr. Peak was shut down. The fire couldn't have come at a worse time for Peak. It was WWII and the local draft board was hounding him. After the fire, the board took Mr. Peak away and he left the ruins of the movie and his home in the capable hands of Mr. Acker.

The Peak house was the same one that Homer Roberts grew up in later. It was during the winter of 1944 that my dad had driven to Stonewall to the bank and he parked his 1935 Ford in front of this old movie house. My brother Gerald and my dad thought it was a palace. To me it was a nasty burned out hull of a building. Somehow dad already knew the bank in Ada was in charge of this property and it wasn't long before a willing buyer and a willing seller met face to face. To sweeten the deal, Mr. Acker threw in the rental property next door to the movie—a store that rented for $25.00 a month to a guy named Shorty Grinstead.

Mr. Acker urged dad to buy the Peak home but he didn't. Instead he bought an old box-type frame duplex whose west half was already rented to two old maid teachers. The ladies quickly developed a distaste for their new unwanted neighbors—us. They finally moved. Another positive development was we had the Ackers just across the street.

The Ackers were excellent neighbors. Mrs. Acker and my mom became good friends and Charley became Gerald's Algebra tutor— saving him from flunking Mr. Duke's algebra class. Meanwhile, Mr. Acker taught me a lot about lawn care—I guess he saw my future as being somewhat different than Gerald's. About 60 years have passed and while my brother now hopefully knows his algebra I know a lot about lawn care. Go figure. Time has removed a lot of people and landmarks in Stonewall but I still like to drive around over there. No one takes much care of Mr. Acker's lawn these days and the old house we lived in burned as did the old Main Theater. I still remember well in my mind, scenes of kids riding bikes down the gravel streets in that neighborhood and I can still see Mr. Acker tending his beautiful yard— his wife looking on from her window. For sure I remember the many good things Ackers did for the Bullard Family.

Have a good week and be sure and go to church this Sunday.
Wayne Bullard, D.Ph.

169

10-11-12
Doctoring up at the VA

My friends know I get my medical care up at the VA in Oklahoma City. The best part about their care is that it's free—at least to me. I also have to admit that the care I receive up there is very well organized and over all is better coordinated and effective compared to the hit and miss care I used to experience in private care. Recently after suffering a chronic pain in my side my primary care guy told me I needed to go upstairs and see the surgeon. He said I had a hernia. So, in due time my appointment came about and I drove back up to the City to see what he thought about it.

I was ushered into an exam room and standing there was this girl. I first thought that it was another one of those "take your daughter to work" days, but no, it was my doctor. Most of the time these people toss you a gown and tell you more or less to get ready but such was not to be the case this day. "Let's have a look," she says and enthusiastically proceeds with her examination. "Uh, I think my boss needs to look at this," she says as she skips out of the room. She didn't close the door very good and that hallway seemed pretty busy to me so I hopped over and shut it myself. "Well, I guess they forgot me," I said to myself after some time had passed and no one returned. So I got dressed.

The "boss" came in (eventually) and did his own exam exclaiming that I would have to have surgery but first had to get an OK from my heart doctor. So far I haven't heard anything from them so my surgery may just drift away into cyberspace—which may not be such a bad thing. Sometimes it's hard to keep things rolling up there (especially in surgery) which is a problem not unique to the VA.

Meanwhile, my wife is getting along pretty good these days with her Tulsa doctors. Her cardiologist is Steve Scott up in Tulsa. Steve is an MD from Stonewall, son of Bruce and June Scott over there. We go up this week for another exam for Pat's knee from Dr. James Slater who is the son of another Stonewall graduate, the former Betty Boone. I don't think James ever went to school in Stonewall but I credit his mama's "Stonewall" brains with getting him through medical school. It's a small world after all and I find it interesting that kids from these small schools continue to do well in the professions. Now I know that people (some anyway) are reading this to see how Pat is doing. Well, she is still sort of slow getting my breakfast and I hope the doctors can fix her knee and will soon get her back up to speed.

On another topic: I think it won't be long before our frosty football field is deserted in favor of round ball—played inside and by the stove. I've already seen a 6th grade basketball game over at Moss so the handwriting is on the wall. I spotted some frost in my own yard Monday morning—probably as early as I've ever seen it in my rather lengthy past. Looks like the cold fronts of October have dampened visions of global warming once again. This was the earliest frost in a long time and the low temperature edged out a 121 year record for this date. Perhaps this will be the year we'll have beautiful fall foliage before winter sets in. We'll see. I guess if I really want to know what lies ahead in January I could go get some persimmons (as I have done in the past) pop 'em open and see what the seed looks like. It will either be a perfect little spoon or fork at the center of the seed. The spoon means a mild and short winter while the fork is bad news—long and cold.

Regardless of what the persimmons or even Al Gore say about the coming winter, let me wish you a happy weekend and remind you to go to church this Sunday.

Wayne Bullard, D. Ph.

waynebullard@sbcglobal.net

10-18-12
Going To The Cotton Bowl

The older you get the harder it is to get to and enjoy the Cotton Bowl AKA "The Red River Rivalry." It's hard to get a room down there too, so I usually exploit one of my last and only friends, Virgil Guy to put me up. You know how my wife is, she thought having a fractured knee was too painful and wouldn't allow her to make the trip this year. So daughter Lesli and I just decided to go without her. We invited two of our friends, a girl named Mika Strong and her little girl, Abbey along for the trip. We made a day trip out of it.

It was still dark as we left Saturday morning and went our usual secret shortcut around loop 12 to streets called Spring and Lagow where we received special parking protection rights from other special friends down there who have the added advantage of living right next door to the Cotton Bowl itself.

A burly female guard told us to stand by to be searched. She didn't really search me and just ran this wand thing around and about. I figured she was just trying to protect us from some crazed UT fan smuggling in dynamite to blow up the whole Cotton Bowl. If they had it would have saved them a lot of embarrassment. The game that took place was something to behold with Mack Brown calling in his lawyers in the 3rd quarter to negotiate a good exit plan from his job. Even the Texas Longhorn Band toned down their act a little. Had I given it much thought I would have brought them the sheet music to Boomer Sooner. I figured if their team was dancing to our tune, their band might as well be playing it.

Other than the big game, I guess the Texas Fair, like Oklahoma's, has degenerated down to a God-like worship of food. Especially bizarre foods like deep-fat-fried butter sticks; snickers other sticky unhealthy foods. I decided to jump right into the festivities and bought some Texas Buffalo Wings. But that didn't work. I think the guy sold me some of those food things they use for display as they were so hard I couldn't bite them. That was OK, however, the sauce on the wings was hot and nasty. I went back for another small fortune in coupons and I was able to purchase an enormous potato which wasn't too bad. I was a little suspicious anyway. I figure if these people are so unreliable and crooked that they can't be trusted to handle money (coupons only, thank you) why should we trust them to cook us a potato.

After a few more unhealthy food choices and foolish trust placed on unsafe rides, it got dark and we headed back to our friends and car on Lagow Street. Our car was still there, the only one there in fact. A big party was underway nearby (no doubt funded in part by the windfall provided by our parking fees) and you can imagine mine and my party's astonishment when this somewhat thin, yelling and laughing woman came hurdling across the liter infested parking lot— running directly to me. The happily high woman was very excited to see me and proposed that the two of us embark on a night of exciting partying with her providing the entertainment and me providing the financing. I figured she knew a party boy when she saw one. Lesli broke the magic spell by yelling, come-on Dad, get in this car and let's go! "He yo dad? Well you just get in the car and go on sweetie!" Tyrone, standing nearby was encouraging me to upgrade my standing in his community by buying him a beer. I gave old Tyrone a little beer money and bid my farewells as I leapt into the car and said—drive.

My great Chevy Chase adventure had ended and we made it all the way to Durant before we drove into the storm. But that's another story. Just wait 'till next year. Be sure and go to church next Sunday— especially if you've been to Texas lately.

Wayne Bullard, DPh

11-01-12
Tossing your Turkey

Thanksgiving is a nice time of the year with our families gathering but I still remember the time we tossed turkeys in Allen—and it's time I write about it again. Back in the middle of the last century (1970s) merchants were always dreaming up ways to get people to town and spend money—such as cash drawings and big sales and such. It was this type of dreaming up promotions that caused our banker, Vernon Burright to come up with the bright idea of a turkey toss. His accomplice, Harve Butler and several other good old boys felt it was a good idea too and it wasn't long before 36 turkeys were purchased in far-western Oklahoma.

For my out of town readers, let me explain: The "Turkey Toss" consisted of taking live turkeys to the top of the Farmer's State Bank and after a few good swings (to notify the crowd and the turkey that something was about to happen) the turkey would be tossed into the crowd. And a good crowd it was. Whoever caught the turkey got to keep it and boy were they ever ready—the crowd not the turkeys. KTEN-TV showed up and taped the unusual event and soon the deed was deemed a great success even though the turkeys were pretty tame and mild. Harve and Vernon were very pleased and said: "You ain't seen nothin' yet, wait 'till next year."

Time flies by and it wasn't long before Vernon had sent to the far west for 36 more turkeys—"the meaner the better," he said. The turkeys were transported, fed and exercised by old Harve, who had a dog kennel out where Sam Johnson lives now. Each of the birds was swung around by the legs and made to flap. By the time Saturday had rolled around the birds were feeling pretty good about themselves. So were Vernon and Harve.

At 2PM of the big day I stepped outside my drug store to view the fun. The highway was closed. A rather large and noisy crowd was on hand and so were the cameras of KTEN-TV, capturing the moment for posterity. A bunch of rowdy little boy's josled for better spots among the eager adults—they wanted in on the fun too. Harve had reported to me earlier that "man, these birds are a lot livelier than last year's turkeys. We're going to have some fun today," he went on. The first turkey was introduced to the blood thirsty crowd below. When it finally was released it flew low over the crowd leaving a trail of blood—and it wasn't turkey blood. The turkey decided to land on Dutch Kraetti's pink and charcoal grey DeSota parked across the street in front of the Food Center.

An alert Roy Hinchey quickly jumped upon the trunk of the pristine DeSota while the turkey flapped up and onto the porch. Roy pursued but eventually slid off the porch suffering a few bumps and abrasions while the turkey took to the air and was last seen going west at a low altitude. The escaped turkey was never caught and remained at large for the next year or so before disappearing. Turkey #2 was a little fatter and was unable to maintain altitude as he flew over the groping crowd. This was the one that landed on the little boy's group— several were left bleeding. One of the worse injured was the little Humphreys boy—a real turkey fighter. Some say this one was finally hauled in by Jr. Dicketts but later escaped—just like #1. The carnage continued as I went into my drugstore to doctor on the little Humphrey kid. Boy was he ever bloody. The other turkeys fought well too and several found freedom that day before the event ended and while a lot of people suffered wounds, nearly all said they had a good time.

"Wait 'til next year," an exuberant Vernon said. But there was to be no next year There were murmurings and threats and our next meeting quickly turned into lot of denouncements and talks of lawsuits and the animal rights folk were there too. We agreed (to save our hides) to never do this again and instead just give away 36 frozen "Butterball" turkeys with no toss. They agreed not to have us all sued and locked up in jail. It wasn't much fun however and we soon gave that up too.

Vernon moved away after that. Some said he moved because he couldn't stand the excitement of living in Allen or perhaps he had a broken heart over the cancelled turkey toss. And while the famous short-lived annual turkey tosses have faded from our memories, Vernon and Harve have not. They just don't make 'em like that anymore— and I still miss 'em.

Have a good weekend and be sure and go to your church Sunday.
Wayne Bullard, DPh

11-04-12
No news is bad news

Every morning my dad got up early to open up the side door of his grocery store in Centrahoma. He made sandwiches for a small posse of cowboys that mostly worked out on the Cody Ranch. I also got up to fetch the little roll of newspapers the Mistletoe Express tossed out onto the side of SH-3. That was 70 years ago and I was Centrahoma's paperboy.

I only had 6 customers and 2 extras. For a while I thought I was paying for just six but after I learned I had to pay for all eight I became a lot less generous with them. After that my grandpa (W. W. Armstrong) and my dad had to fork over a nickel each. My dad, a person known to be cautious in his spending complained that his should be free but he would pay anyway—even though I read "his" copy.

Which brings me to one of the points of all this—the content of The Oklahoman. Newspaper editors in general and the Oklahoman in particular complain bitterly that people just don't read papers like they used to. Well, that's right. Before and during the war (WWII) people depended on the paper for their news. They (the news writers) wrote extensive and comprehensive stories in those days about people like Herr Hitler and his ambitions and when the war clouds got heavy the people were well informed and able to make intelligent political decisions—as they must do in a democracy. Even common people who weren't "well educated" were well versed on what was going on and such knowledge helped this nation to win the big war, WWII. Newspapers helped shape our lives.

The newspapers of today have fallen way short of the mark. Our nation has been in war (one that's cost thousands of lives) that puts our young people into battle for something we vaguely call "freedom." When Jay Leno goes "Jay Walking" we laugh at how little people know about current events. This is partly because the front pages these days do a poor job of informing readers and as a result fewer people read them. You have to hunt for actual news stories in papers such as The Oklahoman these days and in general the front page looks more like a copy of "Grit" than that of an important daily.

Newsmen seem to be obsessed with shaping our social values while ignoring or doing a poor job educating the public about important economic, domestic and foreign affairs which voters in a free democracy need to grasp. A case of "bullying" in Oklahoma City currently draws a lot more ink than do the life and death political issues in the Middle East.

Recently the circulation department of the Oklahoman cut off some large chunks of Oklahoma because (so they said) delivery is difficult. Years of tight-fisted penny-pinching against the "paperboys" who get up in the middle of the night and see to the delivery of their product has resulted in a shortage of route managers and workers. It seemed easier to just shut down outlying routes than it was to take care of their loyal readers who helped make the Oklahoman one of the greatest dailies in America.

I have always been a loyal reader. Even during the 4 years I spent in the Military and away from home I would search out a copy of "The Oklahoman" in San Diego or San Francisco. I was a happy camper. Later, I was pleasantly surprised when I was transferred to the East Coast to find the Daily Oklahoman on sale in the big news stand in Times Square—easier to buy than in Allen, Oklahoma. I found myself plotting during the 4th quarter of the OU/KSU game (in Gaylord Stadium) how I could get my Sunday paper after the game. However, so far I can't figure out how to get my Oklahoman here next Sunday. But I'm thinking about it. What's my advice to you? Send an email or letter to their circulation department. Be sure and go to your church Sunday.

Wayne Bullard, DPh

11-21-12
Be careful what you dream about

Some of you may not know that last week was a big event in my life. I had my hernia repaired. And what an epic surgery it turned out to be. Several weeks earlier, a cute little VA doctor whose name tag identified her as Teresa had "supposed" that the surgery would be done through a small incision in my belly button and that I would be numbed up before a few quick stitches were made to repair the pesky little problem. "Put to sleep?" Probably not she gushed as it is indeed a simple surgery and as quick as a wink I would be sent home to Allen where in a day or two I would be as good as new—riding my bike. I was pretty happy.

A lot has happened since then to wipe the smile off my face. I went up on the appointed day and was quickly introduced to a group of different doctors—ladies and gentlemen of the medical profession who had different views and techniques when it comes to hernias. I never saw Teresa again. Folks on the 7th floor act as though she may not have ever existed. I was a little bit worried as I was taken through the double doors at 6AM on that fateful day and told to take a seat. Thus I found myself sitting in the herniated waiting room with a few other hernia sufferers. We had little idea what we had gotten ourselves into.

The VA is well organized and I was amazed when a girl with the big El Marko came in and asked me to show her some ID and then point to where my surgery would be. A large "X" was placed on my left side. We had been led into the operating area and IV's had been started. To get through the screeners one had to be able to repeat their social security number several times and remember their date of birth. A pretty lady came by and said "I'm going to put something in your IV that will make you sleepy. It won't make you go to sleep, just relax you." I never knew what hit me.

I woke in a different room and upon demonstration that I was indeed awake, I was discharged. One minute had passed. I wondered if I had had the surgery yet, as I walked down the long halls up at the VA. "Wow! I thought as I rode in the wheel chair—these guys are really good. This operation doesn't even hurt." Pat eventually got my prescriptions filled and we somehow made our way back to Allen—and when my incision woke up, I did too. My first night home was not to be without its perils either. It's amazing what "drugs" can do to one and to their dreams.

First night home I awakened at 1AM with a strange woman in my bed. It wasn't my wife either so I got up and looked. It was one of my neighbors. I asked my wife what she is doing in our bed. "I don't see anyone, just lie down and rest." The neighbor woman never moved and actually was well behaved, not bothering me a bit. I just found it weird that she chose this time to come stay all night. The next morning my wife convinced me that the lady had never even stepped foot in the house and I eventually realized that it was a dream. I won't name the innocent victim of my dream but may view her with some suspicion forever into the future even if she did just come over to see if I was OK.

I am healing pretty well and the doc says that after 2 weeks I can drive. He never said how long it would be before I can do the splits or jump the hurdles again but I may ask him my next visit. Be sure and lock your doors at night—you never know who may crawl into bed with you. I hope all of you are having a nice Thanksgiving this season and have a great weekend. Be sure and go to church Sunday.

Wayne Bullard, D.Ph.

waynebullard@sbcglobal.net

.

12-06-12
Christmas Time and Bucks

This past Sunday the First Baptist Church had their annual "Hanging of the Green." The well attended event was followed by a Christmas Dinner served in the Fellowship Hall. The food and fellowship was great but the best part for me was the presence at church of so many young couples with little kids. The usual and traditional songs were sung and the Christmas Story told in word, deed and song while the decoration of the "Candy Cane Tree" was a highlight for the little kids. It wasn't on the program but one tot decided to do his own dance of interpretation of the music — up on the stage and for the pleasure of the audience. I never did get to thank him for his novel and impromptu dance moves but I think all found them highly entertaining.

One can't think of Christmas without thinking back to their childhood and my mind went back to grade one in Centrahoma. We had quite an elaborate program that Christmas in 1940 and everyone had parts. Ina Klinglesmith, our teacher, made sure everyone participated and had the costumes needed to play our parts. Everyone knows you just can't find anyone better than your first grade teacher. They are just somehow very special people.

I got along real well with my second grade teacher for the first few days but after she took a paddle to me over a disagreement we had over class rules I started thinking maybe all teachers aren't first grade teachers. And they aren't. I read in Sunday's paper about a lady down in the DFW (Dallas) area who as a second grade teacher tried to introduce a little discipline into her small charges lives. It seems the lady rewarded her kids with play dollars, called "Bucks" for certain things. For instance, kids who went to the bathroom and took care of business during scheduled breaks were paid two "Bucks." It isn't clear just what you could do with these "Bucks" but apparently they were highly sought after by the kids.

If a kid needed to use the bathroom at any other time it cost them two bucks. One little boy, with a special needs kidney stood up to see if he could go to the restroom again but upon remembering it would cost him two bucks sat back down. A little later he wet on himself that brought humiliation of the sort that can only come about in a room full of seven year olds.

The little boy's mom upon learning of the dilemma was (naturally) furious. An explanation by the teacher brought no resolution to her worries so she took it to the administration who instructed the teacher to stop the program immediately. Thank goodness Ms. Lewis, my second grade teacher, never charged us any money (imaginary or real) for having to go to the restroom but that could be because she never thought of it. Besides, I'm not too sure a trip to the restroom at Centrahoma would be worth more than a nickel, much less a dollar. They were outdoors.

I keep in touch with just about all of those special Centrahoma schoolmates who shared those first 4 years of school with me and when I think about them now I often picture them dressed up in little Christmas uniforms, standing on the stage and singing Christmas songs—not as the old folks that we pretend to be nowadays.

There will be lots of Christmas programs in the coming days in Allen, especially up at the school. Be sure and watch out in the local papers and make note of them. Your attendance is greatly appreciated and noticed by the kids and you'll find its well worth your time. Don't forget to go to Church Sunday.

Wayne Bullard, DPh

12-13-12
Leave Your Gun at Home, Son

The sign on the door at the local pharmacy reads: "No Firearms Allowed." It made me remember the old western song, "Don't Take Your Gun to Town, Son." One of my friends asked me "why don't you want to carry, you used to pack a pistol?" "Well", I replied, "I used to need one but now I don't." I was lying through my teeth. I had already thought this out completely. I'm a lot older than I used to be and my life is complicated enough already. For instance, I have my glasses to keep up with. I keep getting new glasses because I break or lose them once in a while plus my eyes change so I have lots of glasses. Some change as the light changes. Some are prescription sunglasses (I hate those). I have several pair of squinty reading glasses I buy at dime stores. I spend a lot of time these days just looking for my glasses and trying to remember after I find them if they are mine or someone else's. Of course, I have to help my beloved significant other whose glasses seem to be lost a lot lately too.

There are other things that need my attention lately. I carry a date book these days. I don't actually know just where it is right now but it contains vital information as to my next doctor appointment, my wife's appointments and all my engagements. It's hard to remember all that stuff when you're 65 years old—Oh wait, I'm 77 now. Then there is the matter of my heart pills. I have to find and carry those pills everywhere I go—not all that easy to remember either when you consider I'm really looking for my glasses. I'm pretty good at hanging onto my wallet but my keys live a life of their own—able to move about and relocate at their will. And how many times have I had to turn the car around and go back for a cell phone? It's good I'm not deaf—yet. I've learned to dial my cell-phone and wander all over the house till I can hear it. I could go on but I think you get my drift now about carrying a gun. Do I need my wife nagging me with questions of "Where is your gun?" "Was that it you laid on top of the car before we drove off?" I tell you it would just be another thing.

Meanwhile, if I packed and had to leave my pistol in the car while I go into a store, what good is it? And how much more would I have to endure the criticism of my wife when I arrive home with an empty scabbard? The lost gun? Suppose some criminal type finds it and slays their spouse with it and pins the rap on me? I've seen those Perry Mason movies. I'm no idiot. So I'll just leave my gun at home.

One last point about why I won't bother with a carrying permit. The world is due to end on December 21, 2012. This can be a good thing if you think about it. No more income taxes. No inventories to run. No more budgets or resolutions to make. My unbelieving wife already sent out a bunch of Christmas cards but I know it's a waste of money. I feel a lot of relief about gifting this year. You know how hard it (was) to find a nice gift for the wife. No more worries! I'm not paying any utilities either but I plan on maxing out my credit cards. Sure hope those Mayans are right.

Not that it will make any difference after December 21, but they legalized Marijuana in the state of Washington. Perhaps that old movie "Sleepless in Seattle" should be replaced by "Stoned in Seattle." The State of Washington has plowed some new ground (at least in this country) by making smoking Marijuana legal. I think they did this to ease their transition at the end time. No one said whether the end would come on Daylight Savings Time or Standard. While Washington State residents hope to smoke their way through the end of the world, others surmise they may be doing some other kind of smoking. Oh well, I hope each of you are having a great time of Christmas spirit in spite of all this and be sure to go to church Sunday. Christmas greetings go out to each of you. If there is one.

Wayne Bullard, DPh

12-20-12
Christmas In The Desert

I always try to tell a Christmas story for this time of year. A few times I have told of Christmases past that weren't so good. Of course, my publisher Bill Robinson thinks those stories are best and seem to be his favorites. Since then I have told of the Christmas of 1943 that we made an early morning Christmas trip to Grandma's on Goat Ridge down in Leflore County when gas was so hard to buy. On that cold morning my mom decided to make it into a real challenge by pulling out the choke on our old Ford so she would have a place to hang her purse. I have written of the lonesome time in New York that I was stranded in port aboard a Navy Ship in the duty section when the ship's cook went on a "crying drunk." Christmas dinner was bologna sandwiches on cold and somewhat stale bread. Well, I think you get the drift.

Last Christmas, my brother-in-law, Fred Ellis in a spree of story topping told of his Christmas in 1963 and it is hard to top—even by my standards. In 1963 Fred and Kay, Freddie's parents had been on the move, looking for greener pastures. That Christmas had found them in Phoenix, Arizona. A few years of moving a lot, working different jobs had not actually improved their financial standing very much if at all. Fred had been between jobs but when December arrived he had landed a good job doing maintenance work on a downtown high rise while Kay got on as a nurses aid at Scottsdale Hospital. Times were good all of a sudden.

The last weekend before Christmas Fred and Kay cashed their paychecks and headed for the shopping malls. Seven year old Freddie had his heart set on a bike and 11 yr old Susie had ordered a new doll of some fancy sort. When the happy family left the mall to head for the supermarket they were almost effervescent at their good fortune. Santa was on his way. Life is good.

184

I never understood just how this happened but the old Buick, packed with toys and goodies was alone out in the grocery parking lot when the thief (or thieves) took it—cargo and all-away. I think a cop later gave them a ride home. They had their groceries but all their Christmas presents were taken. The police later found the car but it was empty-- no bike and no baby doll. There were no credit cards out in that sunny desert place for Fred and Kay to use so Christmas found Freddie without his bike. Somebody, hearing of the robbery got the kids some other presents but for sure not the bike Freddie had counted on. But someone gave little Freddie one toy that year. A secondhand toy car with four flat wheels that made it hard to play with but with a little bit of 7 year old imagination he made it work that bleak Christmas day nearly half a century ago. He still remembers the clunking noise the little car made when he tried to roll it.

When I relate one of these stories my readers always come up with something a little better and write it to me. Please feel welcome to do so this year too. Meanwhile I hope for each of my readers a Merry Christmas—no robberies—no little cars with wheels that are flat on one side—and that you get to be with your loved ones. Be sure and go to church this Sunday.

Wayne Bullard, DPh

This picture was taken in Coalgate in 1947 of Pat's dad, Fred Ellis on his favorite horse named Pat. This horse was born on St. Patrick's Day and had a perfect clover shape on his side.

185

12-27-12
Cutting back

Well, here we are, still alive and living our lives. The Mayan calendar was either wrong or perhaps we've all been "left behind." Those of us who maxed out our credit cards or perhaps went the other way and didn't buy their wife a Christmas present are really up against it. However, there may be some bright spots down the road. It looks like we may not go over that thing called a "Fiscal Clift" after all. The president hopes to present his own spending cuts just as soon as he finishes up his vacation there in his birthplace Kenya—oh I meant Hawaii. Sorry. The Republicans say that President Obama is to blame in the first place for this "Clift" in his failure to cut federal spending. But they fail to take into account what the President has already proffered.

My Utah correspondent, Dick True pointed out to me recently that Obama has already (contrary to what the Republicans say) offered some cuts in spending--$100,000,000.00 dollars as a matter of fact. I have trouble comprehending a million dollars and a billion is way out there but when he offers to cut a hundred billion dollars out of his federal budget, I am impressed. That is real money. We were taught ratio and proportion over at Stonewall in the 8th grade to help us solve math problems and also to help us get mathematical projections in perspective—so I checked it out.

My Utah correspondent spends about $20,000 a year on groceries, utilities, gasoline and whatever it costs him to live. Pulling a hundred billion dollars off the federal budget and taking it in perspective to and proportionally to $20,000 comes out like this—six cents a year. So if my buddy wants to tighten his belt accordingly and help out he needs to spend less, to the exact proportion that President Obama is proposing to the federal budget—well he needs to spend only $1,999.94 next year not the full $20,000. Problem solved?

For news here on the home front, old glory is waving once more from the intersection of SH-48 and E. Broadway. It's our 3rd flagpole this year. Early this year the pole was run over by a car driven by a woman. No further comment there. Later this second pole was believed to have been whacked over by an 18 wheeler cutting through town—illegally. So now we have number 3, a brand new pole, new flag and a new base and I think it's the finest looking one yet and many thanks to our city manager and others who saw to its replacement. Pole #3 was set back east a bit and has a better built up base to help it stay upright in the face of traffic. But what we really need is for people to just be more careful there.

It was another "rare" white Christmas this year. My company is all gone and the biggest thing I have to show for the holiday is me. I've gained about 5 pounds in 5 days. The Christmas day snow moved in about 1PM and some said it was only 2 inches or less. It was hard to measure in the high winds and besides, who wanted to get out in those 25 degree winds and try to measure it anyway? Not me.

Sunday morning services at the Baptist Church were well attended as the children's classes sang Christmas Songs (of course) to us last Sunday. These children did an excellent job singing in presenting their inspirational program. After the Christmas Sermon by Pastor Chad Kaminski, the praise team led by Jeff Ray presented a medley of Silent Night and Oh Holy Night.

Monday, Christmas Eve night, I attended the 10PM candlelight services at the Methodist Church. As usual it was an outstanding and meaningful program for those who attended as well as the presenters. Special thanks to Rev. Bob Langston, the pastor and Soloist Crystal Johnson, for jobs well done.

I wish all of you a very happy New Year and hope you can attend your church this Sunday.

Wayne Bullard, DPh

01-13-13
Keystone Pipeline

It will be interesting to see when and if the Keystone Pipeline which is being constructed and laid from Hardesty, Alberta, Canada to the Port of Houston is ever completed. The line is currently coming by the eastern edge of Allen through Hughes County and is employing hundreds of people. Completion of the line would be a giant step forward in marketing new energy sources in Canada and in the USA. Meanwhile, the pipeline is in its early stages of construction and the tank farm in Cushing is still being expanded. Producers are still finding their products discounted as production exceeds what local storage, refiners and pipelines can handle—such is the glut of oil these days.

Pipelines are considered by people who know about such things to be a safe and reliable way to transport oil products. They help keep down heavy truck-transport traffic on back roads and country bridges. It's a cheap and reliable way to get the product where you want it. So why do people oppose pipelines? Well, you have to read between the lines—they weren't that worried about the Ogallala aquifer or of spillage in a creek someplace. There is something else. That something else is called global warming.

The global warming crowd's theory goes that working to make petroleum products more expensive and scarce will promote the further development of wind and solar power—thus saving the planet. We'll also have to admit that their fight to complicate and or hinder the energy industry is working pretty well. Their actions do indeed force up the price of gas at the pump. A lot of global warmers also hold an almost religious belief that their fight is just and correct—that burning oil produces carbon dioxide (true) which is not only harmful but evil.

Implicit in this is their theory that burning of hydrocarbons is actually unnecessary—that we can produce enough energy from wind and sun. This bunch of zealots also preach that there is a sinister plot by the "powers that be" to deny people access to more efficient engines (that get 200mpg) and these people's interest in keeping us from using hydrogen engines and other magic fuels that can be produced on a factory assembly line. These people fight oil wells, pipelines, cheap gas and fracking in their noble hopes of saving us from ourselves.

Someone needs to revive Albert Einstein's works and words about energy and physics and have all of us sit down and revisit our old 9th grade general science classes. The energy crisis needs to be approached with good sense and a lot of logic. Or to put it another way, let's settle down here.

Have a good weekend and be sure and go to church Sunday. It'll be energy put to good use.

Wayne Bullard, DPh

waynebullard@sbcglobal.net

01-17-13
Flat Tires and Stickers

Fort Supply Oklahoma was established in 1868 as a supply depot for Gen. Phillip Sheridan. A town still remains out there--a 7 by 7 block square plat on SH-270 in Woodward County. I didn't know any of this on the early morning hour that late September day in 1964; I just wanted to get home. My family and my parents had just finished a fun trip to Wyoming to visit my older brother, Gerald. We'd had a great time racing around up there trying to see every sight but it was time to get home and go back to work.

We hadn't slept all that well in the "smelly" town of Garden City that night and this morning we were bucking the high winds just north of Woodward when I felt the flat. Thank goodness, I thought to myself, we have a good spare. I pulled over and went into the routine of jacking up the car and found I had parked in the worse thicket of goat-heads and stickers ever. Never-the-less I soon had the car jacked up and the wheel off when I found the spare was flat. In the distance I could see the top of a water tower. I knew it was Fort Supply and I wondered if anything at all could be open on this windy and cold Sunday morning. About then Pat reminded me that not one car had come by while we had been stopped. Well, Fort Supply looked to be close by.

I pulled a bunch more of stickers out of my socks and pants. They were tough but soon I was rolling the wheel down the highway. After a few minutes of slow travel I noticed a truck barreling down the highway — going my way. I moved over and put out my thumb. He stopped and I threw the tire into an open side door of the semi. He hauled me into town and sure enough there was a café-gas station that had a sign out front announcing "Flats Fixed."

An old boy short on teeth and IQ plugged it and aired it up. I asked if he could give me a ride back and after the obligatory spit he said,

"No." I went inside and found a local teen with a pickup without front fenders (didn't have any back fenders either) who offered me a ride and away we went. I gave him a dollar, put the wheel back on and drove back to Fort Supply where I had my old "friend" fix the other flat. I was pretty pleased with myself for being done with this chore and wondering when I would heal up from all those stickers. "Thank goodness," I said to my wife (who is hard to impress) "that we are back on the road and have a spare this time." She said, "I'm impressed."

I went on about 30 miles or so and the car weaved. "Must be the high winds" I said as we cleared another mile of red dust from an adjacent wheat field. But I was suspicious we were going to have another flat. Just ahead was a station and I pulled in and sure enough, my newly plugged tire was low and hissing like a Texas rattler. I went in and asked if they fixed flats. "This is Sunday." I don't know what made him think I didn't know what day of the week it was and I was getting progressively more homesick. I went out and took off the "leaker" and when I got the last lug tight on the spare and let the car down it pooched. Yes it was going flat too.

"Ah ken sale yew sume tares," the gas guy said. Yes, he had a deal for me. I bought two tires that Sabbath morning from this "unborn-again" merchant. "I never heard of "Road-Boss Tires" before. Then I said, "Put 'em on." After buying two inter-tubes and finding there was no such thing as free installation in this dust bowl I paid the money and we came home to Allen. I probably should have gone directly to church when I got home and asked God to forgive me for the evil plots I hatched up in my mind against both of my tire guys. It included hanging them up by their thumbs.

Hope your tires all stay up and you have nothing but pleasant thoughts for your fellow man. Be sure and go to church Sunday—it might help you deal with flat tires and evil thoughts if you have a flat.

Wayne Bullard, DPh
Wayne Bullard@sbcglobal.net

01-24-13
Love Those Old Cars

Once in a while you hear some of us old "coots" talk about how good those old cars were. "Better than those plastic things we buy these days" so we'll say. Well, they did have style and I think most people are thinking of those cars back in the 40s and 50s—those that came after WWII when no cars were even made for 4 years. But the demand far exceeded the supply for 2 or 3 years. You had to get on a waiting list. It was in such a setting late in 1946 when a train hauling "hundreds" of new Chevys wrecked just east of Calvin. New cars scattered everywhere some bent up but the insurance company went ahead and auctioned them off. The need for a car was so great that most sold for more than sticker value of about 800 dollars.

If you were on a waiting list you didn't have any say about color and the "extras" back then were a radio and a heater. You could save 8 bucks if you would skip the heater and about 12 bucks on that AM radio. Eventually Detroit caught up with demand and that's when consumers started getting more selective. However, quality control was "out the window" up there in Detroit with labor problems abounding. So sometimes doors didn't always close just right and engines weren't always just real good.

But the Bullard's were lucky. We were on several waiting lists but our first new car was a 1947 Nash Ambassador. It was not the car Dad wanted but the day the Nash Dealer called from Ada our old car had been laid up for 6 weeks waiting on parts. We were afoot. That afternoon Gerald, Sue and I were busy tearing off the shipping paper from the upholstery inside and the car turned out to be a great and trouble free car. Should have stuck with Nash. But so much for that idea.

Our next car, a 1949 Chevy was really a nice looking car. Smelled great and had a radio with push buttons, a heater plus the stylish sun visor (another $18). We took a trip to Wister that weekend to visit grandma and show off our new car. We were between Calvin and McAlester when the car "jumped" out of gear. Dad found he had to manually hold the car in gear with his hand. The next week Service Chevrolet in Ada advised us: "Yeah, some of 'em do that—you'll just have to live with it and hold her in gear. It may get better later on." It didn't. My dad mentioned that sometimes the horn honked when we turned left. "Yeah, we're hearing a lot of that too," the service manager said. My brother and I had a devil of a time figuring out routes home late at night so we wouldn't have to make any left turns. Stonewall sounded like Tijuana with all those horns.

Our troubles had just begun. In 1952 I borrowed my dad's brand new Ford he bought that day and already had about 50 miles on it. I had a girl friend to impress and wanted to take her to the McSwain that night. I got as far as Mississippi and Main when the car stalled that cold January night with a wind chill factor of a million below zero. I finally got it fixed but we missed the movie and nearly froze to death. My girlfriend was so impressed that she made it a point to never date me again. I'm not over it yet.

The worst was yet to come. The new '58 Chevy I bought to impress my bride- to- be blew up. Legal threats caused a reluctant GM to change out the engine, the transmission and repair numerous other major flaws. In 1964 I blew out two tires one hot Sunday in the parking lot at the Baptist Church on a brand new Buick. I was backing up. I watched helplessly as a one week old 67 Chevy bought here in Allen had its engine disintegrate and being laid up 3 weeks. Union problems led to metal fillings in the engine: "Thanks guys." I don't have space to go on with this and mention my run-away cruise control on my Ford Wagon. Nor will I mention the 89 Buick that would catch afire if you drove through ice slush.

I tried out a foreign pickup once—it was awful. In all fairness to US car makers let me say I quit having quality problems with my cars in 1991. I prefer good old domestics anyway so I'll stick with cars that are made here in America.

Have a good weekend and if your horn honks when you turn left, just think of it as a safety feature. Be sure and go to church Sunday.

Wayne Bullard, DPh

waynebllard@sbcglobal.net

01-31-13
Hitchhiking in Oklahoma

Hitchhiking in Oklahoma was pretty common back when I was a younger person. It was impolite to pass by a pedestrian on the road without offering a ride. I can remember a time riding to Allen from Lula in my Grandpa Will Armstrong's wagon and how we encountered several people who were invited to "hop on." They would ride down the long dirt highway for a ways—to their destination and just hop off. Another time my dad pulled over his car on SH-3 just out of Stonewall and invited a young guy to get in but when he saw how crowded the car was he said, "no thanks, you got enough."

Most of those courtesies faded away as it became more commonplace for the hitchhiker to not only accept a ride but perhaps take your cash and your car. This brings up Max Milner, one of about a zillion little boys who were sons of Jonas Milner. Jonas built the first brick house in Allen at the NW corner of Baltimore and Gilmore Streets and there are many stories of this legendary family. The other day I got an email from Max Milner with one more story. Here it is—and thanks Max for sharing.

About 1957 Max Milner was hitchhiking from Ada to Norman one fall day to see an OU football game. As luck would have it, one of his rides let him out on a lonely stretch of road some 15 miles east of Lexington. There were but few cars traveling by and Max began to worry if he could be on time for the kick-off. Then a sleek Chrysler Imperial hurled toward him and quickly passed him. The car had zipped past doing some 80 or 90 miles an hour as it stirred up the red roadside dust. About 300 yards up the road the big heavy Chrysler suddenly began to brake hard, causing the tires to squall and smoke as the rear end fishtailed slightly before coming to a stop. Then the shiny new vehicle weaved evenly in reverse as it rapidly backed to him. When the car stopped a window whizzed down and the well dressed passenger, beside his driver, shouted out, "Max Milner, what in the world are you doing way out here?" Max recognized the man as Judge Orel Busby and grinned as he related he was trying to get to the football game at OU. The Judge smiled as he told Max to get in, they were also going to the game.

A lad, Jonas Milner and a child, Orel Busby had moved with their families to Indian Territory near Allen from northeast Arkansas and became close friends. Later, the son, Orel Busby was a member of the first graduating class of East Central College. After college, Orel went to Konawa where he taught, became principal, and then was elected 'The Boy Mayor of Konawa' at age 21. Orel went on to graduate from the O U Law School and practiced as an attorney in Ada prior to serving two terms as County Judge for Pontotoc County, Oklahoma, and then as District Judge. In 1932 Orel Busby was elected Justice of the Oklahoma Supreme Court. He served for 5 years before resigning to re-enter private law practice and to operate the 4-B Ranch properties west of Allen.

Orel Busby, the Milner Family Friend, was engaged occasionally over the years by Max's dad, Jonas Milner. Jonas had 3 wives. Unfortunately, as each wife died, Jonas would marry a younger woman as he had outlived each of them. As a young lawyer, Orel Busby was hired by Jonas for various legal services. Socially, Jonas had also been hosted on occasion at Busby's Lodge between Ada and Allen. Max also appeared before Judge Orel Busby in the discharge of guardianship of a minor when he turned 21. As did all four minor children of the late Jonas Milner. Was perhaps, Orel Busby the namesake of another lad around Ada, Oral Roberts?"

Thanks Max for the good story and I hope you and all the other readers have a great week. Don't forget to go to church Sunday. You too Max.

Wayne Bullard, DPh
waynebullard@sbcglobal.net

02-07-13
Mayor Ed Koch

I remember many years ago (back in the '50s) being in New York City. I liked to walk around the towns I visited when I was in the Navy and take pictures—and I hoped NYC was a great place to take pictures. But when I went walking in most parts of town it wasn't so pretty. My trip over to Washington Square Park didn't work out well either. The famous gateway, so often pictured in movies and travel brochures (inspired by Paris' Arc de Triomphe) was covered in liter, broken glass and graffiti—ugly words and racial slurs. I kept looking for a picture to take and I guess I didn't take any since I don't have any today.

Nearby Greenwich Village was sinking fast too. This historic part of town housed artists and such but it had degenerated into a litter-strewn slum looking a lot like Guatemala City. Not too many weeks earlier I had made a pilgrimage to Bunker Hill. My ship often tied up in Boston and the Bunker Hill monument was in sight. But my trip failed. Druggies were busy, thugs were everywhere and the historic monument was also covered in gang signs and other graffiti. No pictures.

I was back up there in New York City several years later and things were no better. In fact the place had gone broke and the federal government told the city to get lost as it refused to bail it out. Then the big power outages hit in the 70s and rioters looted out neighborhood stores before burning them to the ground. There was a bad feeling about the city. In January of 1958, a buddy and I were walking through Times Square when two loud booms sounded. Gunfire! A masked man holding a pistol crumpled, dropping his money bag and the gun. He was dead. We ducked inside a nearby store for a few minutes. Such were conditions in the heart of New York City's Times Square.

I guess the people up there finally got fed up. They elected a guy named Ed Koch, Mayor. They felt that he couldn't do worse than the other Mayors. Koch was detested by the left-wing NY press and minority groups fought his every step. But the new Mayor cut expenses and spent tons of time out in the subways talking with people and bucking them up. He not only got the budget fixed by cutting out the political "Lard" he did something that really caught people's eye. He literally cleaned the town up. He not only reduced crime by an astounding factor he got rid of liter. He attacked Washington Square and removed actual tons of broken glass and other liter on the grounds. He scrubbed the nasty subway clean and took all the obscene gang writings and "art" off its cars.

NYC today is clean. Not as squeaky clean as some foreign cities but it looks pretty darn good these days—a place you can take a picture. Greenwich Village and Washing Square areas are once again tourist attractions and desirable addresses as its hardworking people stay busy keeping their home-town clean. Of course, the press and liberals finally defeated the Mayor and he was kicked out. Koch passed away last week but it'll be a long time before the people of NYC forget the mayor that got rid of liter and once more made their hometown a great place to live—and visit. Mayor Koch was 88.

There is a lesson here. Allen needs to get busy too. We need to clean up our own streets, parks and yards. Let's see if we too can return our home town to a place we like to call the "greatest place on earth."

Have a good weekend and be sure and go to church this Sunday.

Wayne Bullard, DPh

waynebullard@sbcglobal.net

02-14-13
Pat and the hospital

Last week was pretty busy for my family. Pat had her right knee replaced. Last Sunday I drove her up to Tulsa where I had a hotel room reserved for us. Lesli and granddaughter Meegan went along to help too. Early Monday morning I checked her into St John Hospital in Broken Arrow and eventually that morning she got the new knee. Daughter Traci had arrived from St Louis and it was a good thing—even a dedicated husband like me needs all the help he can get at these times. Nurse Brenda had seen to it that we had a suite with an extra bed so we could spend the night if we so pleased. We did please to do so.

Nurse Brenda turned out to be an old lost cousin and it was a real pleasure to meet her and find out about this wing of the family and what they had been doing. She was the chief nurse over the surgery up there at Bone and Joint and I really appreciate her looking after all of us last week.

Meanwhile I had shifted my command post to the home of my son Steve in Jenks. Back in her room I checked to see this suite and found it to be a couch which worked well for the person staying the night which turned out to be Traci—surprise! On Wednesday we took Pat out to Steve's and on Friday night we came home. Allen looked pretty good and all went well. Pat was soon relaxing in repose up in her bed looking like the Queen of Sheba and treated as such. Like I said, it's good to be home.

It's still winter-time in Allen and we need to look after our neighbors and see about them. Sometimes a trip to the store or post office is needed and greatly appreciated. This time of year is also time of the playoffs. I was glad to hear that our girls won and our boys are still in play. I wish them a lot of luck. On yet another sports note I was able to get away and watch the 22ned ranked OU women play the #21 OSU women up at Lloyd Nobel. OU won the contest by 19 points and all I got to say about that to the numerous OSU fans hanging out in Allen is "tough."

Thanks to each of you that called, penned a note, brought food (especially that) during this time. Just try to remember (those that may have intended to bring something) it's never too late. I like to remember what our editor, Bill Robinson, said the other day. "Those times that the wife ails are really the time a man suffers." In keeping with this thought process, last week I heard a current public service message on the radio advising about prostate cancer. It basically announced that when a man suffers with the prostate "It's really the woman who suffers." I don't really understand that but it must be true—it was on the news. I admit that I missed the point of this message.

Take good care of your knees and you ladies might need to have your prostate's checked. Have a good weekend and be sure and go to Church Sunday.

Wayne Bullard, DPh
Waynebullard@sbcglobal.net

02-21-13
Getting Older

Harry Shelton tells me I have a new reader. This one is a minister in the congregational church over in Rupert, Vermont. Harry, an old Navy buddy lives across the line over in New York State in a nice little town called Hoosick Falls. Anyway, welcome Mary Beth—who knows, maybe I'll make you my Vermont correspondent.

A little girl at church recently looked me over and pronounced: "You're old aren't you." That got me to thinking. I have a birthday this month and I'll be 78. That will make me about the oldest one in the "Cemetery" class down at the Baptist church. A class that is actually called "The Men's Class" but we nicknamed it for sadly, or not, our next promotion is across the highway to the cemetery. Yes, I suppose I'm getting old.

Fellow Oklahoman Will Rogers who died the same year I was born (1935) had this to say about getting old.

1. When you are dissatisfied and would like to go back to your youth, think of algebra.

2. Eventually you will reach a point when you stop lying about your age and start bragging about it.

3. The older we get, the fewer things seem worth waiting in line for.

4. Some people try to turn back their odometers. Not me, I want people to know why I look this way.

I've traveled a long way and some of the roads weren't paved.

5. You know you are getting old when everything either dries up or leaks.

6. I don't know how I got over the hill without getting to the top.

7. Never kick a cow chip on a hot day.

8. Never slap a man who is chewing tobacco.

Here are some points Will made concerning his philosophy of life.

There are 2 theories to arguing with a woman….neither works.

Never miss a good chance to shut up.

Always drink upstream from the herd.

If you find yourself in a hole, stop digging.

The quickest way to double your money is to fold it and put it back in your pocket.

There are three kinds of men. The ones that learn by reading. The few who learn by observation. The rest of them have to pee on the electric fence and find out for themselves.

Good judgment comes from experience and a lot of that comes from bad judgment.

If you're riding ahead of the herd, take a look back every now and then to make sure it's still there.

After eating an entire bull, a mountain lion felt so good he started roaring. He kept it up until a hunter came along and shot him. The moral: When you're full of bull keep your mouth shut.

Have a great weekend and be sure and attend your church.

Wayne Bullard, DPh

waynebullard@sbcglobal.net

04-04-13
Easter Sunday, Basketball and Voltaire

Some of us are critical of our fellow man no matter what he does. I heard someone say (it wasn't me, honest!) Sunday morning that they wished all these people would come to church every Sunday. Well, that's an eternal thought I guess, since I've been hearing it all my life. But there was a hint of criticism in the statement. However, by now and at my age, I'm just glad to see 'em there at all. Easter is a time of hope and quest and you could see it in the faces of worshipers last Sunday morning as they celebrated the resurrection of Jesus and expectation of their own rebirth to eternal life. A guy named Voltaire, a man never known to be very kind in his remarks about preachers and such once said: "The world embarrasses me, and I cannot dream that this watch exists and has no watchmaker."

Easter Sunday was also the day the NCAA scheduled my Sooner girls to play in the sweet sixteen in Oklahoma City. So it was after church Sunday we headed the car NW towards downtown Oklahoma City and the Chesapeake Energy Arena—where the girls were to meet and play Tennessee to see who advanced to Tuesdays game with the supposed winner of the Baylor-Louisville game (Baylor, of course). The OU game was a mess. The shorthanded Sooners team of 8 was quickly reduced to seven by a well-timed trip that sent Morgan Hook crashing to the hardwood, face first. I waited for free shots and perhaps an ejection as they dragged her semi-conscious body off. But no foul was called giving me a hint as to how the refereeing might be going. Hook was said to have suffered a concussion as the already reeling Sooners struggled on. Ticket holders along with Sherry Coale watched and waited in vain for Nicole Griffin to involve herself in the melee but she remained on the court only as a spectator.

The girls were lucky to get by with only a 15 point loss as the fans resorted to wondering about how bad it was going to be for Louisville on the second bill. Brittney Grinner wandered around the arena during the OU game giving interviews and posing with Kevin Durant and in general being the center of celebrity attention. When the Louisville women came in they were largely ignored and looked a little pitiful and insignificant sitting down on the far end by their little band—waiting their turn to be slaughtered by the Grinner.

The Louisville band lived up to expectations, which were very low, but their women came to make a statement as they limited Grinner to no buckets the first half. Baylor had it carried to them and in spite of a furious comeback attempt lost the game on a controversial referee call at the end. I still am not sure just how Baylor managed to lose that game but on a cheerier note, that's the last we'll have to see of Brittney—who just might be the best woman's basketball player I have ever seen.

Lastly, we are getting some good rain—something we ought to appreciate. Climatologists tell us the summer will be hot and dry and if we don't start off with more water in our lakes than what we have, there will be some hard times this summer. I enjoy hearing from readers and continue to be surprised at who and where they are. People who are from Allen seem to be everywhere and they read the newspapers. Be sure and have a good weekend and go to church Sunday.

Wayne Bullard, DPh
waynebullard@sbcglobal.net

03-07-14
Chickens Blending In

I pushed the button on the poolside elevator and as I went in, this chicken went with me. We both turned and faced the door, waiting for it to close. When we got to my floor, the chicken got off with me and disappeared down the outside hallway. She seemed to know where she was and I asked no questions. I decided then and there I was going to be keeping a close eye on the chickens in Key West. Perhaps they were reincarnated humans getting another chance for life down in Florida. I was at the Doubletree Hotel at the time about 9 years ago. I remember it well because it had a rather large pool out back, elevators that opened to the outside, and that chicken.

I told myself I didn't drive all the way to Key West to look at chickens and tried to put their odd behavior out of my mind. After that I tried not to notice the chickens that seemed to be all over Key West. The next day, try as I might, I couldn't help but notice them. At an outdoor restaurant two joined us for lunch. Before I could shoo her away a curious hen had hopped up into the adjoining chair, straining her neck to see what I was eating. Signs around the place advised us "Please don't feed the chickens" I didn't. I asked the scowling waiter what the deal was on the chickens. He replied, "I hate them but down here the idiots have passed a law protecting them. We can do nothing."

The waiter was right. The people of Key West are idiots. It seems that several years ago someone brought chickens to Key West and then just turned them loose. Pretty soon chickens were just wandering all over the place and Key West residents ignored them—for a while. Finally the city council passed an ordinance to deal with the problem and hired a chicken catcher. For one thing, the city fathers failed to realize that chickens not only have rights but they have feelings too. Liberal thinkers started harboring the fugitive chickens and said "Chickens don't like being denied the right to walk the streets and to exist. They didn't like having their feelings hurt and or to be killed and eaten." Besides, after a month at work the "catcher" had only caught two chickens and had them in his back yard—not knowing what to do with them. The city fired him and someone let the 2 chickens out.

In 2 years the chickens had again, doubled in population and the city decided "No more Mr. Nice Guy." A new and faster chicken catcher was put to work. But what do you do if with them if you can't kill 'em or eat 'em. A prison camp was provided, goals set and a plan was underway. The plan? A census was taken and a population cap placed on the chickens by the "Nazi-like" police of Key West. A minimum of 200 roosters and 500 hens would be rounded up by Gestapo chicken police annually and the hapless chickens would be loaded up and hauled away. But to where? Labor camps? Murdered? No. The chicken police haul them to a secret place on the mainland where they are supposedly going to live out their lives in luxury and freedom. It remains to be seen if the liberals will tolerate this outrageous violation of chicken rights but I understand a meeting of "Save the Chickens" will convene next Wednesday in the dining area of the local KFC. Meanwhile, I saw the "hotel" chicken once more before checking out and heading north. She was getting on an elevator. I guess it lived there.

Have a good week and be sure and do a good deed for a chicken this week. By all means be sure and attend your church this Sunday.

Wayne Bullard, DPh

waynebullard@sbcglobal.net

Main Street Centrahoma about 1939 - John Thomas 2nd from right

03-14-13
Pigtails and the Horseback Rider

I was watching TV news on channel 4 and what I saw set me to thinking. This time it was an irate parent giving the Oklahoma City School Board the what for over school uniforms. It turns out she was pretty much against it and most other plans the school had thought up too. Sadly, it's just part of the paranoiac-divisive society we live in. Not so many years ago had one spoken of the "School System" they would mean the board of education, the teachers and the parents all working together to try to educate their kids. After all, didn't they elect the board that hired the teachers who taught their kids? It was a joint effort.

A teacher would have to get pretty far out of line just a few years ago for a parent not to stand solidly behind them in discipline, what they taught and how they did it. I like to retell a story about my friend for life, Roy Byrd down at Centrahoma in about 1945. The leadership and cooperation with school staff in this little story still serves as a good example to our school patrons of today.

The story starts on an old school bus heading north 4 miles to take Roy home at the end of the school day. Ethel, his mom had told him to go to Smith's Grocery downtown and pick up a 10 pound bag of sugar and bring it home on the bus. Earlier that morning, the driver, Ode Heck, had to get on Roy for pestering a pretty little girl. He kept touching or pulling her pigtails—an act she at least pretended not to like. Roy continued his romancing of the girl that day and was finally moved across the room by his teacher to give everyone some relief. At the end of the day Roy took himself, his books and his 10 lb. bag of sugar he had charged down at Smith's and got back on Ode Heck's school bus.

Pretty soon Mr. Heck had to ask if he was bothering that girl. The little girl retorted that sure enough, Roy Byrd was pulling on her pigtails—again. Mr. Heck stopped the big bus and told Roy to "get off." As Roy rose to get off he handed the sugar and his books to his brother, Troy to take on home to mom. Mr. Heck told Roy, "What you carry on the bus, you carry off the bus." Roy trudged off carrying his heavy bag of sugar. The bus drove on leaving the 10 year old alone on the lonely 4 mile stretch to home, discovering that 10 pounds was heavy for a boy his size. Roy walked a ways before looking back and saw a lone horseman going his way. He knew it was his dad, Leroy Byrd, so he took a rest and waited.

Leroy, as was his way, rode up, stopped and extended a hand to his boy and lifted him and the sugar up behind him and the horse resumed its journey. Not a word had been spoken. Finally the father asked his son, "Why are you out here walking?" Roy explained that Mr. Heck had made him get off. Leroy asked his son to explain why he was put off the bus. When Roy got through reporting all that had taken place, the horse stopped. Leroy reached back and took the boy and set him down on the ground. Not a word was spoken as Leroy and his horse continued on except this: "Don't forget your sugar."

Roy, now an old retired teacher himself, is a good speaker and sometimes is asked to speak at meetings of teachers. He tells this and other stories to emphasize how important it is for the whole community, especially the family, to be involved and helpful in the education of a child. There is a good lesson in there for the patrons of today's sometimes failing schools. It's good to be a good leader but you have to be a good follower once in a while.

Baseball and softball season is here. Be sure and support our teams and your kids and their teachers in their pursuit of education. And of course you need to take your kids with you to church Sunday.

Wayne Bullard, DPh

03-21-13
Centrahoma Rising

My brother Gerald and I (he's the one that lives up in Wyoming) were driving down SH-3 toward Coalgate some years back when he said, "What happened to Centrahoma? Did they move it over?" "No," I replied, "they built a new highway and bypassed it." "Turn around and let's go see it," he said and I did. There wasn't one business open. Up until a few years ago you could buy gas and pop at the gas station but it was shuttered. Also gone was the old grocery store our parents operated so many years ago. Since we had moved in October of 1944 the handful of businesses we had left behind were not only shut down but gone. The few remaining houses were occupied by people we didn't know or were vacant.

The row of old rock and brick buildings that I supposed had housed businesses at some time or other was gone too. The roofless old structures made dandy places for kids with BB guns to bird hunt and sparrows were plentiful. My bloodthirsty brother felt it was his duty to kill as many as possible. But the town looked to me like it had rolled over and died for sure. The last effort (I knew of) made to revive Centrahoma was made by Garvin Moore, a grocer who took over his dad's old store back in the 50s. Garvin's efforts were fairly successful but when he moved away the town's pulse ebbed and when the city council stopped meeting and filing the necessary papers the new streetlights were removed and the town ceased to exist (again) as an incorporated City.

Years went by and Centrahoma continued to wither away but it wasn't until last year that someone decided to do something. Brothers Jerry, Duck and Dan Daffern, longtime Centrahoma residents—urged on by Jerry's twin brother Duck, decided to go to work and see if the little Coal County Community between Coalgate and Tupelo could be incorporated—again. Now, Dan is the Mayor and it appears he is doing a good job. But what is a town without a business district? Not much they decided and since Centrahoma isn't served by even a coffee shop, much less a restaurant they decided to get to work providing for that need. Now it seems success is theirs.

When my family drove up last Saturday evening to check it out I saw the brothers, Jerry and Dan out front taking a break in the pleasant spring evening. I was surprised to see what the inside of the old remodeled gas station looked like. It was all attractively re-done and smelled like a new house. The original station was an old 2 storied building in 1940 when we moved into the back of our grocery store and I wondered how old it was by now. Whatever its age, it's all made new now and there is another new dining area nearly completed under the old service shed.

We all ordered the fish dinner which comes with a bowl of special flavored pinto beans, slaw, hush puppies, French fried potatoes and the best tasting fish I've ever eaten—cooked by an expert named Lola. Delicious desert and drinks are included. I wondered what they breaded the fish with. It had an unusually good flavor and—well, you'll just have to drive over there and try it. Just take the Centrahoma turnoff north and look for the sign "Whistle Stop." The hours are 6am to 2pm Monday through Thursday and 6am to 8PM Friday and Saturday. Tell the Mayor that I sent you. Maybe he'll make me an honorary citizen or something.

Be sure and go to Church Sunday.

Wayne Bullard, DPh

Gerald & Wayne, Centrahoma 1940

13-28-13
The Slippery Slopes of Branson

Spring break in Oklahoma has been a "tricky wicket" this year. One Allen family seeking a good ski slope for their family found some tall mountains. How tall were they? Well, at least 3 of them (the people not the hills) got altitude sickness and had to find oxygen bottles. My family, not being much smarter sought the spring break climate of Branson. Not only are the hills sort of short over there but they are reportedly alive with the sound of music. The last thing I grabbed going out the door to get into my daughter Lesli's overloaded Ford was my sunglasses. It was, after all, a bright and shiny day. That was in Oklahoma.

I didn't need my deluxe Walmart glasses in Missouri, however. The cold north winds soon blew out the light of the sun, ushering in an ugly looking bunch of winter clouds—clouds that would soon dump a load of snow on spring-break-loving vacationers. One day of Silver Dollar City pretty much did me this time and I retired to my less than sumptuous digs at the Castle Rock Hotel that also hosts this humongous water slide park—all located indoors and kept at 84F (so they claimed). The next day I may have been the only 78 year old man going down the killer tube or the rushing river with a bunch of people whose average age was about four. For some reason I felt pretty much at home—intellectually. As it turned out water-sliding with 4 year olds was a pretty good thing to be doing as the snow began to pile up outside.

I sat around a lot in that water park and at times just baby-sat with my street clothes on. This little boy came up carrying a life jacket. Looking me right in the eye he said, "Put this on me." I did so and asked him, "Who do I look like, your grandpa?" He looked me up and down and said, "Yeah."

Of course there isn't a level spot in Branson either to park or drive so that slick night when Les and I decided to go out and find a steak no one would go with us. There were problems both driving and parking but it wasn't as bad as you might think. The City had knocked itself out clearing streets and parking lots and by the next morning there was not a street or parking lot in Branson hosting any snow. They had cleared it all away. But it was an excellent day for the water park, again.

That afternoon we drove around to the Pierce-Arrow Theatre and enjoyed their 2 hour show. They had a good crowd. I hadn't seen them for a while and they had refreshed their stage, added or changed routines and even Cecil had new acts—even changed his name. We had a good time escaping the dreary freezing drizzle that afternoon.

We gave up the dreary looks of Branson to return to the cold-windy weather of Allen. We were greeted with 40 MPH wind gust, dark skies and snow flurries Sunday morning as people hustled to church. I was thinking "This is as good a day as any to stay in and skip church" but I didn't and after enjoying the good conversation and fellowship down at the bright and cheery church house, I was glad I didn't. And speaking of fellowship, I have enjoyed hearing from readers. One transplanted Allenite, Mr. Gleason of New Jersey called me last week and we had a good visit. Graduating from Allen in 1943, Mr. Gleason went right into the service to fight in the war but his name is on the war memorial twice—he made both WWII and the Korean War. We had a great visit remembering a lot of names of people that live or have lived here in Allen.

Be sure and go to church next Sunday. It's Easter you know.
Wayne Bullard, DPh

04-11-13
On Being Young

There was so much energy in the great hall you could just feel it. It was a little surreal, thousands of high school kids crammed into the convention center—all yelling and jumping around like it was a rock concert or something—but it wasn't. It was the FCCLA meeting at the Cox Convention Center in Oklahoma City and we were honored guests of the Allen FCCLA Chapter and honored we were. Current officers were ushered in with a bang followed by a "Pants on Fire" motivational speech by Laymon Hicks of Tampa, Florida. Hicks pretty much set the feisty crowd on fire as he set the tone for the day.

In the midst of the chaos there was a lot of order and purpose. It was a good setting for high-school aged kids to get a grip on their ambitions, setting new goals and finding ways to achieve. For me it was a good time to observe and see how many of our young people are responding to times that are often described as tough—about kids said to be at risk. I heard a well-known national news anchor last week describe this same group of kids as "lost" because of bad economic times. He pointed out that many young college graduates were working at menial labor and being victimized by the "system." It was a gloomy outlook, he said.

We had the same predictions many years ago—during the 30's –something called "The Great Depression." The economic setback had been so severe during that time that some people actually starved to death and many of our young men were deemed to be unfit for military service because of malnutrition-related health problems. That generation was also frequently described as "lost." In a short time this same generation had overcome this worse economic failure in history—the same people that rose to the occasion and won World War II and then came home and built the greatest economic machine in the history of the world. They were the same ones who gave us the internet and went to the moon—and back. They built the interstate highways and we soared to new levels of prosperity and freedom—becoming the envy of the world.

Our kids have fought their way through all sorts of social and family disruptive influences, withstood the annoying decay of TV and Hollywood which seems to have poisoned the very essence of America with their attacks on morals, God and Country. If you listen to the "Main Stream Media" you would not only hear that these things are happening but a done thing. You would hear our kids are illiterate and our teachers are graduating people who can't even read. Yet, somehow through all this, our education system is still the envy of the world, producing workers that still outperform all others.

Yep. I saw a lot of good things in Oklahoma City last week. I saw thousands of good looking, clean cut kids working for a better future for them and for America. I saw our own Allen delegation excelling and taking charge of things—winning elections and succeeding. I saw many teachers, teachers like our own Katrina Lewis, working above and beyond the call of duty seeing to it that our kids at least have a good crack at freedom, success and prosperity—just like we did. I have great hopes for this generation.

Have a great weekend and be sure and support our kids, their school and their teams. They deserve it. And be sure and go to church this Sunday.

Wayne Bullard, DPh
waynebullard@sbcglobal.net

04-18-13
Global Warming For Dummies

"Global warming is settled science" so we've been told the past 20 years or so. "Failure to believe in global warming just means you are ignorant and stupid," so the enlightened ones say. Only thing is, I'm hearing less from global warmers lately. Something has gone terribly wrong with global warming and their main cheerleaders have been left out in the cold. Like the religious groups that retreat to mountain tops as they predict that on a given date the world will end--they've been victimized by "an inconvenient truth" or to put it another way— nothing happened. We're all still here. It's 2013 and the temperatures forgot to come up. Sorry.

Oh it's true that we are still pumping carbon dioxide into the atmosphere by the ton but sadly, the results have been less than catastrophic. Perchance the carbon dioxide is being absorbed into the vast oceans or perhaps we just figured wrong. Or perhaps it will kick in later, say about 10 or 1000 years from now. All I know for sure is that everyone needs to calm down. Even those who are getting rich buying and selling carbon credits need to look for some other way to make a living.

Last week as I drove down SH-1 toward McAlester I saw what seemed to be a major car wreck or some sort of snafu just outside of town. An ample number of police vehicles with their lights flashing were alongside the road. Yes, it was the demonstrators out where the famous Keystone Pipeline crosses. The small colorful group was yelling and waving signs lettered with words like "CAN'T DRINK OIL--WE ALL LIVE DOWNSTREAM." Meanwhile, 79 year old Nancy Zorn of Warr Acres had gotten up early and after putting on her purple pant suit made her way to the pipeline too. Nancy brought her bicycle lock and chain which she used to chain herself to the big digger. Nancy had the lock and chain tightly around her neck and after the Atwood Fire Department was unable to saw through the hardened steel without threatening the integrity of Ms. Zorn's neck she graciously took off her shoe, removed the key and unlocked the thing. Everyone, including Nancy and the entire Atwood firefighters heaved a big sigh of relief and Nancy was placed in custody and transported to jail. Her bond was believed to have been set at $250.00.

Another of the Oklahoma City delegation, Gregory Dickson said he was worried about the pipeline not actually doing anything for the economy and about its adverse effects on the environment. Contentions are that the oil shipped through the pipeline would contain sand which could erode the transmission line and lead to oil spills. However, officials on the scene said the sands are removed from the oil first and only oil will be piped through the pipeline.

The main purpose of the protestors seem to be to slow down global warming by forcing us to cut back on our use of fossil fuels to propel our cars , warm and light our homes and to power industry. These activists are simply trying to save us from ourselves. My point here is these people aren't very well versed in the science of global warming either. Don't you suppose before we chain ourselves to a heavy piece of machinery or otherwise make a fool out of ourselves, we ought to wait for the facts of the case to be sorted out by the grownups?

Meanwhile, going on to other "inconvenient truths" the weatherman says we might have one more freeze this spring and that it won't be caused by man-made pollution—just Oklahoma weather. Have a good weekend and be sure and go to church Sunday where talk of hot air, global warming and Carbon Dioxide is kept to a bare minimum.

Wayne Bullard, DPh
waynebullard@sbcglobal.net

04-25-13
Traveling in Arkansas

My wife was reviewing an upcoming trip with me last night and asked if we could take a little icebox for our picnics. "Sure, I responded, perhaps we can have a picnic or two on the road." That pleased her for me to say that since I don't always like to stop by the roadside and eat. It also reminds me of a trip we made in '09 to Alabama. I ran across some remarks I made about that trip which were unpublished and since my computer has been on the blink this week and I have nothing else to offer my publishers I will just submit that little bit of journalistic backwash.

"We had been a little slow getting on the road that summer day but every bag was finally packed, the lists checked 2 then 3 times and a spectrum of toilet articles and numerous medications for whatever ailed or potentially could ail us was in the car. We were headed to Hot Springs on this our first leg of the trip. All was well as we cruised into Arkansas on US-270 just east of Hartshorne at 70MPH when my wife rose up in her seat with the same gusto I had observed in a man stricken with a fatal heart attack and said, "Oh my Gosh, I forgot the mustard!" I slammed on the breaks and left tire marks in the road slinging stuff from the back seat to the front. After collecting my wits and getting my speed back up to 33MPH I said, "What do we need with mustard?" "To go on our sandwiches I'm going to make down here someplace so we don't have to stop and eat."

For the next 88 miles I looked for mustard in a part of Arkansas that exists only to make Oklahomans feel better about their own state and themselves. All business such as little grocery stores were closed down due to the Walmart induced recession. Finally I came to a little town of about 500 that had 2 gas stations, a super market, a dollar store and a dollar general. All appeared to be very busy. We went in and blew a dollar on a jar of mustard.

We drove on but I wasn't really in the mood to stop and eat in the car or by the side of the road. I finally made it to Hot Springs and there, as if by magic, sat a Red Lobster, A Chilis, an Applebees and a host of other watering holes. I pulled into Applebees. I set the sack with the mustard back on top of the unused camera and we went in and ate. "We'll eat sandwiches in the hotel tonight"she said—not giving up.

A lot of her family was from Hot Springs so we drove aimlessly about town gawking at the defunct old hotels that once housed profitable and busy bathtubs filled with fat tourists soaking in hot and healing mineral waters. Later, we drove up a 15MPH road to the top of some mountain there downtown with a commanding view of the aforementioned spas and as if that wasn't enough, we rode to the top of a tower ($6.00 each) so we could get an even more breathtaking view of what I mentioned earlier in this paragraph—giving it the old Clark Griswold quick look and then leaving Hot Springs— tired but happy. We drove further east to a Hampton Inn in a place called Forrest Hill. After we got settled in I noticed that Pat had made me a nice sandwich there that evening in the Hampton—and yes it had mustard on it.

We will be making a trip soon to a place called Deland. It's in Florida I hear and one of my "favorite" granddaughters (at least that's what I tell her) is graduating from college there. I'll try to let you know how that all works out and how many sandwiches with mustard I eat—although I really enjoy a little mayo now and then. Meanwhile, let's hope for spring to come on and get here. Don't forget to attend your church this Sunday

Wayne Bullard, DPh
waynebullard@sbcglobal.net

05-02-13
May at last

At last it's May and after the coldest April in years. In fact it is said to be the 2nd coldest in history with areas in Alaska and the rest of the country running about 7 degrees below normal on average. But that's what weather does—it changes. The trick is to not get too concerned over it—we have people in this country who will do that for you, passing laws and figuring out ways to profit from weather changes. They are called liberals and that's all I'll have to say today about global warming. Besides, I've been out of town.

Pat and I drove up to Tulsa last Sunday afternoon. Even with spring being so late it was a beautiful drive up scenic SH-48. Well, they say beauty is in the eye of the beholder and that's why I choose scenic "48" as my way to get to Tulsa on my frequent trips up there. In Tulsa we attended a reception for a guy named Odai—Bishop Francis Afotey Odai from a place called Accra, Ghana. Odai is a preacher of many talents and of many ministries. He is an "overseer" of several other pastors in Ghana as well as being a pastor of a large church there in Accra. Odai has a television ministry in Africa as well as coordinating church planting and the much needed ministry of digging water wells for the people back in the bush.

Southern Hills Baptist Church in Tulsa is involved in these ministries with members of the congregation going on all sorts of mission trips over there—trips that involve church building, the water well digging and more especially medical missions. One of the things that caught the eye of my daughter in law, Courtney Bullard and husband Steve was the plight of young girls in the big city of Accra.

Migration to the city from the bush is ongoing and in that migration are thousands of little girls who go to the city thinking of a better life. Once there reality takes over and they realize there are no jobs, no food and no shelter. Their dreams of a better life turn into a nightmare as they fall into the hands of pimps who cast them into physical abuse, slavery and prostitution. It is a brutal and mean fate and there are thousands of these young teens who are owned and exploited by these evil men.

That's why Steve and Courtney founded something called "The Pearl House." This organization provides food, shelter and ministry to these "rescued" girls in a place called "The Pearl House." There is a story related to why Courtney named it "The Pearl House" and it showcases the love and respect Pearl House People have for the girls they rescue from the streets. In Accra, Pearl House workers literally go out into the dangerous streets and rescue these children and take them to the Pearl House, a sanctuary that can meet their physical needs for food and a clean bed as well as their spiritual needs. This ministry has been described as "One of the most extraordinary philanthropic humanitarian endeavors of our generation." In the book of Matthew (13:45-46) there is a story of a jeweler who was looking for the finest pearl. When he found a pearl that was more beautiful and valuable than any jewel he had ever seen, the jeweler sold all he had and bought that pearl, his pearl of great value.

You can find out more about this work by going online www.thepearlhouse.org or by writing to The Pearl House at PO Box 738, Jenks, OK 74037. I hope all of you are having a good week and can make it to your church Sunday. A lot of good stuff happens there and you need to be a part of it.

Wayne Bullard, DPh
waynebullard@sbcglobal.net

05-09-13
Religion In The Military

Listening to an address by Accra, Ghana's most known church spokesman the other night, he was asked "what are the biggest problems you face in your Ghana Ministry?" Without pause Bishop Odai replied it was "Voodoo and Islam—these are the worse evils in Africa." I thought the answer might be not enough money, or a shortage of workers or something along those lines so his answer surprised me. I thought to myself "Thank goodness we don't have to worry about stuff like that here in the good old USA!"

But perhaps it's later than I thought. Our own President Obama's appointee Mickey Weinstein who now heads up the President's head of Military Freedom Foundation has ordered the powers that be in the military to develop court martial procedures for those who share their faith. I wondered just what they were talking about anyway. Well, it was about this order from the military that will make it a crime—a "crime" that possibly could result in imprisonment for uniformed military who tell others about their faith—in particular Jesus. Weinstein told reporters that people supporting the gospel of Jesus were traitors and should be charged as such.

Mickey Weinstein, the atheist, is passionate about his belief or should I say, unbelief in God, depending on how you look at it. The edict has members of Congress—well, some of them anyway—in a stew. The military has always had a strong presence of religion in their ranks since the time of George Washington. They hire and commission the Chaplains as officers and they have played such important roles in the great wars this country has conducted for the causes of the very freedoms that Weinstein is even now declaring illegal and traitorous.

The very office of Chaplain would by necessity have to be abolished since their job is not only to counsel and comfort armed force individuals whether they be wounded or troubled in some manner, but are paid to share their own faith. By law they would have to be discharged and removed. Talk about muzzling the "Ox" as the bible sometimes calls preachers!

One article I read mentioned what an uproar all this was causing but I haven't seen it. Very little press time has been given to this radical ruling designed to purge religion from the ranks of the military. Twenty years ago there would have been chartered buses and trains heading to Washington crammed with irate preachers and loyal laity ready to take to the streets or whatever to preserve rights of our military personnel to exercise their "Freedom of Religion." Just think, if their freedom to speak and worship can be removed that easy, give a thought to yours.

Sadly, many Americans are unconcerned about their rights anymore—most don't even realize they have them or consider them so important. "I don't go to church anymore, let someone who does worry about this" may well be their thoughts. More than likely most Americans haven't even heard about this at all. So many citizens have quit reading newspapers or paying any attention to the news that a large chunk will never know about it anyway—such is the state of our republic these days.

Enjoy your weekend and be sure and go to church This Sunday.
Wayne Bullard, DPh
waynebullard@sbcglobal.net

05-16-13
The American Road

There's no better way to go look at America than to take to the highway and well, have a look. I needed to go look at some of my grandkids anyway so Pat and I left out on a cold Friday morning heading northwest to St. Louis, Mo. East of Tulsa we saw a large cloud bank and pretty soon our sun had disappeared. As it turned out, the ball of heat was to go missing for 3 days as we kept driving bravely down I-44. But just what could it do? Snow? Here it was, May 3rd — the grass is green, the trees leafed out and it's supposed to be summertime, ain't it? Before we got to Joplin the ground was covered with a few inches of snow and it was starting to blow in clouds across the highway. The temperature dropped from 45 to 33 and did it pretty fast.

We splattered our way on into St. Louis in time to attend a stage production of "Twelve Angry Men" starring....who else? My own grandson Alec, among others. Before driving out of St Louis the next week we visited a few sites of interest including the transportation museum which has a great display of old trains and automobiles. Later on, like on Wednesday morning after winning a few games of dominoes we pointed our trusty car East once more and were soon bouncing along some very rough Illinois highways — by far the worse roads we drove on so far this trip. We lunched in Paducah, spent a night near Nashville and drove next to Lake City, Florida for another night at a Comfort Inn. The next day we slipped into Deland, Florida for Lindsey Bullard's graduation from Stetson University.

There in Deland we grouped up with a lot of in-laws, friends and relations for several good meals and an exceptionally good time. In time, we remembered her graduation and all of us made a pretty good crowd of our own. Airline schedules on the following Sunday caused a lot of hasty exits by the Reeves and other Bullard's leaving Pat and me looking at our bug splattered car out in the 92 degree heat of Florida wondering what we had done. But we had a schedule and were soon packing up and hitting I-95—south. This time we took the new graduate, Lindsey Bullard, with us. We were off to visit Colton Bullard down at Coral Springs.

Colton can't live by himself nor can he speak or do much to take care of himself. He is autistic. Colton lives in a small group facility with a few other boys he has lived with now for a few years. He is well cared for and I think enjoys his life as much as is possible considering the circumstances. Colton was glad to see us and we him. Seeing my grandson again was well worth the long drive. Our visit passed quickly as we enjoyed that quality time in the beautiful outdoors of Coral Springs. We all spent the night in a nearby Comfort Inn in Lantana, Florida. We arose the next morning and drove Lindsey back up I-95 to Deland. Later, we headed on North in the general direction of a place called Dauphin Island, Alabama wondering how far we'd get and where we might discover another place to spend the night. That was a sort of hassle before we landed in Marianna in the Florida panhandle. A good bit of seafood later that evening from Ruby Tuesday's put me back on good speaking terms with my tummy as we prepared to go on to the Island the next morning.

Two or three have asked if I planned on seeing Cousin Gator down at Immokalee, Fla. but I decided to leave Gator be and instead concentrate on this other cousin, Jimmy Bullard. We share similar political views and I'm pretty sure, he will be free to put us up a few days and even supply some bologna sandwiches and good conversation. Later we'll visit Don and Cathy Ellis in Brewton, Ala. before heading back to Allen. Have a good weekend and be sure and go to your church Sunday.

Wayne Bullard, DPh
waynebullard@sbcglobal.net

05-23-13
On Coming Home

It is good to be getting back from our recent and long driving vacation. I really did enjoy seeing friends, kin and being able to attend events with my grandkids like Pat and I just did but let me say again, it is good to get home. As a matter of fact, the older I get the better it is for me to get back to my own house, my own bed and my own home town of Allen. I remember the last time I was gone for what seemed like a long stay and after getting home I was so very glad to be back. I was greeting people like I hadn't seen 'em for months instead of just a few days — although my enthusiasm exceeded theirs.

But my tepid reception back reminded me of one time in the Men's Bible Class (AKA Cemetery Class) down at the First Baptist Church when I was gone — out of town. My friend Lane Ritter, of Atwood came to class late and noting my absence asked "Where's Bullard?" Class sage and orator Donny Johnson said, "Didn't you hear? Old Bullard died last week. We buried him Thursday." Everyone supposedly just looked at Donny and let it go.

I heard of the fraud later that week and jumped Donny about it. "Did you really tell him that?" I asked?" "Yeah I did" he replied. I didn't know whether to be amused, amazed or mad at him but curiosity took over and I asked him, "How did he take it?" "Pretty well," Donny replied. That's sort of how my recent absence was taken — pretty well. One always would prefer being missed when away but whatever, I am glad to be back. Oh well, the next Sunday Ritter seemed glad I wasn't dead after all. Although I pointed out to him the lack of flowers at my funeral and food for the bereaved of my table.

Last week I mentioned attending Lindsey's graduation and that was a lot of fun seeing her and visiting so many old friends and meeting some new ones. This past week I visited my cousin, Jimmy Bullard of Alabama. Jimmy lives in Sylvan Springs, not too far from

Birmingham and lives part time in his beach home on an island called Dauphin. I always find the Gulf an interesting and beautiful place to visit and we had a great time touring the scenic wonders and historical attractions in this little corner of the earth just south of Mobile. It was sort of relaxing just watching the coast and getting to visit. It was so peaceful, however I sort of wished something exciting would happen as I kept my eye on the coast with my binoculars.

Well it did, sort of. But I missed it. A man with a boat that hadn't been in the water in years decided to launch and test it out—and he did. Loading his wife and two year old boy in the little 20 footer, he left harbor to see if he had all the leaks fixed. As it turned out he didn't and the bilge pump gave out pretty soon leaving him too far out to make it back to safe port. He made it to the beach where we were and was barely able to get his family to safety—including the 2 year old. I tell this story partly to reassure my boating friends that there are dumb people in Alabama too—just like on our lakes in Oklahoma. The lesson here is to make sure your boat is safe before setting your toddler aboard and moving to the deep waters beyond.

We went to church Sunday with the good folks at First Baptist Church of East Brewton. Yes, they have an old men's class with a no-promotion policy too. Being less innovative than me they had failed to name it "The Cemetery Class" yet but I did what I could to help them out on that. I'll head out in the morning toward Allen and see where I get. Hope all of you have a good weekend and attend your church this Sunday.

Wayne Bullard, DPh
waynebullard@sbcglobal.net

05-30-13
Memorial Day in Allen

It was that time of year—Memorial Day. It signals to Americans the beginning of summer. It's a time when people pull their boats out for the first time and head for the lake. It's the end of school, and the beginning of cookouts and trips. Memorial Day however, means more than time off and fun. It is a time to remember our freedoms and those who lost their lives defending our freedom. It is a time to honor the dead.

A long time ago my family journeyed to Leflore County for something called "Decoration Day." Hundreds of people gathered in the shadow of Wolf Mountain where the terrain and people meld seamlessly into the geography and culture of the Ozarks in a place called Ellis Cemetery. An all day "Singing" was conducted with spirit and enthusiasm in the small chapel on the grounds. The singers never missed a beat as the large crowds roamed about; decorating the graves with flowers while they kept their eyes peeled for anyone they might know. Many horse-drawn rigs were parked north of the chapel and picnics were laid out where-ever shade could be found and as I remember it, a good time was had by all.

Traditional observance of Memorial Day has diminished over the years. It seems many Americans have either forgotten or were never taught about the meaning of this day. Many now think the day is for honoring any and all dead and not just those fallen in service to our country. And that's OK. In Allen we are lucky to live in a part of the country where a lot of folks still pay their respects to honor the men and women who have paid the ultimate price for our freedoms.

Last Monday a good sized group gathered in the Allen Cemetery to pay their respects to our war heroes. I think veterans from every war from WWII, Korea, Vietnam and those in the Middle East were present at the service. Shelby Greenhill sang The Star Spangle

Banner—allegiance was pledged to the flag and prayers offered before Aaron Finney made a fine speech to the crowd. Aaron, a veteran of the war in Iraq, is an unapologetic patriotic American who loves his country deeply and you could feel it in his eloquent words.

The Allen Masonic Lodge graciously hosted a lunch following the ceremonies which was greatly enjoyed by the crowd. It was one of those days that make me proud to be a veteran, and an American living in Allen.

I hope each of you have a good weekend and can attend your church this Sunday.

Wayne Bullard, DPh
waynebullard@sbcglobal.net

06-06-13
The Worst Hard Times

A few months ago my friend for life Eula Tilley, loaned me a good book "The Worst Hard Times." This book, written by Timothy Egan who now is the weekly generator of an article called "The Opinionator" in the New York Times. The "dust bowl" book is a comprehensive look at an epic event in our part of the world that lies just east of here during the horrible and dirty 30s. This New Yorker wrote a very thought provoking book that took me back in time and made me wonder (a little bit) why anyone even lives in Oklahoma.

One thought often leads to another and my mind traveled back to a Sunday afternoon a long time ago.—an afternoon I recall with vivid clarity. I was sitting in the back seat of my Aunt Oma's '41 Chevrolet listening to her and my mom talking. It was an important talk and it was about living in Oklahoma. Oma asked, "Why do you want to keep on living here in Oklahoma? It's nothing but blowing dust, mud-holes and poverty. Go with us to Richmond and start a new life— get a good paying job and just leave this all behind."

Looking all the way back to that time in 1942 I don't know why my family chose to stay in Centrahoma. It was probably the easiest thing to do at the moment. We were getting by living in the back end of our grocery store and making a living. But the future did indeed (in retrospect) look pretty bleak from a financial standpoint. Quite often one of our good customers would come by and tell us good bye—joining an almost infinite string of Oklahoma tagged cars and trucks heading down the legendary highway 66 to the promised land—California. Whatever the exact reasons, dad chose to stay.

It's a question that still comes up. "Why do you live here? Why do you stay?" Now it's not the economics or the dust, it's the pesky tornadoes. Growing up I looked hard and long before I ever did see a twister and I was about grown before I finally did. The things usually come in and leave quickly. The big F-4 that ravaged the area just west of Stonewall in 1959 was an exception—it was not only big, it was very visible. Now the tornadoes seem to be bigger (and very visible) and worse than ever. To aid and abet the things we have HD TV which allows the storms to get right in our living rooms and reduce us to levels of curiosity, wonder and terror on a scale unknown in 1942. Look no further than to Oklahoma City last week when the tornadoes and panic came to town.

So now I have seen interviews with national news organizations featuring Governor Mary Fallon (and others) where they explain (again) why Oklahoma is such a grand place to live and raise a family. But it is indeed a hard thing to explain and understand. Perhaps it's the nature of our people? Perhaps it's the scenery. Maybe the reason we stay has to do with heritage and kinship. I think Okies have itchy feet that make it easy to leave for new frontiers sometime—easier than staying? Or is it easier to rotate your home like many do between California and Oklahoma? Not really. People tend to move around to follow their work or to put it another way—they move because of economics.

I know from experience it is a hard thing to leave your extended family, your traditions and the familiar grounds we call Oklahoma. And I'm pretty sure I'll not be moving because of a tornado. My daughter asked me where my place of safety was but before I could answer she said, "Oh, I know; it's in your chair out on the front porch 'cause you don't want to miss anything—especially a tornado. I guess she has me right on that. Speaking of missing something, make sure you go to church this Sunday. You don't want to miss that either.

Wayne Bullard, DPh
waynebullard@sbcglobal.net

06-13-13
A litter bit goes a long way

As a kid it was often my job to take out the trash—except there wasn't a real good place to take it. But we had a "burn barrel." What we couldn't get to burn we had to haul off. I would think you could get most of the year's accumulation of ash and other unburnable stuff in a large wheelbarrow. One evening my brother Gerald and I were just "shooting the breeze" when I asked him; "Where did Grandma Bullard put all her trash?" "They didn't have any," he replied. "Surely they had some trash," I retorted—"they bought a few things at the store didn't they?"

He explained it to me. The few paper bags they carried home were used over and over for storage as were their copies of "The Kansas City Star" which arrived 3X a week. Cloth bags of flower, green coffee bean sacks were also used up in making clothing or just reused like toe sacks—nothing was wasted.

Last week, the Black Rock correspondent for the local news outlets, Rod Bailey wrote me something along this line. It was a story of a little old lady and a check-out girl at the store. The young

Mana Sue and Wayne
Wash Day in Centrahoma 1942

cashier told the older woman that she should bring her own grocery bags because plastic bags weren't good for the environment. The little lady apologized explaining, "We didn't have this 'green thing' back in my earlier years." The young clerk said, "That's our problem today. Your generation didn't care enough to save our environment for future generations."

The clerk was right. We didn't have the 'green' thing back then. Our milk and pop bottles were all returned and they were sent back, sterilized and recycled—over and over. We didn't have plastic either—just those brown paper bags. We reused them for numerous things such as book covers for our schoolbooks. None were thrown away. But she was right. We didn't have the green thing back then.

Back then we washed the baby's diapers because we didn't have the throwaway kind. We dried clothes on a line, not in an energy gobbling machine burning up 220volts of coal and gas produced electricity. Wind and solar power really did dry our clothes back in those days. Kids wore hand-me-down clothes from their brothers or sisters and nothing was tossed away. But like she said, we didn't have that green thing. Back then we had one TV or radio in the house— not a TV in every room. And the TV had a small screen—not like those big ones you have to have today. In the kitchen we blended and stirred by hand—we didn't burn electricity to do everything for us. When we packaged a fragile item for mailing we used wadded up old newspapers not Styrofoam or plastic bubble wrap.

We didn't burn up gasoline just to cut the lawn. We used a push mower. We got enough exercise by using human power which meant we didn't have to go to the health club to run on treadmills that operate on electricity. We used a glass, or a dipper or a drinking fountain when we were thirsty instead of a plastic bottle or throw-a-way cup. We refilled writing pens with ink instead of buying a new pen and we replaced the razorblades in a razor instead of throwing the whole razor away. We walked a lot in those days—lots of us rode buses and kids rode bikes instead of turning their moms (and grandpa) into a 24-hour taxi service in a car that cost more than their house did. We didn't need help from a gadget that receives its signal from 23,000 miles in space to help us find a burger joint either. And we don't need advice from a smart-aleck who can't make change without the computerized cash register telling them how much. Speaking of smart-alecks, thanks Rod. And to my readers, be sure and go to church next Sunday.

Wayne Bullard, DPh
waynebullard@sbcglobal.net

06-20-13
Growing Old is Hard to Do

There are a lot of things I don't like about growing old. In fact, just recently I discovered that I am no longer growing old—I'm already there. You know this when you walk through the cemetery and you have more friends resting there than you have walking the streets of Allen. Another thing I've noticed is that people have become strangely inhibited. They like to hide their identity by not looking like they did just a bit ago back in time. A law needs to be passed so they would have to wear name tags. It would also help if the name plate also had a picture of them. I would think it would help even more if the picture was taken while they were yet in school.

My Salt Lake City, Utah correspondent, a "somewhat past middle aged" old sailor named Dick True managed to remain in his middle age longer than me—so far. In fact just the other day he sent me a list of things I should have learned (but haven't) by the time we leave middle age—which as I said, I have.

If you are too open-minded, your brains will fall out.

Age is a very high price to pay for maturity.

Artificial intelligence is no match for natural stupidity.

If you must choose between two evils, pick the one you have never tried before.

Not one shred of evidence supports the notion that life is serious. It is easier to get forgiveness than permission.

For every action, there is an equal and opposite government program.

If you look like your passport picture, you probably need the trip.

Bills travel through the mail at twice the speed of checks.

A conscience is what hurts when all of your other parts feel so good.

Eat well, stay fit and die anyway.

Men are from earth. Women are from earth. Deal with it.

No man has ever been shot while doing the dishes.

A balanced diet is a cookie in each hand.

Middle age is when broadness of the mind and narrowness of the waist change places.

Opportunities always look bigger coming than going.

Junk is what you keep for years and toss 3 weeks before you need it.

Experience is a wonderful thing. It enables you to recognize a mistake when you make it again.

You shouldn't weigh more than your refrigerator.

Someone who thinks logically provides a nice contrast to the real world.

It's not the jeans that make your butt look fat.

Marriage is like a hot bath. It ain't so hot once you've been in it for awhile.

I apologize for that last one—it's a Donny Johnson saying. Don't blame Dick True for it.

Have a good weekend and be sure to go to church Sunday.

Wayne Bullard, DPh

waynebullard@sbcglobal.net

06-26-13
Drinking the Water

I read in the Oklahoman the other day that the Oklahoma City Tap Water finished in first place for quality of taste. I wondered which faucet they drew the water from as my experience in drinking OKC water is not that great. The water tastes like it came from a muddy lake somewhere. Oh wait. It did. Oklahoma City gets its water from a variety of places including Lake Atoka and Canton—both are muddy lakes. But you have to hand it to them; they work hard to have enough.

Allen is very fortunate to have good tasty water. The soft water it pumps out of the Gerty Sands is also very clean and tasty. Our water wasn't always that way. For many years Allen folk drank salty water from polluted wells. You could run your bath and find worms swimming around. It was pretty yucky containing some mineral complexes that made it slick, strange and hard to swallow. In fact, most of us hauled our drinking water from outlying wells—wells that also weren't all that pure and safe.

The Allen Chamber of Commerce then did something (1965) that turned out to be one of the best things to happen in these parts—they filed a class action suit on behalf of the town against this privately owned water company that supplied our water. Although the strange tasting Allen water was found to be "safe" to drink, the fact that water customers were driven to other sources for "tasty" water meant some residents were carting home untested water. We had cases of Amoeboid Dysentery in Allen caused by an out of town contaminated well. Another popular watering hole, the artesian wells near the Francis turnoff was also contaminated but it didn't cause any of those types of infections.

The Chamber won the right for the city to buy the water company and the town trustees were placed in charge. I was a Court Appointed member of the board reporting to Judge Busby. He wanted to be sure we made reasonable progress toward getting good water piped in. Citizens voted a big bond, drilled wells and built a new water system from scratch, bringing not only good water, but reliability. Water systems that are allowed through neglect or accident to go down, frequently expose the system to pollutants getting in and contaminating the system. It's very aggravating these days to have the water go off and on requiring flushing and even boiling by customers before they drink it. Thanks to city employees and especially our water commissioner, Harry J. Ellis, it's been years since we had an outage of water (that I have known about) and we can have confidence that when we get up each day that we will have good, clean water in abundance. Thanks, Harry Joe.

Finally and on another subject, there is this: I got to go to another fish fry recently—this time down at the Church of Christ. It was good to see Donny Johnson sharing his chef skills with Tommy McFerran at the occasion of a retirement party given in Honor of Dr. and Mrs. Jim McDonald who have moved to the old "Goat Ranch" just south of Allen. Both retired from teaching this year, down in Denton, Texas. We're proud to have these folks as our full-time neighbors and friends. I think close to a hundred people turned out to welcome the McDonald family to the Allen Community and of course, to eat fish.

Have a good weekend and don't forget to attend your church this weekend.

Wayne Bullard, DPh
waynebullard@sbcglobal.net

06-27-13
Can You Hear Me Now?

A huge outcry has been heard across the nation as we learned that Obama's buddies are listening in on our phone calls as well as reading our email—especially those messages to Pakistan and Tripoli. The cry has lessened some in the past week as Americans learned that this eavesdropping may have saved our bacon a time or two from terrorist attacks. Still, Democrats remain pretty mad at George Bush (CNN says he started this stuff so he is responsible) while Fox News viewers are angry with Obama for taking this to new and unheard of levels. You have to wonder how Obama gets anything done just sitting there listening on his headsets all the time.

One segment of our population that didn't get excited at the news of this loss of civil liberties and privacy was the older folks that live in Stonewall. I grew up over there (my number was "17"), and I know. You may have thought that life was simpler in those by-gone days but they weren't. You had to know what you were doing. You had to know to crank the phone while it was hung up before you picked up and listened for Myrtle. Nothing happened until she made it happen.

Our calls were monitored (for quality and content) by Mrs. Morris. Although the big walnut (or was it Oak?) switchboard was pretty enormous, Myrtle knew every number, each circuit and monitored calls because she needed to know when we answered (so she could quit ringing) and when we finished so she could pull the plug. I knew one high school boy who went to the Main Café to call his sweetie on the payphone so Myrtle couldn't listen. Unfortunately, he didn't know she operated the payphones too.

Myrtle Morris was resourceful and taught me how to operate the board knowing my curiosity would cause me to stop by to give her a break so she could go to Earl Cradduck's for some groceries. Sadly, I learned she had taught others to do the same thing for the same reasons.

I thought I was the only one at the time. The best part of filling in was I got to listen in for a little while.

The fact was we never minded her listening in and knowing so much about our lives. In fact kids called her to chat—sometimes on the pretexts of asking her what time it was. After all, she had a large man's watch hanging on the board. I remember calling "17" one time and Myrtle said, "Your mom has gone to Ada." Her finger was on the pulse of Stonewall and I think we were all pretty happy to have it that way. And while we are pretty sure Obama is listening in, I don't know anyone who calls him up just to chat or ask him what time it is or where their mama is.

Be careful what you say and who you call or email and be sure and go to church next Sunday—after all, you must know by now that God listens in too.

Wayne Bullard, DPh
waynebullard@sbcglobal.net

07-11-13
Digging 'taters on Goat Ridge

Summertime is special. For kids It's time for vacations, trips, camp-outs and doing things—school is out and it's time for swimming and free time—a time to make memories. I've had some pretty special summers when I was a kid— but the summer of 1943 was a pretty memorable one for me and my brother, Gerald. I've mentioned before how that my brother Gerald and I were often banished to my grandparents down on Goat Ridge in Leflore County every summer. Dad said we were to help him on the farm. Gerald felt they were just trying to get rid of us in that early summer of 1943. And I remember it very well.

We were raised by a man (our dad) who owned a movie theatre—thus we learned to make sense of things by relating things to movie plots. For instance our arrival on J. T. Bullard's farm that summer caused Gerald (in later years) to compare our visit to the events in the movie "Bridge on the River Kwai," starring William Holden and Alec Guinness. In the movie the slave driving POW Jap camp commander literally works the Allied POWs nearly to death building this bridge the Japs need to win the war. In our situation, we arrived just in time to "help" dig potatoes. He had what seemed like thousands of acres of potatoes which were ready for harvest and he took his obedient mule and plowed them up, but not perfectly. You still had to grunge around for them. In Gerald's view, grandpa was the Jap Commandant. We were the allied POWs. In our roles we carried large buckets and dug out the potatoes. When our bucket was full we struggled to the nearby wagon to unload.

We finally got the potatoes dug. It took about 6 days. My Uncle Jack was home for his last summer before graduating from Fanshaw School the next spring and going off to war. Things improved drastically after the potatoes were dug with daily trips to the 'Bluff

Hole,' a clear water, perfect swimming place. One day melted into another and time passed. Another casualty of the war was up on the ridge too. My Aunt Inez and her little 3 year old girl, Gail were there. Her husband, my Uncle Tracy, was already gone to the Army and they were another pair of displaced ridge dwellers. There was no running water or electric up there but we didn't mind. In the evenings the family gathered on the long front porch. Jack would get his guitar out and Inez liked to sort of coordinate things. We would sing songs like "You Are my Sunshine," and such as that.

Gerald was worried. He confided his fears that we might be stuck there— forever. "We came down here on one way bus tickets" he reminded me. I spoke with Grandma of my concerns and she said she was sure that we would be going home soon and not to worry. "You'll understand all this in the sweet by and by," she said. Then I heard a familiar and welcome noise. It was the rattles of my dad's old 1935 Ford. He was coming to get us and he did. He also had news. Gerald and I had a new sister. Linda Kay had been born on July 3 and I suppose she wasn't as big a surprise to my mom as she was to me. When Inez let me know that she knew, I asked her how. "I just know," she said.

We went home to Centrahoma that day and met the prettiest little girl baby I had ever seen. Linda grew up and became a beautiful woman and remained a very pretty lady all her life. But that dread disease, cancer, took her from us about two years ago. Now when her birthday rolls around every July 3rd I miss her a little more as I think of that day on that front porch 70 years ago down on my beloved Goat Ridge. It tempers us to remember that life comes to us with a mixture.

Have a good week and be sure and go to church Sunday.
Wayne Bullard, DPh
waynebullard@sbcglobal.net

08-01-13
Time to Promote?

Kids do get older and down at the Baptist Church we have Sunday school promotion day coming up on August 18. I suppose all churches and schools do this. I think these promotions are carried out because the ever-growing little kids sit in those little-bitty chairs at small tables where they are talked to by teachers who may well be using baby talk. Thus, kids are promoted because they get larger and will no longer fit in the little chairs so they move them up to the next class where the chairs are bigger. I know this is true as they continue to teach the same lessons to the older children as they do to toddlers.

While they may be noticing that their kids are getting bigger, the teachers can now tone down their baby talk in favor of more normal talk which seems reasonable to me. Our young teens need bigger chairs too but still require a lot of "simplicity" and games in Sunday school. In fact they often have to be feted with Church Camps, mission trips to far-a-way cities and require lots of food. Older teens and young adults, AKA young married couples are often herded into separate classes behind closed doors. No one knows what they study or talk about in there but I guess it's OK since I don't hear any complaints nor see a lot of dropouts. Thereafter the classes are segregated by gender and the chairs stay the same size for the rest of the pupil's lives. Fortunately it's pretty easy to tell the men and women apart—unless your Sunday school is in San Francisco or someplace like that. But I also understand that Sunday school is not all that big a thing in San Francisco.

Beyond gender, classes are often broken down by age. Age discernment is tricky and even the pupil is sometime unable to tell if they are "old" yet. Yes, it's a tricky wicket sometimes requiring the Wisdom of Solomon. That may be why our church just allows them to go where they wish. Our church has its somewhat famous

"Men's Class." No one seems to know or dare say just what age a man should be to sit in this prestigious class but a few things are clear. It is your last promotion in the church. Thus the name "Cemetery Class" is sometimes used as its nick-name as we all well know our next assignment is across the highway in the cemetery. At least that's where they haul our remains to. Of course we all have higher and better hopes than that and fully expect no less than Heaven to be our ultimate spiritual destination. Just sayin'. Some other things The Cemetery Class believes in are the inerrancy of the Bible, a strong national defense, low taxes, a generous social security, that Christ died for our sins and of course, catfish dinners. Not necessarily in that order.

Philosophy as well as bible history is scrutinized closely each week as each Sunday school member finds himself 7 days closer to this "last" promotion. Plato, Socrates, and the Apostle Paul might find himself right at home bantering about the writings of Solomon in the great books of Ecclesiastes, Psalms and of course, Proverbs. We may not always be right and accurate but we have a good time trying to find "truth." So what does promotion day mean to the Men's Class? Absolutely nothing.

I hope you have a good weekend and are sure to go to your church Sunday. Who knows? Maybe your church has a place for you too. Or you might try slipping in the "back door" to the fellowship hall and give us a go. Visitors are always welcome in the Cemetery class.

Wayne Bullard, DPh

waynebullard@sbcvglobal.net

08-08-13
The Good of Global Warming

A lot of good has come from global warming, if you will. We may not have reduced much of that carbon dioxide but we sure cleaned up the atmosphere in general. I noticed this on my frequent vacations here and there. For instance I remember back in 1968 and in 1969 on visits to NYC and Los Angeles. Even using a "smog" filter on my camera hadn't helped that much. New York and LA were still ugly with smog. Visits to the same locations in recent years revealed a much different view. In Los Angeles I could now see the mountains. It was beautiful. First time I had ever seen 'em and then in New York City the air was also cleaner—smelled good too. Two years ago I found myself atop a point out in the Painted Desert in New Mexico. They have signs lamenting that you can't see very far now because of the haze. To aid visitors they have sketches showing what it would look like without the haze. This particular day I could see it all. I asked a ranger about it and he said he didn't know why it was clearing up as the Navajo Electric Plants were still going full blast and were still burning coal.

We no longer seem to have rivers catching on fire from pollution. Those problems have been dealt with. I give the "Global Warmers" a lot of the credit for all this. I wrote an article back about 20 years ago about a Leflore County creek called "Little Caston." It was a clean water stream fed by cold springs out of Wolf Mountain. Beautiful Goggle-Eyed Perch made for good fly fishing and the stream was so pretty it sort of hurt your eyes. But that was a long time ago. By 1990 the water was full of chicken and turkey poop. They called it litter. Drew Edmonson, The State Attorney General at the time was suing the state of Arkansas on behalf of several of these rivers and the State of Oklahoma's loss of them to pollution. It may have been a little late for Little Caston but after striking some sort of deal with Arkansas the pollution has been abated somewhat and the last time I looked the creek was clearing up.

All that being said, we have failed to reduce CO2 very much—the global warmer's original goal. What should have been a scientific debate about just what is and isn't connected with this warming has turned into a nasty political argument. National Geographic had a story last year that made about as much sense as anything I've read by them about the warming. They pointed out how much CO2 was being released by the formerly frozen lakes of the arctic that had locked in substantial amounts of this CO2. So much in fact it made the CO2 releases of mankind look puny. Trying to "re-cork" the bottle may be too late. Passing laws now to reduce the gas is foolish and they make us look foolish trying to destroy the economy bringing immediate hardship to mankind which in turn would make it even harder to deal with global warming.

We need to tread softly in this matter. Banning coal and such are already playing havoc with electric bills and they are about to get a lot worse. But global warming may not. Many scientists think the era of warming is about over having been unable to find evident warming the last 20 years. This summer has been the shortest in history for Alaska and thawed areas are rapidly freezing back up and it's still August. Many think Sunspots play a bigger role in earth-temperature change than does Carbon Dioxide.

And this: There has been a rumor that there is a supreme being like a God or something which is said to have created all this—the earth, solar system and the universe. Perhaps it's the "Intelligent Being" many speak of. Well anyway, that's the way I lean on all this. I am a "Panologist." I think it will all pan out. Have a good weekend and stay cool—go to church Sunday.

Wayne Bullard, DPh
wayneBullard@sbcglobal.net

243

08-15-13
Vacationtime for Obama

My grandpa J. T. Bullard who was raised up in a hard work and little play ethic, migrated to Oklahoma around 1903. In later years his idea of a generous vacation time for his 7 boys and 2 girls was a wagon trip to the "Push" (aka Fourche Maline Creek) and camp out for a few days while doing some serious fishing. I'm not even sure he completely approved of that. One thing for sure, years later after I came into his "radar" he had taken to eyeing presidential vacation time with an evil eye.

He was the only person I ever had heard of that didn't like Franklin D. Roosevelt. For one thing J. T. felt FDR spent too much time on the road—the railroad in particular. FDR made a lot of trips for those times and traveled in a private rail car which I'm sure was more comfortable than the "Dinky" that ran through Allen during that period. Grandpa especially begrudged Roosevelt's vacationing up on the east coast at Hyde Park or down in Georgia at Hot Springs.

Truman didn't vacation much and I don't recall J. T. complaining about old Harry. But then came along a guy named Dwight D. Eisenhower. Nothing was more worthless and time wasting than golf and "Ike" loved to play golf. Many was the time I would see grandpa listening to his radio and when the announcer got around to talking about the President's golf game he would just shake his head. "I can't understand why we pay him so much money and let him live in that fancy White House just so he can play golf," he would say. I couldn't help wondering today what grandpa would think of Mr. Obama.

B. Obama just left out for Martha's Vineyard up in Massachusetts for 8 days more of vacation. He took the presidential plane leaving behind all the high profile debates over the budget, government surveillance and his health care reforms. He will spend the next few days not only playing golf but going to the beach, playing basketball and it's said he will be shopping at the Bunch of Grapes bookstore.

He brought Michelle along (she wore a yellow summer dress) while he wore Khakis and a blue shirt. Also, he brought Bo (his dog) and 70 secret servicemen. I don't know how the secret service got up there but one was carrying 2 large mesh bags of presidential basketballs. The 70 guys are staying in 70 hotel rooms, each costing $345 bucks a night. It didn't say where the dog will sleep but he was flown up in his own special plane called an Osprey, a hybrid aircraft which takes off like a helicopter but flies like a plane. It is a large 4 engine troop transport. I hope Bo enjoys his high dollar ride.

Tight finances may have put a little squeeze on the president. He previously stayed at the 28-acre Blue Heron Farm, but it recently sold to a rich architect, Baron Foster of England. This time he is making do in the $7.6 Million mansion owned by a businessman friend from (where?) Chicago. It has a nice basketball court too but sadly, the place is on a public road.

Nearby residents will find their "public" road closed. Local newspapers warn residents not to complain to the City but just call the White House about not being able to go home. Jay Carney, White House spokesman, said that people shouldn't sweat it so much, that the president needs and is looking forward very much to some down time with his family and friends. Oh well—Just let grandpa spin in his grave.

I hope all of you have a good week and when you travel don't close any public streets for 8 days. Don't forget to go to church next Sunday and thanks to those who write. I enjoy hearing from readers.

Wayne Bullard, DPh.

Waynebullard@sbcglobal.net

08-29-13
When You're Teeth Turn Orange

A few days ago as I drove down the highway my tongue found a rough spot on a big jaw tooth. It had broken off a little chunk and we all know any problem with any tooth is bad news and will mean a trip to the dentist. Not just any old dentist either but a dentist up at the Veteran's Hospital. I called them and the sweet voice that called herself Barbara told me to come in on Wednesday at 8:30 am.

Eventually the day arrived and it was a hard day indeed. I soon found myself reclined in a dental chair and a strange woman with a bright light hovering over and looking in my mouth. "What's that on your teeth?" she asked. "Nothing," I replied as I laid there in the lowest bidder chair. "Your partial, is it always this color?" she asked in a voice that couldn't have been more stressed than if she was asking how long I had had aids.

I had no idea what she was talking about. Before a dental visit my teeth are always well brushed, flossed, spit shined and sparkling like jewels. I try to create the impression that I spend most of my waking hours cleaning and tending to them. She put her hands back in my mouth pulling on my partial. "Hot ooo uooin air?" I tried to ask. "Trying to remove your partial," she replied. She quit and I popped 'em right out for her. My eyes also nearly popped out too. There, as bright and orange as any orange crayon was my lower partial. She called for her supervisor. I wondered to myself what would happen to me for was this a disease that had turned my partial orange? "Are my other teeth orange too?" I asked anxiously. "No, just those," she answered and not sweetly. She handed the partial off to her disgusted supervisor like they were a stool sample.

They both left taking it to another room where they said they would try to clean it—leaving me alone to ponder my fate—as well as the color orange. When they returned about 3 minutes later with the same expression on their faces as the doctor has when he is about to tell you that you have 1 week to live. "Have these teeth always been this color?" "Did you have them made this color on purpose?" I tried to explain that they were tooth-color when I left Allen this morning and they turned orange on the way up here. "I swear!" Being used to working with mentally handicapped and shell-shocked veterans, they dismissed me with a hand gesture and an eye-roll. Finally the resident took the equivalent of a shop grinder and ground the orange off. I have no idea why they were orange. They had never been orange before and haven't been since—thank the Lord.

One good thing—they put me in for a new partial. Said mine was worn out anyway. I'm just glad they didn't lock me up. Later, my wife asked, "You get your tooth fixed?" I told her I did and she asked if I got a good checkup. I tried to explain about orange teeth but didn't have much luck. She then said, "Why don't we go see our new granddaughter in Tulsa?" "Well, one reason may be that we are in Oklahoma City right now." But we went and much to our surprise the granddaughter was prettier than ever and had grown. She didn't have any teeth. Of any color. I think that was a good thing.

Have a good weekend and go to church this Sunday. And use caution if your teeth ever change color.

Wayne Bullard, DPh
waynebullard@sbcglobal.net

09-04-14
Mother of the Year

I wrote a story some time ago about a mother in Lebanon who had been voted mother of the year and elected to public office in the nation's legislature. Why was she so worthy? She had encouraged 3 of her boys to dedicate their lives to the Palestine state by becoming suicide bombers. One by one as they got old enough, they had strapped on the explosives and took as many Jews as they could with them to glory as they journeyed to their own reward of virgins. The point of the story wasn't irony or humor but to point out the values, or lack thereof, in the tormented area we call the mid-east.

Another story caught my eye today. In a town called Eaton, Pennsylvania a woman in a sports bar interrupted her evening by going to the restroom and having a baby. She took the new baby, who was born alive, put him in a plastic sack and hid him in the water tank of the toilet. This person then returned to her "date" in the bar and continued to enjoy the wrestling match on the TV. Her boy friend noticed she was bleeding and offered to take her home — and did. The next day a cleaning crew somehow found the boy and called police. An autopsy showed the baby was born alive, and the woman has been found and arrested. We can be proud of the fact that, so far, unlike the Muslims in Arabia, no one has nominated her for "Mother of the Year."

We live in strange times and to some extent among strangers. An unusual mix of Arabs, various racial groups and vested interests such as labor unions in Detroit have brought that once great American city to its knees and into bankruptcy. Much of the city has been burned out and abandoned over the years as run-a-way crime has frightened away the working middle class that once inhabited the city. Most chose to flee to the suburbs (or in many instances just move far away). Detroit has lost over half its population over the past few years and will soon be unable to pay retired city employees their pensions. Muslem calls to prayer can be heard over loudspeakers throughout the city as thugs patrol the streets seeking mischief. One might think they were in Baghdad or Haiti.

You can't help but wonder if this could be the fate of other American Cities. Well, yes it could be. While the circumstances may differ, the causes and problems are the same. It is said that Los Angeles is not too far off from being in the same shoes as Detroit as perhaps is the whole state of California. One development is this: Liberals—, who are thought to be the root cause of most of this, are making sounds like "We can't afford to let these cities fail." So we need to hold our pocketbooks tight here. The people who lead these cities into this mess have and had no intentions to allow these cities to sink. They fully expect those taxpayers in other cities throughout this grand land to pony up and pay the tab, making sure no pension checks miss a beat. They may well do it too. And if they do we can expect other cities which are operating in the red to just keep plowing ahead. Just keep on spending. After all the bills will be paid somehow and with someone else's money.

To quote a man telling his wife goodnight: "Sleep good tonight honey, I've got bad news in the morning." Be sure and go to church this Sunday for the good news and have a good weekend.

Wayne Bullard, DPh
waynebullard@sbcglobal.net

09-12-13
Traveling the West

We left Allen the other day to look at some more of America. After all, I'm retired and that's what old retirees do isn't it? My wife loaded up quite a bit of stuff in case the house burned while we were gone and now we wouldn't lose anything. Got off a little late but eventually found ourselves out in Western Oklahoma looking for a place to grab a bite to eat. We were on our way to a place in Newcastle, Wyoming where a brother named Gerald lives. Meanwhile, I was still hungry and I pulled up to one place—looked homey and rustic but the sign on the front caused me to keep moving. "The Rusty Bucket" is no place for me. Sorry, that's just the way I am. Finally remembered that the McDonalds in Woodward was the best McDonald's in the state (my opinion) so I kept on going.

No one had told me that there were only Mexicans in Woodward these days and you can imagine my surprise when all the help there was no longer little fresh-faced well-scrubbed Anglo Saxons but had been replaced with adult Mexicans. It might have been due to school starting and they needed some adult replacements. I didn't ask. But it wasn't long that the new arrivals had my food out and it was good. We left the place happy and full and I tuned my radio to Fox on Sirius Radio. Fox news was featuring several political figures including John Kerry who did a lot of bloviating engaging in his political puffery. Wow! Got to use those two big words in one sentence. So we drove uneasily on, pretty sure President Obama would soon have us entangled in another war.

We always stop at Slapout for snacks and souvenirs. So, how did Slapout (population 2) get that name? Back in the '30s an old boy put in a small grocery store out there on the highway. The place was nameless but his stock was so thin and unreliable he often had to say he was "slap-out" of whatever it was you needed. Locals named the store "Slapout" and the name stuck. We drove on to Garden City where the air is thick with commerce. Commerce in Garden City consists of feed lots and lots of flies and stink.

The next day we went on up the highway toward Gerald's house in Newcastle up in northeast Wyoming. We made it OK and we toured a lot of local places of interest—some oil wells he still works and 2 of his movie theaters. We looked at the "Dogie" there in Newcastle and the "Hot Springs" Theater over in Hot Springs, SD. Both are very historic and well known in the area. It was fun to poke around this little bit of history.

Of course, visiting Mt. Rushmore is a highlight visit in that area. Gerald's place is probably 65 miles from Rushmore so we spent quite a bit of time just looking, touring all the museums and exhibits of the four famous faces on a mountain. Why were these four Presidents selected to be on the mountain? There was Washington, Jefferson, Lincoln and Theodore Roosevelt. Washington was selected because he was the father of our country. Jefferson made the list because he used his eloquence so very well laying out the laws of liberty. Lincoln is up there because he saved the union and made America a free country for all—regardless of race. Theodore Roosevelt had great vision and color as he set the tone and policies that set the course of America as a leading power in the 20th Century.

We left Newcastle this morning and drove toward Yellowstone Park. The drive through Wyoming and Montana is spectacular and we made a stop at "The Little Big Horn National Monument." I thought this would be a quick stop but it took a while. The park contains a museum which tells all about the battle. I already knew Custer got killed up there in his famous last stand but I pushed onward on the 4 mi loop that shows the field of battle where Custer and his entire command were wiped out. I was glad I stopped and didn't begrudge the time. I am pressing onward to a place called Yellowstone.

Have a good week and don't forget to go to your church Sunday.

251

10-03-13
Wearing Clean Underwear in Centrahoma

I am pretty good at keeping up with my personal hygiene. I shower and put on clean clothes—especially underwear every day. I got to thinking about this the other day after my second trip up to the VA in less than a month. The first was to my dentist which prompted me to write an essay about how hard I work keeping my teeth clean, especially my lower partial. I related that prior to a dental visit I always brushed my teeth extra good and gargled with Listerine until it burned. So it was with much shame and regret that I received criticism from my dentist. Seems my partial had turned orange and we never did figure out why. Never did that before nor since but my oral hygiene was put to question.

I was just getting over that medical snub when it came time for my every-9-month eye exam. I really don't know what to do to impress an eye doctor about my good daily hygiene except to clean my glasses extra good before I go in. It wasn't enough. "You have a lot of crud in your eyes" the pretty lady doctor said, looking me right in my supposedly cruddy eye. "Crud" I replied. "Yeah," she replied. "lots of you guys have cruddy eyes. It's just little bits of stuff, perhaps dried up ocular fluid and a little bit of just environmental stuff." Shamed again, I pled to her: "What can I do?" "Go buy some Johnson's Baby Shampoo and wash your eyes out real good every night when you shower," she replied. Well, I did and I do. Now I possibly have the cleanest eyes in Allen.

Now I wonder where else I might fall short. My mom had her suspicions of my personal hygiene habits when I was in lower grade school—well, upper grades too. She often looked at my underwear as I left for school. When I complained about this violation she said, "You never know when you could be hurt in an accident at school and when you are I want you to have on clean underwear." Finally it happened. I got beaned by a baseball when I was in the 3rd grade and was toted into my classroom, laid on the teacher's desk and my head wound treated. Not once did anyone ever look to see if my underwear was clean and it was then I began wondering about my mom's priorities in life. I think she was more concerned with her own image as a mom than she was with mine as a clean son with fresh and clean underwear.

My mom, my Aunt Ruth and Pearl Downard were good buddies and Pearl was my 3rd grade teacher so I tried to toe the mark in her class but often failed. One day F. R. Heck (who would be elected High Sheriff of Coal County a few years later) stumbled over something one morning and in his fall uttered ""the word "S**t". Miss Pearl was shocked. She stood F. R. by her side, obviously angered and disappointed in the boy and said, "Class, you heard this awful word F. R. just said. It's an ugly word and I know none of you would ever use such a word and I am just sorry you had to hear it." In an effort to make Pearl feel better about F. R's verbal shortcomings I held up my hand and told Ms. Pearl, "My Aunt Ruth says "S**t" all the time."

Ms. Pearl reported my un-asked-for feedback (I overheard it) but nothing ever came of it—from mom or Aunt Ruth. Apparently it wasn't as serious as being found wearing dirty underwear. Nevertheless, I felt the best I could do from then on out was to keep my mouth shut in class and make sure my underwear was indeed, always clean. I failed miserably on the first things but did well on the 2nd. Have a good weekend and be sure to go to church Sunday. And you may wish to make sure you have on clean—well, you know what.

Wayne Bullard, DPh
waynebullard@sbcglobal.net

10-24-13
Medical Advice, Sudsy eyeballs
& German U-Boats

My haphazard articles of "One Pharmacists' View" started long ago when I inserted medical advice in my ads about medication problems. I sometimes strayed off into editorializing about other concerns that struck my fancy. I got letters and emails. One advised me to stick with medicine and leave my other advice out. Another advised me to get more into politics since in his opinion, my medical advice "sucked." More recently, in response to an article in which I related that my eye doctor up at the VA prescribed Johnson's Baby Shampoo to be used to clean up my eye she described as full of crud a reader wondered if it's what the eye beheld or what might actually be in the eye. I was inundated with email (2) about this and am sad to report that one eye is now sore. So you "I told you so" guys can be happy.

I am often corrected about the "facts" I write about. I try to get my facts at least 80% correct leaving me a little room (20%) for parable. My story some time ago about my mom pulling out the choke on the family '35 Ford at Christmastime in 1943 when gasoline was severely rationed, set off a little talk—about the war and the rationing that went with it. So here we go on another tangent—rationing.

After the war started on December 7, 1941, it took a little while for America to realize what a pickle it was in—commodity wise. America had been a land of plenty. You could buy anything you had the money for in those days and we thought of ourselves as exceptional. Suddenly, after the outbreak of war there was talk of rationing. German U-Boats roamed our shores at will, sinking ships carrying coffee and other stuff from South America. Meanwhile the Japs had cut off our supply of rubber from Indo China, leaving us with only 8% of what we had to have.

A lot of people rushed out to Sears and bought themselves an extra set of tires—while they could. All car manufacturing ceased and showrooms were soon empty. Buying panics during Christmas resulted in rationing on gasoline, coffee, sugar, meat, butter and fat. Why fat? Well it was used in the manufacture of explosives. Tires were simply unavailable. Synthetic tires were not invented at this point. What tires there were went to the military—the same military that went around and seized those tires the hoarders had bought that Christmas.

Scrap-iron drives provided an unbelievable amount of iron and steel for the defense effort as well as a lot of "Pop" money for kids who gathered it up for a penny a pound. Roosevelt set the national speed limit at 35 and while many didn't pay much attention to it at first, we all did when our tires wore out. A lot of people had to put their cars up on blocks (no spare parts) for the duration and they gave their gas stamps to their pastors to help out their church families with emergencies. I think it helped out with church attendance. Our old car's tires had so many "boots" (crude patches) in them making our ride so rough that we did well to make 35mph.

Ordinary folk (like us) got a windshield sticker with an "A" while more important folks sported a "B" sticker. The "A" would get you 4 gallons a week most of the time, a "B" was worth 8 gallons a week. The Coveted "C" was for doctors and other VIPs. Rationing ended in September of 1945 but it was about 1948 before you could walk into a car-dealer's showroom and buy a new car in any color or shape you wanted. Food items such as sugar and coffee were soon plentiful as were the long missing Snickers and Milky Way candy bars.

Be sure and go to Church this Sunday—God never rations his many blessings. And be thankful we live in a land of freedom and plenty.

Wayne Bullard, DPh
waynebullard@sbcglobal.net

10-31-13
Baseball and World History

The World Series started last week in Boston and my old friend Harry Sheldon up in New York State shared a baseball story with me the other day. It concerns a third-string catcher named Moe Berg and just why Moe was invited to go on tour in baseball-crazy Japan in 1934—with Babe Ruth and Lou Gehrig. The answer was simple. Berg was a US spy. Speaking 15 languages (including Japanese), Moe had two loves: baseball and spying.

In Tokyo, garbed in a kimono, Berg took flowers to the daughter of an American diplomat being treated in St. Luke's Hospital—the tallest building in the Japanese capital. He never delivered the flowers. The ball-player ascended to the hospital roof and filmed key features: the harbor, military installations, railway yards, etc.

Eight years later General Jimmy Doolittle studied Berg's films in planning his spectacular raid on Tokyo. Berg's father, Bernard Berg, a pharmacist in Newark, New Jersey, taught his son Hebrew and Yiddish. Moe, against his father's wishes, began playing baseball on the street. His father disapproved and never once watched his son play. In Barringer High School, Moe learned Latin, Greek and French. He graduated magna cum laude from Princeton having added Spanish, Italian, German and Sanskrit to his linguistic skills. During further studies at the Sorbonne, in Paris and Columbia Law School he picked up Japanese, Chinese, Korean, Indian, Arabic, Portuguese and Hungarian—15 languages in all plus some regional dialects. Moe Berg loved his language studies.

Later on during WW II, he was parachuted into Yugoslavia to assess the value to the war effort of the two groups of partisans there. He reported back that Marshall Tito's forces were widely supported by the people so Winston Churchill ordered all-out support for the Yugoslav underground fighter, rather than Mihajlovic's Serbians.

Not finished yet, Moe penetrated German-held Norway next and located a secret heavy water plant—part of the Nazis' effort to build an atomic bomb. His information guided the Royal Air Force in a bombing raid which destroyed the plant. There was still a lot of concern of how advanced the Nazis' were in development of the A-Bomb. If they were successful, they would win the war. So we sent in our baseball player again.

Moe went to Switzerland under the code name Remus to attend a German physicist (Werner Heisenberg—a Nobel Laureate—lecture) and find out how close the German's were to this A-Bomb. Moe posed as a Swiss graduate student carrying in his pocket a pistol and a cyanide pill. If Moe found that Werner was close to building the weapon he was to shoot him and then swallow the cyanide pill. Moe, sitting in the front row, determined that the Germans were nowhere near their goal. Later, Moe walked Heisenberg back to his hotel and complimented him on his speech. Awarded the Medal of Merit—America's highest honor for a civilian in wartime, Berg refused to accept, as he couldn't tell people about his exploits. After he died, his sister accepted the Medal and it hangs in the Baseball Hall of Fame in Cooperstown.

One more quote from Moe. "Maybe I can't hit as much as Ruth, but I speak more languages than him."

Have a good weekend and be sure and go to church Sunday. Even if you just speak one language.

Wayne Bullard, DPh
waynebullard@sbcglobal.net

257

11-28-13
and Then its Thanksgiving

You know, time has a way of moving quickly and catching you unaware. Yes, another Thanksgiving will be here next week. A time for your family to gather up, eat some delicious food, visit and enjoy each other's company. Or at least that's the way it should be. We often forget about the homeless, people in poverty and those who find themselves alone—without family or friends—perhaps the ultimate poverty. Look around and see what you can do this Thanksgiving. Give a hand up to those in need of material or friendship. And consider this when your family gathers: Put away those smart phones. Nothing says "rude" louder and with greater effect than a person pulling out one's phone and retreating into a "cell phone coma" than choosing this little idiot box over precious family fellowship.

There used to be an old philosopher in Allen by the name of Charley Vandeveer. Charley, a barber and Furniture Store operator, was a constant source of new and unusual philosophical sayings. One day I walked into his store and he was sitting alone staring off into space. He looked like he had received bad news. "What's wrong, Charley?" I asked. "Oh I was just sitting here thinking and it came to me—I'm 40 years old and I'm not ever going to amount to anything." Later after he had cut my hair I was able to cheer him up considerably with a joke or two. But as the day went on, I wondered if I should consider my own status and perhaps go ahead and admit: "I'm not ever going to amount to anything either."

My Salt Lake City correspondent, A. R. True sent me something to think about last week about growing older and not being able to do anything about it. And like Charley, I guess I can forget about ever amounting to anything.

Your kids are becoming you…but your grandchildren are perfect! Going out is good…coming home is better.

You forget names...But it's OK because other people forgot they even knew you!

You realize you're never going to be really good at anything.

The things you used to like to do you no longer care to do but you really do care that you don't care to do them anymore.

You sleep better in your recliner with the TV blaring than in bed. It's called "pre-sleep."

You miss the days when everything worked with just an "ON and "OFF" switch.

You tend to use more 4 letter words..."what?"..."when?"...???

What used to be freckles are now liver spots.

Everybody whispers

You have 3 sizes of clothes in your closet...2 of which you will never wear.

Have a good weekend and if you're still under about 75, go ahead and try to amount to something. And don't forget to go to church this Sunday. You might learn how to amount to something down there.

Wayne Bullard, DPh

waynebullard@sbcglobal.net

11-07-13
Global Warming Gives
Us the Cold Shoulder

Since the beginning of time there have been people who think they know when the end of time is coming. Many had a following of believers who usually wound up on a mountain-top or someplace with their group and count down the minutes to the end together. Of course it never happens. Surprisingly, these people usually take it well, explaining why it didn't happen and so forth and go home with their heads held high and are never heard from again—but not liberals.

I see that Mayor Bloomberg (another liberal end of timer) was in London the other day and in the course of a speech lamented how backward and uninformed many people are and made the following statement: "In parts of America there still remain people who don't believe in evolution or even in global warming." Before you think too much of that just remember that liberals in this country often state that all people having some sort of difference of opinion from them are "backward and ignorant." Not everyone accepts as "settled science" that global warming is, as some think, good reason for taking political actions such as are presently being taken.

One problem with the global warming theories is that they have not, over time, panned out. The "warmers" cried wolf long ago and nothing happened. In fact, this summer the UN released a massive new climate report that throws cold water over the theory and its time tables. Quite simply, the report states that Global Warming has been on the pause button since 1998. No warming, particularly in the Northern Hemisphere (where it has actually cooled) has been recorded. The 2,200 page new Technical Report attributes this to a combination of factors such as natural variability, reduced heating from the sun and the ocean acting like a "heat sink" to suck up extra warming in the atmosphere.

Now the debate is just how long this cooling will last? Possibly a long time says Anastasios Tsonis of the University of Wisconsin. He points to the repeated periods of warming and cooling in the 20th century. Tsonis goes on to say that there are a lot of climate models out there but they don't agree with each other and they don't even agree with reality. In fact, the IPCC (Panel on Climate Change) admit that none of the models predicted the hiatus—or to put it another way, no one saw it coming. Professor Tsonis criticized the IPCC for ignoring so much of the new research that studies have turned up regarding climate change as they still claim that human activity is responsible for 95% of global warming.

Judith Curry, chair of the School of Earth and Atmospheric Science at Georgia Tech, says the IPCC is taking a big credibility hit over the cool-down and they're stating that the cooling is now, or shortly will be over. "The IPCC has torqued the science in an unfortunate direction." She further complained about them using explicit policy agendas to achieve their own political goals. These twisted "facts" do not inspire confidence in the final product—which now drives our politics and energy policies toward items such as the Keystone pipeline and the production of electricity.

In a related story last Friday, President Obama issued Executive Orders to several government agencies to take immediate steps—steps that will cost billions more—to cope with the effects of the oncoming disasters associated with global warming. Guess he didn't see the UN memo.

Have a nice weekend and enjoy the cooler than normal fall weather. Be sure and go to church Sunday and take your coat.

Wayne Bullard, D.Ph.
waynebullard@sbcglobal.net

12-05-13
Doing Thanksgiving

The wife and I drove up I-44 to St Louis 2 weeks ago and visited with daughter Traci Runge and her family for a few days. While there (also one of the reasons for going) we attended a musical performance by her 3rd through 5th grade choir. About 80 of the kids marched in singing and entertained the large crowd for about an hour with seasonal songs. Nothing like hearing a bunch of little kids singing well to start your holidays off right. Traci teaches music at the school.

Grandson Alec was also in a musical play called "Thoroughly Modern Millie." The production was originally produced for Broadway by Michael Leavitt and was performed by the Westminster Christian Academy there in Balwin. It was a great production and it's always a pleasure to get to see your own grandkids (which we knew were talented anyway) perform and we really enjoyed the visit up there.

We left Balwin (St Louis) Monday morning and drove to Branson where we stayed until Sunday and drove home. Tim and Lesli Costner along with their two daughters, Emilee and Meegan drove up from Allen and shared a condo with us as did Charles and Eula Tilly of Norman. Steve Bullard, wife Courtney and daughters Francesca and Charlotte spent a few nights too with 5 month old Charlotte being the star of the show. Shopping and show going took place and a few contests in dominoes as well. Shows attended included "The Dixie Stampede "Dickens' Christmas Carol" and "It's a Wonderful Life."

We had a good time and drove home Sunday. We were somewhat tired and worn Monday morning as we ventured out into the thick fog to keep an eye appointment in Oklahoma City for Pat. I couldn't see my "shortcut" in Holdenville and had to make a detour through town. It was fairly difficult for two old "codgers" such as us to see, which makes one wonder why we didn't just stay at home. Well, you could see enough to drive (however unsafe it was) and we made it just fine.

Our wrong turn in Holdenville was followed by another or two which made me wonder about the human brain. In my wondering let me say there definitely is a difference between male and female brains.

I depend a lot on my wife to provide a balance in the arguments as to whether we should turn off or go straight. She claims that I am not apt to be asking directions anyway so we probably shouldn't even have the navigation device in the car (which is run by a bossy woman who doesn't yet know they moved the highway over in Atwood in 1965). There are, for sure, some basic differences in men and women's brains—which any wife can attest to.

A brain scientist has recently found some of these differences. The brain lobes are interconnected and talk to each other. Well, that may explain those voices we hear but I think the good doctor had something else in mind. Connectors on males run from front to back of the brain while the female connectors mostly run right to left. Which is to say women's left and right sides of brain are hooked up better than their counterparts. This gives women more verbal skills which means they talk a lot more. It also gives them more intuition. Note: Intuition can be defined here as "gut feelings." Another way to put it is: "Thinking without thinking."

Women also have better memories and remember faces better than men. Who knew? Good news on one front for the verbally challenged, poor memory males—males are better map readers (I tried to tell her) and have better muscular control. Well.

Have a good weekend, dress warm and go to church this Sunday and if you don't know where the church is, ask a woman.

Wayne Bullard, DPh

Main Street Downtown Allen 1938

12-12-13
News from Allen and Beyond

In case anyone of my readers live under a rock or have been in a coma for a spell just let me say this: OU defeated OSU in Saturday's bedlam game. This game is called "Bedlam" for good reason. It's hectic. Channel 5 (KOCO) television in their pregame program in front of the frigid T. Boone Pickens Stadium said "OSU deserves the victory this year. They have earned the Big-12 Championship and it looks like they will get it this afternoon!" The cowboys stood to not only get the glory and a Choice BCS bowl to play in, they would have the chance to earn an extra $6 million bucks. At least that's what she said.

Sometimes you don't get what you "deserve" and sure enough, they didn't. In a few hours Sooner fans were celebrating yet another victory while cowboy fans went home on suicide watch. They always have such expectations of their team but it often fails to live up to their expectations. OU defeated the hopeful upstarts 33-24. Stoops will take his team on an unexpected trip to New Orleans and play Alabama. Gundy will assemble his Cowboys in the Cotton Bowl and have it out with Missouri. As always, OSU fans can be assured they have my complete sympathy pertaining to the tragedy.

I mentioned that Advocate readers expect and receive news that just isn't always available in other papers. Allen varsity teams, both boys and girls starting off with lots of young and inexperienced players are looking good. Be sure and get out and support these kids this winter. The popcorn is good and hot too. In other news a male cheerleader at OSU attempted to trip an OU player. I am so shocked. OSU officials promise punishment will be handed out to the "criminal" OU fans are mostly passive about this outlandish act.

Overseas this week we find President Obama in Africa attending to the Mandela funeral and he has already messed up by shaking hands with Raul Castro, the communist strongman from Cuba. Republicans are screaming. Continuing on, it comes as no surprise that the annual wave of stealing the Baby Jesus and Mary and Joseph images from church nativity scenes is sweeping the nation. So far local police have learned of no such crimes in Allen—in fact there may not be any of these kinds of nativity scenes in Allen. I think they were all stolen last year.

Canada has made new territorial claims on the North Pole. President Putin of Russia announced he is beefing up artic defenses. All this time I thought it belonged to the USA. I make a motion that we avoid any problems with Canada and Russia by "Quit-Claiming" any rights we have up there while reserving all the mineral rights.

There's no way to keep up to date without news from New York. Cops raided a home up there, injuring all three of its occupants as it did so. They broke down the door, pepper sprayed the woman of the house, her son and her daughter. Exactly what all happened next is not clear but the 3 family members said they were beat up and hospitalized from the "police brutality" that ensued. Tragically, the family parakeet, named Tito, had his cage tipped over and Tito was slammed to the floor where an overweight police officers (probably the one who thought up this raid) stepped on Tito. Tito was examined by an expert and pronounced dead. The unnamed lady victim has now hired a lawyer and is suing the police department for killing her bird. Nothing about her kids who are now out of the hospital. Police have filed no charges and do not expect to. I don't know what a parakeet costs these days but looks like the police up there are going to have to cough up some cash and buy the lady a new bird.

I hope you are enjoying this Christmas Season as much as I am. Meanwhile, don't forget to go to church this Sunday. "Hanging of the Green" has been rescheduled for this Sunday at First Baptist Church.

Wayne Bullard, DPh

12-19-13
Christmas Rush

Christmas, which has been creeping up on us has now gathered steam and is practically here. Many will be traveling to visit kin, and others, like us, will be staying at home and receiving them. I think I prefer the latter. Last week we drove to Tyler, Texas to attend the graduation of our granddaughter, Julia Runge. Julia graduated from the University of Texas at Tyler with honors and we wanted to be there. There was a cold rain falling all the way and parts of North Texas was still in a mess from the ice storms that swept through. But we made it fine and had a great time. After Commencement we all gathered at a restaurant called Bernard's' for the celebration meal. We drove back Saturday.

Most of us made it through the sleet and ice without incident but I have to admit I did take a spill in my driveway and about "brained" myself. I managed to get up and assured the "not all that concerned" crowd that I was OK and we all went to Calvin and watched our girl's beat Asher in the Pontotoc County Tournament. My wife wants me to go get my head examined but I assured her I am OK. #%@&* Any misspells and typos *@#$% you may see are not my fault. @$#%*# My head is just fine. @##%+.

I ran into two readers in Tyler the other night who said they read my column regularly and said they enjoyed keeping up with happenings up here. Thanks Sandy and Lisa. I always appreciate hearing from my readers no matter where they are. Also, I got a nice letter from Randall Wagner which I gave to the paper. It may be published here someplace. Randall's history with Allen goes way back and in fact, my own history with him is getting to be lengthy.

About 15 years ago Randall wrote me and said he had the Bell from Sunray DX Refinery here in Allen. He wondered if he could just donate it to the town as he had no use for it. I talked to some of the city fathers and it was during the time we were building the new war memorial and we quickly discovered a place for it. In fact, we designed a place of honor for it. We would get a special truck and tote the bell to Allen and make a nice home for it. We were still working on the inscription when they asked me how heavy it was. I called Mr. Wagner to see if the rig we had could lift it or not. He felt that it could. "Where is the bell now?" I asked. "Oh I keep it in my china cabinet." "It weighs about 3 oz."

Turned out we were victims of our own imagination as we drastically down-sized our big plans. A presentation ceremony with pictures took place in the lobby of the Farmer's State Bank after a few weeks and the Bell is in the safe hands of those bank officers. If any of you remember Mr. Wagner, or not, you can cheer up his Christmas a bit with a note or Christmas Card. Randall is in a nursing home. His address is Randall Wagner, 1205 S 4th, Duncan, Ok. 73533.

We have one more edition before Christmas but let me wish each of you a very Merry Christmas and hope each of you stay safe. Don't neglect the reason for the season. Be sure and go to Church Sunday.

Wayne Bullard, DPh.

waynebullard@sbcglobal.net

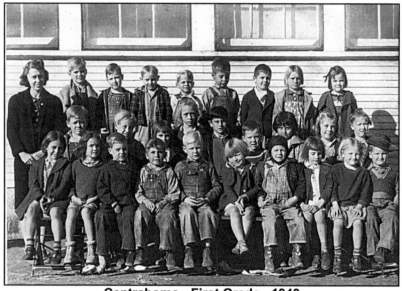

Centrahoma - First Grade - 1940
Mrs. Klinglesmith, Teacher
Wayne is pictured front row, far right with hat.

12-14-13
A Centrahoma Christmas Story

I don't remember too much about the year of 1940 except it was the year I started first grade and of course I remember the Christmas of 1940. I remember that first day of school and I remember the Christmas Program of 1940. The old schoolhouse was odd in that it was wired for electricity on one end—the auditorium part, but the long hallway leading south to the several classrooms was dark. They just weren't hooked up and we had no lights in the classrooms. But it made no difference what-so-ever to me. My attention was on other things.

I remember my teacher, Ruby Klinglesmith. I can remember her soft voice as she rehearsed us pretty hard for the Christmas Program that we were to do. There was no doubt the kindly young woman loved each of her 1st grade students and that we loved and trusted her back. We would do anything for her.

The night of the program finally arrived and a troop of parents assisted our teacher in dressing us for the play. And what a play it was! Some of us were dressed as angels and others as wise men and there was a Mary and Joseph. The baby Jesus was displayed right there on the stage and nobody thought anything about it. Ruby would get into some deep trouble at many schools today with such outrageous behavior as this—promoting a religion—but I doubt if she would have cared. As I recall, the show came off without a hitch—that we noticed anyway.

Ruby was the first of several teachers I had in elementary that started the day out with a flag salute and reading of a bible verse and she would pray for us. Each room had a picture of George Washington and Abraham Lincoln (George's eyes followed you around in the room) in it and the teachers made certain we knew who and what they were. Such was the norm at Centrahoma in those days. It was a very poor community but it had "values" that were known and taught to its children. We sang our songs that night in the brightly lighted school auditorium to a large crowd. The crowd was supportive and happy. I might even add they seemed "satisfied." I know that we up on the stage were.

It's sort of hard to remember so many people living in that area as there were—a community with 3 grocery stores, rail service, bus service, busy post office and a prosperous main street. The good people of Centrahoma didn't know this would be their last "peacetime" Christmas for many years to come, and perhaps their last in rural Centrahoma. A devastating war would be raging the next December and all would be forever changed—including the future of the town and the school by world events.

I still stay in touch with some of those kids that sang songs for Ms. Klinglesmith that night, 73 years ago. My first grade best friends Letha Mae Moore, Roy Byrd, Bessie Key and Jack, Annie Smith and some others still stay in touch by way of these articles I write and I always perk up when I get to hear from them. Ruby Klinglesmith passed away in 2001 at the age of 101. I don't know how many kids that stood on that stage that night are still living but I know many are already gone.

I hope each of you, including the Centrahoma Class of 1952 and all of my readers have an extra good and Merry Christmas and Happy New Year. Don't neglect the reason for the season and be sure and go to Church this Sunday.

Wayne Bullard, DPh.

12-31-13
Happy New Year

Life goes on and the old year goes out with barely a nod as Allen residents turn their eyes to 2014. A few more weeks of winter and we'll be enjoying something called "spring." So far the winds of December have blown cold and brought icy sleet in from the frigid north and now everyone is wondering what January will bring. I know the Farmer's Almanac says it will be colder than normal with some snow and the seeds of the persimmon trees have perfect little forks in their centers—again indicating a cold and bad winter. For those uneducated readers, a spoon inside the seed means a mild winter. If you don't believe me, ask any Indian.

Tradition and habit suits me and that may be why I showed up Christmas Eve Night at the Methodist Church for their Christmas Eve Service. The story of Christmas was presented in music and scripture reading followed by some pretty good coffee and cake in the fellowship room. I appreciate those guys for their faithfulness in these services. There didn't seem to be as many Christmas lights put out this year. I don't know if it was the weather or not but I know the times I had to put my own "stuff" out it was either real cold and windy, raining and freezing or sleeting so I skipped this year. The best part is I don't have to take anything down out there this New Year.

One California church likes to get attention by creating unique manger scenes. This year the figure of Christ was replaced by a likeness of Trayvon Martin lying in a pool of blood bleeding to death. Just why and how they can equate the importance of this widely noted incident with the sacrificial death of Christ is in itself remarkable. Maybe the preacher is smoking a little too much marijuana.

I can't let the year go by without just a word about the Post Office. Our local office is always looked upon as special and does a steady-good job. But this year the Nation's Postal System came out smelling like a rose. FedEx and UPS both do good jobs too but floundered and failed this year with millions of Christmas packages left in their distribution centers—spoiling more than a few people's Christmas. Meanwhile, the USPS hummed right along getting the job done. It might also be noted here that although the USPS is in a financial bind and is raising postage it did make $660 million this year on delivering the mail. So why should they raise the price of stamps? Read on.

Congress has demanded that the Post Office "prefund" their retirement benefits—something no one else has to do—driving them into a negative cash flow. Congress is also trying to re-make the USPS into a private corporation—like UPS and FedEx. I don't know about you, but to me the Post Office is sort of like the armed forces, an institution founded as a service to the taxpayers by our founding fathers. I think we need to leave it alone and let it render this basic service to the taxpayers.

I encourage all my readers to keep a stiff upper lip, don't spit into the wind and keep a good eye out in 2014. And be sure and go to church this Sunday.

Wayne Bullard, DPh

03-06-14
Chickens in Key West and Edmond

I was asked the other day why I hadn't written any more about the persecuted chickens of Key West. Well, as you may know they are not that bad off. My attention came to these birds several years ago while I was visiting this tourist mecca and my family was eating at one of the famous sidewalk cafes on Duval Street. The waiter was all dressed up and the table had a white cloth but that didn't stop what they call a gypsy rooster from hopping up on our table to see what we were having to eat. Our waiter wasted no time scolding and shooing the freeloading guest away.

The man let me know the chickens are "protected" and they can do nothing about them. Later at my hotel I pushed the up button on my poolside elevator and when the doors opened a hen walked in with me. When the doors opened she walked out, seemingly sure of herself and where she was going. I was amazed. She went one direction and I went the other. Obviously Key West was a place where the Chicken could cross the road and his motives would not be questioned. The next day I noticed that chickens were all over the place so I did some research.

Chickens came to Key West from Cuba. In the late 1800s about half the population of this area was Cuban and the kind of chicks imported were called "Cubalayas." Chicken fighting was outlawed in the 1970s and the fighting Cubalayas found themselves out of work. After a few years their owners had died off and in general the birds became Key West's homeless Gypsy chickens. They roamed the town at will and did quite well.

Of course the chickens were seen as pests by many residents and pretty soon the city fathers were being called on to outlaw the pesky neighborhood pests. A chicken catcher was hired, pens were purchased but after one month the catcher reported that after catching a few birds some scoundrels had set them free. He had only 3 to show for his efforts. It was then the city dads discovered they had pro-chicken-freedom-fighters working on behalf of these downtrodden foul—the chickens found they had friends in high places and the people of Key West discovered itself in two camps. You were either for the chickens or against them.

The dedicated chicken-loving-freedom-fighters won most of the rounds and after many feisty battles in city hall here is what they did. A certain number of chickens would be allowed to stay but 500 or so per year would be deported to the mainland and kept in a chicken paradise (at least that's what they told the chickens.) The chicken heaven is located near Orlando and furnishes housing, all you can eat, places to roost and a chicken community center.

Let us fast forward to the present day and go to the City of Edmond. Edmond is a bastion of much zoning, higher-income neat-nicks and liberal Republicans. Some may wonder just what a liberal republican is. They are thought to be conservative in their political ideology but believe in global warming and fresh eggs. A recent story in The Daily Oklahoman blows the whistle on these fresh egg eating chicken lovers. It seems some are harboring their own small herds of laying hens illegally in back yards. The chickens, I suppose, are warned to be quiet and not to cackle whenever they lay an egg but I know it's hard to keep a working hen quiet. Unlike the laid back and content Key West Chickens, the Chicks of Edmond live a nightmare of being found out—all the while doing only what their sponsors placed them there to do. The chicken code enforcers of Edmond needs to lighten up and you can be sure this reporter will keep his eye on this developing story.

Congratulations to our Allen Girls on a great basketball season and as always, let me remind you to go to church this Sunday.

Wayne Bullard, DPh

waynebullard@sbcglobal.net

02-27
The Worst Bad Times over at Centrahoma

I just finished reading a book—Timothy Egan's story of those who survived the great American dust bowl—titled "The Worst Hard Time." It's a well written book and anyone who has an interest in Oklahoma History would enjoy this story of bad times in Oklahoma. I guess it's a story that may explain who we are and perhaps why. It made me think of my friend and publisher Bill Robinson. He loves a story about things that went wrong. Consequently he liked it when I wrote about my worse trips, most messed up Christmas and stuff like that.

I had my 79th birthday this week and it was just fine. Sorry Bill. But I can go back to 1945 which was my 10th and find one that wasn't so good. We had moved the fall before to Stonewall from Centrahoma and I wasn't all that settled about it. Stonewall was a nice place to live with all its modern amenities such as flush toilets, natural gas and hot and cold running water—it just didn't make up for a loss of friends and people I knew. I had spent several days at home sick with flu or some such disorder that dismal war-time month and S. L. Burns, M. D. (our neighbor) came over and gave me a penicillin shot. Next thing you know I broke out and got my first and only case of "Trench Mouth." Anyway I was sick and miserable.

Mom went ahead and made me a birthday cake while announcing there would be no party. "You are too contagious," she said. But mom called an old friend of mine, Mrs. Pearl Downard to come up. "Miss Pearl" as she was known had been my 3rd grade teacher and family friend. I was happy and very pleased to see this lady. Her act of kindness that day brightened up an otherwise "Bill Robinson" kind of day and Pearl made sure I had a happy birthday. Which proves you can still have a happy birthday without eating a cake.

This week I got an email from a very old friend from Centrahoma—a guy named Roy D. Byrd. Roy is a retired teacher from Cameron State down at Lawton who entered first grade with me at Centrahoma. He had finally gotten around to reading a Christmas story I had written called "A Centrahoma Christmas" in the Coalgate paper. I enjoyed his email and wrote him back that I had heard from yet another member of that class that started first grade with us that summer morning in 1940. Letha Mae (Moore) Whitlow had called and we shared our Christmas experiences and she told me she had had a bad fall on the ice right before Christmas and was slow in getting over it. I hope she is doing better now and Letha it was good to hear from you.

There were a lot of people living in Coal County around Centrahoma in 1940 but a lot of them had pulled out or were thinking about it. We were blissfully unaware that Centrahoma Schools were entering their last phase and in a few years the school and much of the community would just vanish. Not vanished yet are the memories of friends I had there that day we moved away—good memories of 27 first-graders standing in the bright sunshine by our teacher, Ruby Klinglesmith— looking confidently to the future.

I hope you had a good week and your future is bright. I also hope that you make it to church this Sunday.

Wayne Bullard, DPh

waynebullard@sbcglobal.net

Don Ellis and Wayne in Alabama

03-13-14
The Road To Alabama

Pat's older brother Don has been ailing down in Southern Alabama for a while now and thus her other brother Fred decided it was prudent for some Oklahoma family to go down there and check in on him. There are six siblings in that family—Don, Pat, Freda, Margaret, Carol and Fred. Fred and his wife Theda volunteered to take their comfy Chevrolet Van and Carol and Pat went along too. I thought about not going with this wing of the Ellis clan but thought better of it and jumped on board at the last moment.

One reason I sort of wavered on the trip is that it's so far. As best I can tell the trip to down near the Gulf Coast is 738 miles. It can be made in one day if you're young and don't have any blood pressure problems, blood clotting disorders, travel phobia or heart trouble. We took two days going and two days coming back. We spent 3 nights with Don and his ever-busy wife Cathy deep in the piney woods of far south Alabama enjoying the company, the southern food and great Alabama hospitality. Don was happy to see us and us him. We spent a busy schedule with that couple and headed back home Sunday morning.

It was good for me to get to spend time with this guy again. I first met Don when I was about 10 years old when we were both kind of new in town. We became friends that day riding our bikes and got better acquainted on those soft summer days on the dirt streets of Stonewall. By that time I had already met my wife, Pat, and since I already knew who she was, I sort of knew who he was. We have been good buddies ever since — Don I mean, not my wife. Oh well, the wife and I are pretty good buddies too. Don grew up and had an illustrious career in the military. During his 27 years of service he served in the Navy, The Air Force and finished up serving his country as an officer in the Army.

Don served his country well in each branch but it was in the army that he served 2 full tours in Vietnam. He wound up over there on another short tour at the end of the war helping the Army get equipment shipped home, salvaging what he could and sometimes having to destroy it. Don saw combat in Vietnam and for his service received several awards, including the Bronze Star.

Don and others like him have been through a lot in their lives in service to their countries and many times we are unable to really convey our gratitude for what these men and women have done for our country. Words often fail us but a simple "Thank you for your service" works pretty well in that direction. And to Don just let me say this: "Thanks Brother- in- law."

It was, as always, great to get back home and it's good to see that signs of spring have started edging in. I'm very grateful for that. I hope your week is great and that you can go to Church Sunday.

Wayne Bullard, DPh
waynebullard@sbcglobal.net

03-20-14
How to get along with or without your cat

Last week I read of a hapless family trapped in their upstairs bedroom by a killer cat. The animal in question was a 22 pound Himalayan housecat which looked like a regular-generic Oklahoma cat. After calling 911 the police along with animal control officers captured the riled up cat and placed it into custody. The victimized family, a grown man, a grown woman and a female child admitted that the cat had been provoked by the little girl when she pulled its tail. The family, feeling guilty of provoking this otherwise innocent cat chose not to have the cat given away or (heaven forbid) put down but instead placed the cat in the care of an animal psychologist. He promises to sort out the cat's neurosis and other issues and restore it to good mental health before bringing it home to live happily ever after.

After reading about this happy cat story I was reminded of Stonewall, my old hometown and also home to a boy named Alfred France. In addition to Alfred (and me) the little town was also hometown to a multitude of cats, none of which had shown any tendency toward reproductive responsibility. Nor had the population of this fair city shown any tendency toward neutering these kitty-swingers whose irresponsible life styles were over-populating the area with more and more cats. One day an old lady had asked Alfred to take her cat's latest production of kittens and just "take 'em off for me and don't tell me what you did." Alfred was good at that and it's a shame the couple with the 22 pound Himalayan didn't know Alfred. He could take a cat out for a ride and make its death appear to be an accident.

One day our neighbor, Mrs. Nance, stopped Alfred on the street and sure enough she had a big kitten problem too. Nance, as she was called, had a .22 rifle and furnished the bullets as Alfred, by now a hardened killer, took the cats, one by one and started holding them up (one at a time) and putting the gun to their little heads and pulling the trigger. Mrs. Nance yelled whoa and fired him on the spot. She entreated me to just take them off. After watching Alfred's Gestapo style executions, I told Mrs. Nance that I just wouldn't be able to help her. I don't know what she did with those little kittens but the last time I was in Stonewall I saw a cat that looked a lot like one of them.

Alfred and my brother Gerald were good friends and buddies. Both worked down at the local movie and operated projectors. I lost track of this cat killer for many years but a year or two ago I helped Gerald locate Alfred (using a computer). Gerald got his address and said he would go to Fort Smith, where Alfred lived and they would have a visit. "Better hurry," I am in the hospital here Alfred told us. He was very right. The next day I got a call from Alfred's daughter in Arkansas. The famous projectionist, story teller, childhood friend and yes, cat assassin had passed away during the night and our big get together plans had come too late.

The town of Stonewall was full of remarkable people and "characters" such as Alfred and I consider myself lucky from the experiences I had growing up in such a community. If you are like me and getting a lot of years on your odometer and want to see some of your old friends before it's "too late" just take my advice and go do it. Also, be sure and go to your church this Sunday.

Wayne Bullard, DPh
waynebullard@sbcglobal.net

04-3-14
Governor Christie's Waistband

I know it's not politically correct and not even "nice" to notice how fat someone is anymore but I was sort of fascinated by New Jersey Gov. Christie's story following his lap band surgery nearly a year ago. He says he has already lost 100 pounds. What I mean to say is, he still looks pretty big to me. It may be harder than it would seem to lose weight when you are running for president while under constant attack by your political foes over closing a few traffic lanes. The good Governor says he had nothing to do with that and it was some underlings doing it on their own and without his knowledge.

Well, the story looks to me like his 100 lost pounds. I'm still not 100% convinced he had nothing to do with closing those lanes and I wonder about the 100 pounds. Christie is doing everything he can to clear up these matters. He just got a report in from an investigative committee that he indeed did not know anything about it (lane closures not the fat) and that he has fired everyone that participated in ordering the lanes closed. The lane closures resulted in terrible traffic jams in an area represented by some of the politicians who wouldn't give him political support in the last election. About that fat? I don't know. Maybe he should step up on some public scales and invite the press. Or perhaps not.

Christie's problems sort of leave The Republicans in a mess as they look over the field of big candidates (no pun intended) for 2016. The democrat's front runner (Hillary) may have already sewed up the Democrat's nomination and that is a problem for that party. As time goes by and The Affordable Health Care Act digs in, both Obama and Benghazi Hillary look a bit more tarnished. In fact, the two Bushes don't look near so bad now as they fade into the past. In fact, a 3rd Bush's (Jeb) name is being floated. Some think he would make a good run but in any case his mom said she wouldn't vote for him. But then I'm not sure the country is ready for yet another Bush.

Anyway, I don't think any democrats will be riding in on Obama's coattails. His negatives are at an all-time high and this time on a subject which younger Americans seem to know little or nothing about—our Foreign Policy. Already striking out on "Obama Care" the President has recently polished up his image as a Caesar at home (governing with a pen and a telephone) with executive orders and a Chamberlain image abroad. His interactions have been very ineffective and embarrassing during the current crisis. When voters look down the road will they be thinking of Obama's snafu's and Hillary's Benghazi tragedies as they ponder "Bridge Gate" courtesy of Governor Christie. Looks like in the end people will want a wide open election, not the crowning for candidates. Paging Governor Huckabee?

I asked my good friend Meegan Costner who also serves as a granddaughter, if she and I were to have a garden this year. She said yes but didn't exactly say she would help get it ready. The weatherman has also been pretty wishy-washy this year too so it may be I will have a "late" garden this year. Anyway I hope to get out and stir up some dirt next week with or without my helper. Our first joint garden some years ago was made a lot more interesting after I found that she was like the two gardeners in the movie "Secondhand Lion." They planted peas, beans, and several things but it all came up corn. We had our little seed bags to serve as plant identifiers but quickly learned that naming a row to be something has nothing to do with what comes up. It's what you actually plant that counts.

I think that spring has finally crept in. At least everyone I know hopes so. Several of my neighbors have already mowed their lawn's weeds, Dandelions in my case and dead leaves. Anyway I hope you are able to get out and enjoy this great weekend. Be sure and go to church Sunday.

Wayne Bullard, DPh

04-10-14
I don't think we're in Kansas anymore

Al Gore rode his white horse into Kansas a few days ago to make a speech. Of course the speech was all about Global Warming and Al fearlessly (and gleefully) predicted the old dust bowl that so afflicted parts of Kansas, Oklahoma, Texas and Colorado (and a few other parts) back in the 30s and 50s would soon be back. He sort of reminds me of an old preacher we had once upon a time over at Stonewall who constantly preached about the end of the world. Even better, he named dates and painted a pretty sorry picture of our future. Guess he didn't think we would make it. Problem was one Christmas he said to us: "Enjoy your Christmas children, this will be your last." That particular Sunday was the day every child in church received a Christmas bag containing an apple, an orange and other goodies. It was close to being my favorite Sunday of the year. My brother Gerald and I were pretty concerned about this sad turn of events.

The poor preacher was disappointed when the moon failed to turn to blood nor did the earth explode and the end didn't come. The preacher was, however, smart enough to tone back his rhetoric. In somewhat similar circumstances as the dysfunctional preacher Al Gore remains unfazed. He just keeps on going. He and his "fellow warmers" named dates, established exact tables of flood tides for cities and have models and gave us the exact time of doom. Unfortunately for Al Gore none of these took place—at least not on the timetable he chose. The CO2 levels have increased but the temperatures and tides didn't. In fact most scientists have noted a long pause in the heating of the globe. The heating that has been noticed since 1903 continued up into the 1990s but as though to confound Gore and his believers, the earth hasn't heated any since. This past winter being the worse winter perhaps ever recorded in modern history didn't help his program either. It didn't even stop him and his zealots from identifying this winter as the warmest on record. I don't know.

Al Gore could strike pay-dirt on his dust bowl predictions, however. The area is known to have severe droughts from time to time and history records some worse than the one in the 30s. But other "experts" say the dust bowl conditions were brought on by poor and incorrect farming methods preceding the drought and that the type of dust bowl as people suffered through in the 30s is not likely to be repeated. Check back with me in about 50 years and I'll give you a more definitive answer. I think the weather will just keep on doing what it does regardless of what I or Al Gore think.

I think everyone has had a great time watching "March Madness." I've heard a few people complain that they are sick of it but not me. Even though it seemed most of the teams I chose (I didn't make a bracket) to win crashed in flames early on. U-Conn boys won out much to my surprise and it now appears that the U-Conn girls may well win their own championship. My main concern is this: Will all this success by U-Conn go to the head of my brother-in-law, Rod Bailey? Bailey, the self-anointed mayor of Black Rock moved to Oklahoma from Connecticut several years ago so I just try to humor him.

I hope all of you have a good weekend and remember to go to your church this Sunday.

Wayne Bullard, DPh
waynebullard@sbcglobal.net

Wayne Bullard
US Navy, San Francisco

04-17-14
The Blue Ghost

The morning was a little bit misty and dreary as I stood there looking out to the Gulf. But the old ship looked good with her fresh paint and red white and blue bunting. Launched over 70 years ago in 1943, the "Lady Lex," as her crew had called her stood proud at the pier. She had been shot up pretty bad in 1944-45 as she battled Kamikazes and Jap submarines from Tarawa to Tokyo. She had done her part in winning World War II and had suffered many casualties and collected many medals to prove it. My old friend, Joe Bryan from Ada was the Chief Pharmacist Mate on the Lexington at that fateful time and one of his duties was to be in charge of the burial at sea detail.

I don't remember how many Joe buried but in one day they returned 34 of their shipmates to the deep—killed by a torpedo that hit just back of the engine room. That had necessitated a long trip back to San

Francisco for quick repairs before returning to "theatre" where she and her crew fought their way all the way to Tokyo Bay for the surrender of the Japanese Empire. Joe finished his duty and returned to Ada where he served his community faithfully operating Bryans Prescription Center and Bryans Corner Drug with his identical twin brother Billy. The Lexington had picked up a nickname before she was towed away to be mothballed—The Blue Ghost. She was tagged with that moniker by Tokyo Rose after the Japanese government had several times declared the Lexington sunk. Tokyo Rose was a famous propaganda agent for Japan who broadcast to American troops and sailors during the war. That was then. Fast forward 10 years.

In 1955 hundreds of sailors were sent to Bremerton, Washington where the Lexington was being refitted and repaired for more service. I was one of those sailors. In fact my entire class of 9 Electronic Technicians from Treasure Island were assigned to get the ship up and running. In August of 1955 the proud ship set sail once again and served proudly in Asia for many years. In July 1962 the Lexington switched coasts serving out the rest of her years in the Atlantic and Gulf of Mexico. Finally, after being a commissioned ship for nearly 50 years the Lexington was decommissioned at Pensacola, Florida. I made a point of attending these services with my wife Pat. It was November 8, 1991 and it was a somber time.

The Lexington was finally towed to Corpus Christi, Texas where she has been turned into a museum ship. On June 17, 1992 she was pulled carefully to the prepared bed of sand that would become her new resting place. Here her tanks were flooded and the grand old ship settled into the sand which would hold her level and steady for a hopeful future.

The reunion of OE Division and its Electronic Technicians from so long ago was to be on April 4, 2014. Six said they would try to be there. In the last weeks leading up to our big get-together, our shipmate Bill Murray died of a heart attack, Dick True's wife had surgery and Commander Youngburg (who no longer is able to drive) got sick and couldn't come. The three of us and our wives met and had a good time anyway. We were welcomed aboard the ship and recognized as former VIP crew. We got to meet and talk with a lot of people that day including several members of the Wiley, Texas High School Band. The others in our group were Don Rudberg and Sally of Bozeman, Montana, C. G. (Chuck) Scott and Flo of Salem, Oregon—The last of the 9 ETs.

It was a great day for us and we are proud to be a little piece of this history. If any of you are interested in more information about the Lexington you can go online and search "Lexington."

I hope all of you have survived this cold spring weather and remember, it will warm up—someday. Be sure and go to church this Sunday.

Wayne Bullard, DPh

Wayne aboard the USS Lexington during the 2014 Reunion

Pat aboard the USS Lexington during the 2014 Reunion

Sally Rudberg, Flo Scott, and Pat at the reunion.

Chuck Scott, Don Rudberg, and Wayne at the reunion.

04-26-14
Squirrel attends Easter Service

I felt pretty good about things Easter morning as I walked toward the main entrance of the First Baptist Church of Allen. After all it was Easter—a time of great hope and celebration of our risen Lord from the dead. It was a time of high attendance and great celebration as people headed to their houses of worship in larger numbers than usual. The choir would be gathering up preparing to sing and there was a steady procession into the building and also out. I saw people run out of the church and I could hear screaming inside. There definitely was something going on inside that wasn't printed in the bulletin.

I didn't know if it was a good idea or not but I ran on inside. Thoughts flew through my head included those of a berserk gunman waylaying Christians this Easter morning and I wished for my pistol. On the other hand I had heard no shots, just sounds of running, yelling and screams. I poked my head around the door, ready to run if need be and people were huddled in corners terrified and yet some were laughing. There was a squirrel in the auditorium

I don't know if it's our nature or our looks or what, but Baptists seem to attract squirrels. We had squirrels in our old church building but they kept to themselves pretty much and we left them alone as they did us. When we built our new church the grateful squirrels moved over with us continuing to keep their low profile. We would hardly notice them being there at all except when they died in places where we couldn't find them. We could, however, smell them for several Sundays.

Just a few weeks ago a squirrel had passed away one Sunday morning and made a point of dying near the stage, up where we park caskets for funerals. I myself had the chore of dumping him outside without ceremony. I was hoping it was the only one—but I was wrong. Our early service Easter morning had caught one squirrel totally unaware and inside so he was quite surprised when we all started arriving early. A squirrel posse had been hastily formed to chase or capture the unwelcome rodent and remove him. But it wasn't working. The elusive animal ran into one of those tall decorative bushes that stand on the stage and there he tried to hide. The hunters had a large piece of white cloth with which they kept trying to catch little Rocky the Baptist squirrel but to no avail.

Pastor Chad was trying to impress some of his congregation with his leadership and bravery. He was right there in the thick of battle when the squirrel made a daring leap to what he hoped would be his freedom. He used the top of Chad's head as a springboard which resulted in the preacher showing the rest of us some dance moves we had never seen before. In fact, we were so caught up in the dance show that we let the squirrel get away again. The posse quickly recovered from their fright and went back into hot pursuit again. The squirrel definitely did not want to leave by the main entrance and finally by propping the back door open while keeping their distance the ad hoc squirrel, the committee/posse was able to get the intruder to leave the building. As he left he had a defiant look on his face as if to say—"this ain't over yet—I will be back."

The early morning church service started 10 minutes late and the pastor didn't give an invitation at the end. I guess he was afraid of what and who might come down the aisle wanting to join up. I hope your Easter was good—that you got to spend time with family and that you got to go to church too. I can't promise that church is always this exciting but for sure you are always welcome to come down and try it. Who knows, maybe we'll have another squirrel release for you, or perhaps just have the same one come out for a cameo? Have a good week.

Wayne Bullard, DPh.
waynebullard@sbcglobal.net

05-01-14
Blood Moon Mania

Up over there, see? My wife Pat and I were shivering in the cold night @ 2AM—it was the time the news said we could rise and see the first "Blood Moon." Yes, there it was. A red, dusty looking moon with just a fingernail of light still showing on its eastern edge. I spent about 2 seconds in a close study of this thing before taking my shivering pajama-clad body back to my warm bed. There will be another moon event this fall and two next year which comprise something called a "Tetrad." My dad loved celestial phenomena and often got up in the middle of the night to view odd events such as meteor showers or eclipses. One night he invited my little brother Jim to rise up with him at 3AM and they could enjoy a meteor shower together on the front lawn. My brother was not that interested in science and in fact smeared face cream on dad's glasses after dad went to sleep.

The next morning Jim asked dad, "how was the meteor shower?" "Oh, it was cloudy and I couldn't see a thing." The story always brings a few laughs to friends and family. But you can bet my dad would be back out in the yard keeping track of this Blood Moon Tetrad. Some bible scholars make a lot out of abnormal celestial phenomena and enjoy linking such to end of the world prophecy. In the last half of the 20th century many made a living off books and preaching about such. People such as Hal Lindsey bravely put times and dates on when the Lord would come and get his people. Some called it the "great snatch" or Rapture. I remember well the Christmas of 1947 when the pastor of the First Baptist Church told his congregation on the Sunday we were to have our "Tree" (the last Sunday before Christmas when all the church kids got a sack of goodies). I listened open mouthed as the preacher told us: "Enjoy this Christmas children, it will be your last." It had been my brother's and my favorite church day. Up until then.

Instead of the Christmas Story that Sunday he preached destruction. We awaited our doom.

The preacher often preached scary and graphic sermons about what was about to happen to the earth and about (here's that moon again) the blood moons. My brother and I didn't see much hope for the bad people in Stonewall or even for ourselves. Some weeks later Gerald roused me from sleep in the middle of the night and told me, "its happening." Sure enough, the full moon was setting in the dusty western sky and was red as it could be. We were pretty worried that night and it was a long time before we even laid back down. We shared the bad news with mom and she took it pretty good and suggested we go back to bed. I thought that she was either the coolest customer alive or just hadn't been listening to the preacher. But I did note that days went by and Stonewall and the rest of our world seemed to be getting along OK and hadn't been destroyed just yet.

My point is this: A lot of people on TV and so forth are making a lot out of this Tetrad—that this has a lot of meaning relating to scripture and the end of the world. But this moon thing is a repeating phenomenon that in previous times has come and gone without well, anything happening. I feel that when Christian "prophets" persist in claiming from time to time that this or that celestial event pertains to events related to the last days, then they may well do damage to the integrity of the Bible message and to reliable witnesses of those in the faith who preach to a world in need of the gospel.

I hope you are enjoying our weather and that you can go to church this Sunday. Also, if you do go outside to view some sort of star event, be sure that no one smears cold cream on your glasses.

Wayne Bullard, DPh
waynebullard@sbcglobal.net

291

05-08-14
Squirrel Truce brings
peace to local Church

Yes it's true. The squirrels did return the next Sunday after Easter. Three perished after a daring Sunday morning Kamikaze attack preceding another attempt at a baptism service. Chad, no long a squirrel pacifist fought back and the invaders perished. One did get away and we didn't expect him to come back. But he did. That night the squirrel reappeared for the evening services. This time he positioned himself on the light combing on the East side of the main auditorium. There he pranced and ran back and forth during the services. Most of us tried to ignore the interloper but some ladies made audible gasps when the rodent threatened to jump on them. He never did. One person who had by this time apparently lost interest in Chad's message took pictures of the playful critter with her cell phone. Turned out good. The pictures not the sermon.

Later the efforts of a Deacon and a member of the choir (sings bass) set a trap which the hapless animal wandered into and was trapped. I understand the kind trapper took the animal over to "Old Town" where it was released to entertain the residents of that area of Allen. So far so good.

Before I move on from this topic I want to thank the people who wrote me about this. The ones (2) who sent Ray Steven videos about the "Mississippi Squirrel" are especially appreciated and I watched them both. Again. I can testify that the squirrels in question were treated in a most humane manner except those that confronted the pastor. While it is regrettable, it is a fact that his new nickname is "Killer." Since I don't want to be accused of milking a topic I now leave this subject and move on to other things.

How 'bout them Thunder Players?" Before these guys came to town I didn't pay too much attention to NBA basketball but these guys have made me a fan. Their game 7 win over the Grizzlies made the arthritis in my shoulder go away—forgotten for a little while. My wife is a different animal. She gets pretty excited and when K-D doesn't deliver I fear for the safety of my TV set. So far she has comported herself fairly well through it all. Strange isn't it—how we get all wrapped up in a team?

I got flagged down last week in my golf cart. The person doing the flagging wanted to know where Chock and Eula were. You see, when they come to town they bring Missy, their pretty little white Schnauzer who in turn demands a golf cart ride. I always try to accommodate. As to Chock and Eula, they brought their big camper down last week and are busy relaxing and visiting friends and relations in Allen. Thankfully they brought Missy with them. And yes, we had a nice ride and yes, we played dominoes (with Chock and Eula not Missy).

Those of you who thought you could settle down and relax last Sunday night and watch a favorite TV program were in for a little disappointment. All the OKC stations were dedicated to showing every little snap and crack of the big brush and grass fires they had up near Guthrie. After a few minutes they had pretty well exhausted all that one could say about a fire of this nature and it became very redundant. Its sad so much damage was done up there but their non-stop coverage was over the top. Sensationalizing every news event, high wind event or storm warning serves no purpose except to cause people to start ignoring future warnings or turning off their TVs. There must be a happy medium in which people can stay informed without being over-saturated with news of this sort. But that's just me.

On a happier note things are looking good in our parks, our boulevard and walking trail. The city has done an excellent job keeping everything mowed and kept up. Even painted the swings and slides down at the park. Thanks guys!

Have a good weekend and be sure and go to church this Sunday. You never know what's next.

Wayne Bullard, DPh.

waynebullard@sbcglobal.net

05-22-14
America's Greatest Generation

The Great Depression of the 30s was one of the hardest times in our nation's history. It was especially hard on the people of Oklahoma. It was a time when nothing was turning out right. It was a time when you could take a load of hogs to the sale barn in Ada (as my grandpa and dad did out at Lula in 1932) and not be able to get but 50 cents a head. It was a time when the rains quit and the dust blew. A hundred men waited and vied for a single job and if they got it they probably didn't receive a living wage. Welfare and Social Security as we know it didn't exist and in spite of government efforts to feed the poor, thousands starved to death. In Western Oklahoma many people, especially school children, died of "Dust Pneumonia" as the dusters often buried cars and even homes. The clouds held their rain in spite of mass prayer meetings on court house lawns and people wondered how it was they had displeased God so much.

I'm not at all sure how this generation of American's would handle such a crisis today. Just what kind of people are we? I know in the 1930s lesser men would have just laid down and given up. But they didn't. They were tough and they had no other options. They pulled on their work clothes and looked for things to do. They looked after their families and they were resourceful. Others, by the thousands loaded up their families into pickups and autos that weren't road worthy and set out for far away areas that might have work. They often had to stop and work at menial labor to earn enough to buy the next tank of 10 cent gas or buy a secondhand fan-belt. Most were headed for a place called California. Many made it. Many stayed. But there are an unknown number of graves along old route 66 reminding us of people that didn't.

One thing for sure, this generation learned to never take what they had for granted. They learned to never waste, to use it up, wear it out, make it do, or do without. Their perseverance and endurance resulted in our living free from want. New farming techniques and land restoration helped the plains people to get back to prosperity and it was during these hard times that Americans showed the world what they're made of. During WWII we found strength to persevere and defend a nation and way of life that some think of today as corrupt and meaningless.

Yes things are different these days. Religious attitudes and beliefs are now routinely ridiculed and the people who practice them are persecuted in the press and in our Universities. Freedom of speech is still there as long as you don't try to express the "wrong" ideas on campus.

One recent and well known case of "free speech infringement" is that of Ayaan Hirsi Ali, a Muslim and an outspoken advocate of women's rights. He was to have received an honorary degree from Brandeis University but the offer was quickly withdrawn when faculty members, students and Muslim groups complained. Of course there is the case of Condoleezza Rice, secretary of state and national security adviser under President Bush. Her invitation to speak at graduation at Rutgers's University was too much to bear and the invitation revoked as the people there didn't want to be associated with a war-mongering-criminal of her sort. There are many other examples.

So much for free speech and a free exchange of ideas on campus. It does not bode well for our future as we look at such close-minded people now running our colleges and universities. You have to wonder just how these people and their minions will fare in the next hard times. After all, doesn't much of our leadership come from some of these same (formerly) great Universities? And you can rest assured that hard times will visit us again. Will they be able to face up to hard times with hard work and resourcefulness or will they simply fold their tents and embrace socialism—the very thing that is wrecking European economies today.

I hope you are enjoying the blessings of liberty in this great country as much as I am and I hope you have a good weekend. Be sure and go to Church Sunday.

Wayne Bullard, DPh

05-29-14
It's A Wonderful Life

"This is a terrible front page," my wife exclaimed! We were driving down the road and she had the front page of "The Ada Evening News" in her hands and reading. "What do you mean, it's a terrible front page?" "It's just full of crimes of the worse sort and all right here at home," she replied. After we got home I decided to see what she was talking about. Well, she was mostly right. There wasn't anything wrong with the paper but every story on the front page was a crime story and it was local stuff. Child abuse, drug arrest, robberies and assaults totally took the Ada paper. It was depressing to read.

It reminded me of a Christmas Classic—"It's a Wonderful Life" that came out in 1946. This great movie only won one academy award. Nor was it a big box-office hit at the time. But it survived over time to be the much watched classic that it is. You who saw it will remember that George Bailey (James Stewart) as a good old boy who owned the local savings and loan. Old Man Potter (Lionel Barrymore) who owned the bank was a bad guy who was always trying to ruin George and take over the town. Try as he may, Potter was not successful—and that was a good thing for more reasons than you might think.

As it was, George Bailey's good nature is what nearly did him in. He provided a job to his incompetent and bumbling Uncle Billy (Thomas Mitchell) who lost a $12,000 dollar deposit in Potter's bank which was found by Potter's equally evil bodyguard and swiped. This drove the Bailey Savings and Loan into immediate bankruptcy ruining everything (at least in George's mind) that George had worked for. Forsaking everything Bailey goes out to the Mill Dam to toss himself into the frigid waters and drown. During this hard time, George is being watched over by God who decides to use a new guardian angel, Clarence, played by Henry Trevers.

It's Clarence's first case and his first job as an angel he is unsure of himself. By this time George has taken his suicide leap uttering that he wishes he had never been born. Clarence rescues George and takes him on a tour of what was originally called Bedford Falls. Now its name is Potterville. George got his wish and he had never been born. He never existed. The rest of the movie shows how much of a difference George Bailey had made in the lives of so many and in general the direction of an entire town. George meets several people whom he had saved from poverty or bad decisions who were now just bums. No one knew him of course, even members of his own family—since he had never existed.

The town itself was full of bars and nightclubs. Drunks were everywhere and drugs rampant. Crime was out of control and derelicts lay around on the streets. His beloved wife, Mary is an old maid, his kids don't exist and no one remembers the Bailey Savings and Loan. Uncle Billy is still in prison for his incompetence and finally Clarence leads George to the point where he turns back to God for restoration and he is. So is his town and his family. Potterville no longer exists but the law is after George because of Uncle Billy's losing the money. But George has friends and in the spirit of Christmas they take up enough money to pay off the demanding Bank Examiner and not only is Bedford Falls restored to its former beauty and wholesomeness but so is George's faith in God and humanity.

Contrasting Bedford Falls with Potterville makes me think of Ada in 1946. It was a town of thrifty hard working citizens with a large middle class of merchants who owned their own businesses, professionals serving a hardworking citizenry and virtually no crime. I remember the first armed robbery (in my life) in Ada. I was shocked. "Ordinary crime right here in our town" I thought. We hadn't seen anything yet. Ada is much changed. Most of our retail business and money is now owned and operated by far-away corporations. Crime and drugs are ever on the rise, church attendance on the downswing, children abused and neglected, it makes one wonder what's next? And I don't see a sign of Clarence anywhere. Pray for our country. Have a good weekend and be sure that you and yours are in church this Sunday.

Wayne Bullard, DPh
waynebullard@sbcglobal.net

06-05-14
Up at the VA

I've been reading about how slow and inept the VA Hospital is out at Phoenix and got to thinking about our VA up at Oklahoma City. Actually they do a pretty good job up there. A few months ago I got a call from a guy up there who asked me when I could come up and get my left shoulder fixed. I had to think a minute. They had repaired my torn rotator cuff in my right shoulder a few years earlier and at that time told me my left shoulder was messed up too but since it wasn't too bad I would be placed on a waiting list. The surgery was "elective." I waited and as it was bothering me I called a time or two but was informed that I was to wait. So I did.

Time went by and the shoulder got better and I forgot about it until I got that call asking me to come up and have it fixed on a Tuesday morning. I told him no I would just pass on it. The shoulder had gotten better and wasn't hurting much anymore. I had a lot of stuff to do in the next few weeks and didn't want to be tied up in rehab for several weeks. That was that—so I thought.

Time passed and I re-injured my right shoulder—lifting something I shouldn't have. But I kept mum. I thought it might get OK and besides who wants to go have surgery anyway? So it was last Friday that I found myself suffering to such an extent that I dialed up my old caregiver up at the VA. "What'd you do to that shoulder," she snapped "You've been lifting stuff haven't you?" She then gave me instructions on how to apply heat and cold and for me to come up Monday and get some X-Rays. I did. She said she would call me. After the Phoenix snafu I expect a prompt call back too.

I drove out to Tinker after that to get an ID card renewed. I was amazed, once again, to notice how much younger the service people are than they were when I was in. We were tended to by a young lady airman who looked to be about 14. She was very efficient and pretty and soon had us on our way but not before we thanked her for her service. Looking around the office out there made me remind myself that we as citizens should be very careful about sending these young people in "harms" way and make sure what we are asking them to do is really worth them risking their lives and limb.

The generation of old Veterans who receive health care up at the VA are rapidly fading away being replaced by Vietnam vets and these we committed to the Middle Eastern wars. I am not comfortable seeing these young men and women pegging along the long hallways of our Veteran's Hospitals with one leg or no legs. It bothers me somewhat more to see a young lady in the same shape. There are no safe places in Afghanistan and an IED doesn't distinguish who it will blow up.

A lot of politicians would have us jump into the Syrian civil war and even confront Putin over the snafus in the Balkans. Really? Do we want to keep on chewing up our prime youth on causes that are not necessary in the national interest? I think not. Troops on the ground are not an option in wars that make little difference to our national interests. Our goal should be to reduce the load at our veteran's care centers—not expanding it because of trivial pursuit.

Have a great summer weekend and be sure and go to your church this Sunday.

Wayne Bullard, DPh
waynebullard@sbcglobal.net

Ruby and J.T.

06-12-14
Genetic Engineering and my Grandparents

My grandpa was a farmer and a good one. He was also an early day genetic engineer with some very sound economic theories too. He was a pioneer in thriftiness and honed it to new and unexpected levels on his farm down in Leflore County. His concept was basically that if you spent little or no money on anything—at all—you had a better chance at turning a nice profit on everything. He was very good at not spending money. He sold melons, potatoes and corn and milk products for cash and placed this cash in a safe place.

Grandma on the other hand was more of a spender. When her daddy died and left her some money she spent the whole wad on a cook stove. A glorious and large monster, it was the best wood burner Sears had and when it was finally set up and put to work was the best stove on Goat Ridge. Grandma also liked to raise chickens. Good looking chickens too. She sent off some money (more than grandpa would have approved) and bought a registered rooster from New England. It even clucked with an accent. The rooster had a glorious career in which he became famously successful in producing some beautiful chicks and his fame was far and wide on the ridge. Grandma was soon selling some of the boy chickens to people far and wide in Leflore County. How she could tell the sex of a baby chick was a big mystery to Gerald and me.

The rooster was something to behold—tall and handsome and full of chicken testosterone, he strutted around the yard bullying everyone around—including me. I didn't like him. He often chased me out of the yard all the time flogging and pecking. What was I doing there anyway? Well, my dad always felt sort of guilty that his dad's 9 children had all grown up and left J. T. without any slave help up on the farm so he sent Gerald and me. Every summer. Later, Gerald would remark that we were like that movie, "The Bridge over the River Kwai." We were the prisoners of war, Grandpa was the somewhat evil Jap Commandant and the farm was the prison camp. Dad however, was pretty sure that living on a farm with no electric, no running water, and a one-hole toilet with a lot of manual labor was very good for us.

The days were long and tiring but there were good times when we were allowed to swim and run about in the piney woods of Goat Ridge or visit our somewhat more civilized kin down on highway 270. It was one of those afternoons when we unexpectedly ran into the large over-sexed rooster about 2 blocks from the house. He immediately attacked me, and Gerald did as he had done earlier, popped him with a BB out of the BB gun. But this time the BB hit the big bird in his comb. For the 2 or 3 who may not know what a comb is, well it is right on top of the head, bright red and in this case was so large it lay down on the side of his head. Like I said earlier, he was royalty. But now he went to bleeding. Bad. Panicked, the big boy ran straight to the house and made a death-bed statement. To put it another way, he told on us. After flopping around a little bit more at the feet of grandma, he expired.

We soon confessed to being the killers. Waste not, want not, grandma always said. The chicken made a somewhat tasty (but tough) meal or two over the next 2 days. The former great relationships we had enjoyed with grandma went down the drain. She was tight lipped and sang church hymns quietly to herself while ignoring us. It was pretty bad. But she got over it. Another younger rooster heroically stepped up and took up the slack and soon grandma and her many hens were restored to a happy state. I think she sent us back to Centrahoma.

Have a good weekend and be sure and go to church this Sunday. And if you go see Grandma, leave your BB gun at home.

Wayne Bullard, DPh

(seated) Great-Uncle Orlan Smith, Grandma Ruby's brother. (standing) Ruby and J.T. in the center with their sons Ernest (left) and Jack (right).

J.T. Plowing

Wolf Mountain

Richard Bullard (above and below), nephew to Cecil Bullard

06-19-14
Alumn Time

It was that time of the year: Alumni time. The time every June that older grads flock back to Allen and get caught up on their visiting and get another look at where they went to school. It's also a good to time look in and see what their old friends are up to—who they married or didn't marry. Some are a little bit mercenary and like to see if their classmates are doing well—financially. Stories are sometimes extracted and exaggerations may occur in the happiness of the moment. Checking up on each other's health is an acceptable practice and well, a lot of talking takes place.

J. I. Jones related one day about two "good old boys" whose graduation dates lay far in the past were visiting in his store one day. One asked, "Have you seen Mary Jane? "Why no, why?" "She is just like this," he said cupping both his hands in front of him. "I don't remember her being all that bosomy" the second guy replied. "Oh no, not that, I mean arthritis." as he cupped his hands in front of himself again.

One of my favorite alumni stories was from a little guy who worked

2014 Alumni Celebration

for Sun Oil. It was a Saturday morning in the Drug Store and we were visiting with some visitors. People used to really dress up for these things and of course there was no shortage of hot air going around but back in the middle 30s this old Allen boy returned home for the Alumni Weekend. It was warm but he had on a jacket and tie—all the time. He looked pretty darn prosperous considering it was in the middle of the great depression and a lot of people were having hard times—and showed it. This guy was driving a big black Buick Eight. Boy was it pretty with its perfectly clean white-walled tires new paint. He made frequent visits up and down the street parking in different locations availing other old classmates and gawkers a better look at his symbols of success and wealth.

At the banquet he wasn't asked to speak but did so anyway. He made a short talk about how he had overcome his upbringing and how he had made so much money but when he got back to his hotel that night he felt sort of dejected. No one had really gone crazy over his exploits and success. No one asked him to their party or home afterwards but tomorrow was another day.

Most Alums' would visit their old churches, if they had moved and again they would get to see a lot of old friends, and they (more importantly) would get to see you. Of course come Sunday morning our subject's big black car (somewhat dusty now) was parked in the parking lot of the First Baptist Church and he found himself a good pew about 6 pews from the front. The church had bought a new electric organ, which they were very proud of—on the credit. The "easy" instalments hadn't been that easy and now they were 3 months behind. During the announcement time the pastor announced the organist would play a medley of music—and she did.

When the pastor took to the pulpit again he pointed out something everyone knew already—this might well be the last time the congregation would be able to hear the beautiful organ as the organ company said if the payments weren't "brought up" they would come get it next Thursday. If that happened, the pastor went on, we will have to drag out the old pump organ which is sitting idle back in an empty room where the dirt dabbers were busy and they would be subject to its wheezing and obnoxious sounds or just get by with a piano. It was pretty.

The well-dressed alum, as if on cue, sprang on his feet. "How much do we owe on it?" The preacher responded with an amount that was a little over $1,000 dollars. "I'll pay half right now if someone or others will pay the other half." He felt pretty safe as he figured there wasn't 50 cents to found in the whole place. The poorly dressed little old lady sharing his pew stood and said: "Sonny Boy, me and you just bought an Organ." Have a great weekend and be sure and go to church this Sunday.

Wayne Bullard, DPh

06-26-14
Riding the Dinky

Do you remember the Dinky? I'm sometimes asked about these little trolleys that ran on a lot of rural railroads and provided passenger and mail service to hundreds of communities. In particular I remember the "Dinkys" that ran locally. One ran from Atoka to Oklahoma City and back each day passing through Centrahoma, Ada and parts in between. The other better known train ran from Dennison, Texas to Coffeeville, Kansas and back again. This one passed through Allen and places like Lula and Tupelo. But what was the deal?

When rail passenger service started losing business the railroads wanted to rid themselves of these expensive passenger trains that rattled up and down the tracks with less than half a load. The solution was tough. The government made them provide this service so to minimize expenses they came up with this diesel-powered trolley. They worked real well. They could zip down the tracks at probably 50 MPH and yet would stop and let rural passenger hop on or off at their doorsteps. The things carried a small post office aboard and a mail sorter. Bags of new mail were dropped off places such as Lula and right here in Allen.

Hughes and Coal Counties suffered losses of about 60% in their rural areas as did Pontotoc in some parts during the depression—an event that defines America. It finally reached a point in the 50s that the Dinky itself was rattling around nearly empty—losing big money. The mail contracts vanished too and the little Dinkys soon disappeared from the tracks that crossed at Tupelo. Eventually the tracks were taken up too.

What brought this subject to our attention was a story out of India. There was a baby girl born on a speeding train, and the child fell through the cracks. The cracks you say? Yes. The train had a toilet mounted over a hole in the floor and the infant fell to the tracks. The train just kept speeding along and the baby was left behind. Finally,

WAYNE BULLARD, PHARM. D.

railroad officials backtracked and found the baby. She recovered suffering only a few bruises and hypothermia. She was mad as heck, one reporter observed. But all this reminded me of the toilet on the Dinky. It was a tin funnel shaped device with a toilet seat on it. The funnel provided a view of the tracks (if one cared to look and my brother and I always looked).

One fellow coffee drinker observed that there were little 3-sided sheds alongside the track where passengers could wait to hear the loud horns mounted up on the front of the Dinky. That meant it was time to get up and stand ready to flag down the train—which would stop and the conductor would put his little step-stool down and assist you (if you needed it) in getting up the steep steps into the passenger compartment. I remember that once inside, the seats were not too comfortable—being wooden-- but the inside of the train itself was somewhat elegant being paneled with what appeared to be cherry wood. With all those stops I wondered how it could ever make it to Kansas and then back to Dennison. But it did.

Riding that old Dinky gave new insight into what politicians like to call "falling through the cracks". Be sure and go to church Sunday but don't expect to see any "Dinky" riders there.

Wayne Bullard, DPh
waynebullard@sbcglobal.net

07-10-14
Sucking Eggs and Visiting the Old Country

I referred to a man once as "*an old egg sucker*." "Why did you call him that?" asked one of my kids. Well, I explained, the term refers to a dog that gets into a chicken's nest and "*sucks*" the eggs. Such a dog was considered worse than useless and is usually given the death penalty. "It's just an uncomplimentary term," I explained. I recalled how that once upon a time over at Stonewall I had "owned" a black dog. I really enjoyed his company but he was caught "*sucking*" eggs. My dad decreed, even without a trial that the dog was guilty, and the sentence was death. As the malefactor who had brought this sorry dog in the place it was my plight to kill him—with a 22 rifle.

My dad told me to just take him down to Buck Creek and shoot him. So I took him—except I decided to not shoot him. He and I were, after all, pretty good buddies. I turned him loose and told him to just keep going. He did. Right back to the house. He was waiting on me when I got home. My Uncle J. C. (a somewhat criminally-inclined man who lived with us at the time) said he would take care of him. But I talked him instead of hauling the dog to Jesse first and after further thought, I ordered the death wagon on to East Jesse and just turn him loose. I hoped he would find a home with "Big Boy Ryan" who lived out there. I don't know what happened to him after that but I was sure it hurt his feelings.

I once asked a man where he had been the previous weekend and he answered "Oh I've been back to the old country." Where? "Sasakwa," he replied. "That's the old country to me." Following that line of reasoning I can say that I too have visited the "Old Country." It was that time of year, the last weekend in June and the Alumni Gathering. Since Pat and I both graduated over there—there we went. We visited with best friends David Alexander, Bob Sparks, Wayne Davis his wife Deloris Davis—all members of the class of 1952.

Stonewall can probably number the superintendents it's had since being founded, on the fingers of one hand—most likely something no other school in this part of Oklahoma can do. Although Stonewall is a "somewhat" poor school district, it has the stability that comes with stable leadership—a leadership that includes vision and stability a school can maximize its assets and become one of the leading schools in the area. I'm proud of what Stonewall Schools have been able to accomplish over its many years, and I congratulate them on what they have brought forth on their campus with their new "Lunchroom" which looks more like a student union than a lunch room, and their re-done gym that feels more like a college facility than a high school.

Energy begets energy, and downtown Stonewall, using a lot of elbow grease, time and money, have restored much of their old business district. The historic building that once housed the bank, the fire station and upstairs Masonic Lodge that was abandoned and falling into ruin. Now the entire first floor is occupied by a Doctor's Clinic. Upstairs, the old Lodge area has some city offices and a large conference room hosting City Council meetings. The great stairway has been refurbished and looks very, well—grand. A new elevator has also been installed. Oh yes, and presiding over this new clinic over there, is our own Mika Strong of Allen. Good going Mika.

Outside the building has been sandblasted and it looks like the red-brick exterior was put up yesterday. New sidewalks and steps and decorative lighting globes set the scene. Maybe I'll make a report on the rest of "old main street" one of these days. But for now let me say that I am very proud of the people of Stonewall who are putting a new face on their town.

Be sure and go to your church Sunday.

Wayne Bullard, DPh

waynebullard@sbcglobal.net

Main Street, Stonewall 1945: back, Wayne, Janice Davis, Mana Sue Bullard, front, Joyce Davis, Linda Kay Bullard, and Sharon Davis

310

07-17-14
How to Keep on Being Married

It was an extremely hot afternoon that July 19, 1958 as I led the new "Mrs. Wayne Bullard" to my green and white 1958 Bel-Air Chevrolet parked in the graveled parking lot of the First Baptist church of Latta. An old high school friend, Dr. Duane Riley, had tied the knot for us and I guess he did a good job. I remember little of what he said but I do know we are still married. But how did you do it? A young man wanted to know some years later. Not being the first to inquire, I set out to tell him.

First of all, I explained, it takes a lot of thought and planning. Some like to say love is involved but that really isn't the case at all. I've known a lot of people who have been married over 50 years that don't even like each other, but yet, they stay together year after year. Is it making lots of money? No. I know lots of poverty stricken people who stick together too. No, it's something else entirely. Something almost spiritual. You just have to understand the wants and needs of a woman to keep them happy. And I know what they are.

First of all, understand that women have a strong need to serve their man and if you are smart you will watch out for these opportunities for service. For example, if I am seated in my den and my wife is way back in the laundry room washing my underwear and I need my coffee cup refilled I don't just hop up and get it. Not if I want to score some points here, I don't. No, I yell until I get her attention so she can bring it to me. I do it for myself but if she sees me doing something she feels is "her job" she will start having feelings of rejection and other fears of inadequacy. While we may chuckle at this as being waited on hand and foot, it's the only way to go if you want to stay married.

Let her do the housecleaning. I know it may be easier to just roll the vacuum out and do it yourself, but when you do, watch out! You running the vacuum is telling her you think the floor is dirty and it's her fault. Leave it in the closet. Avoid dust rags and whatever you do don't jump up after a meal and start loading the dishwasher—especially in front of the kids or visitors. She will be humiliated.

In the rare event you feel you need to eat out, take your wife and baby with you. It's yet another opportunity for you to show your true love. Avoid carrying the infant into the restaurant. Many dads love to help out here, but beware the pitfalls. Carry the diaper bag? Not hardly. Let her make two trips if necessary while you look on protectively, opening doors and helping her get settled and all. She'll love you for it. And listen closely: To avoid a lot of hurt to the mom, don't ever change a diaper if the mom is there to do it. For the sake of the family a man needs to avoid such acts as bathing, feeding and wanting to hold the baby very much. It not only makes her feel more love toward you and pride for herself, it is a good object lesson for the baby too---seeing what daddy's role actually is.

Sometimes a wife has to go out of town for a few days—such as for her mother's funeral or something of that sort. If it is convenient you should go with her, but we all know a man has to work hard to support his wife so most likely you will stay home alone. While she's away, don't go crazy and start doing housework. Stack up the dishes you mess up. Eat a lot of "take-out" and leave the greasy sacks on her coffee table, and when you have to do a little laundry hang up your underwear on her antique chandelier. Leave a few dresser drawers open wide. Garbage? It can wait too.

She'll fuss a little, but there will be a little satisfied smile on her pretty face and you will never see a time when she is more contented. Not only is she back with the man she loves, she can find a lot to do for him.

I hope all you guys enjoy your marriage as much as I have mine and for that let me say, "You 're welcome." Oh, and don't neglect your church this weekend.

Wayne Bullard, DPh
waynebullard@sbcglobal.net

Wayne Bullard on USS Lexington 1955

07-24-14
Landing on Midway Island

A news-story the other day brought back some old memories to me. It was about the emergency landing 2 weeks ago of a Boeing 777 on Midway Island with 348 souls aboard. The landing was made safely after a suspected onboard fire stunk up the inside of the aircraft. The passengers had to wait for a rescue craft to be sent out to Midway and get them back on their way.

My own visit to this lonely island (pop 60) took place back in 1956. Flying aboard an old "Super-Connie" airliner of that day I was not alone. There were about 20 servicemen and over one hundred pregnant women and young children aboard. We were all headed back to America—from Tokyo to San Francisco. Midway was our refueling stop. The old 4-engine prop planes of that day couldn't make it without it. And as a matter of fact this one didn't make it at all. The last I saw it was sitting out on the sands of Midway with a bunch of men staring at a damaged strut. Like the 777, the airline had sent out a relief plane.

We had left Tokyo 3 hours late—sort of like the Boeing 777 had done in the recent story. Our midnight departure guaranteed that many of us tried to nap that part of the trip. Well, not the pregnant women. As soon as the plane cleared Japanese soil they all lined up at the several restrooms on the plane. I noted that when some of them got out of the toilet they would just walk back to the end of one of the lines and start all over again. But to get back to the story, it was when we tried to land that everything went sour.

There is a small gap between where the concrete stops and where the water starts. We landed in the dirt there. Rains had washed a little of the soil away making a pretty good little curb—a curb our right strut couldn't handle. The tires blew and the strut gave way—bending back. The aircraft veered off into the sand making a wild bumpy ride before the pilots got it stopped. Light diffusers from the cabin ceiling noisily popped out, dumping dusty residue on the screaming passengers. I don't think the plans were for us to get off or rest at Midway—but now we did, and most of us made our way to the old wooden terminal.

Well not all of us did. Several women just went out and sprawled out on the grass breathing in and out real funny. The fact that no one had a baby that beautiful morning on Wake Island, is a miracle. One old grizzled Marine informed the uniformed men aboard that we were to take care of these ladies and we did. We finally got to the old terminal which was locked, and was promptly broken into by us. We found food and cooked breakfast for everyone. Actually we had a pretty good time once we discovered none of us were hurt or having babies at the moment. We were just waiting on our rescue and keeping an eye on the flight crew—who probably felt guilty of not being able to make a routine and safe landing, as well they should.

Our last little "snafu" involved the afternoon walks some of us took. Many of us walked around the shoreline of the little island and admiring the gooney birds that live there. It was on the walk back that I decided to cut across the island and noticed what was written on the signs. "KEEP OUT, THIS AREA MAY HAVE UNEXPLODED ORDINANCE."

Just like the hapless passengers on the big Boeing Triple 7, we eventually got to where we were going, but I'll bet they didn't have as much fun or as much to talk about as we did. Hope your weekend is fine and that you find your way to Church this Sunday.

Wayne Bullard, DPh

11-14-13
Veterans Day in Allen

The old run-down building sits there in the center of town—empty. And it looks empty, abandoned and in poor repair. Not a hint that it once housed the busiest drug store downtown providing a center of gathering, a place to enjoy a banana split, or buy some cosmetics or have your prescription filled. It was a brightly lit place that was a centerpiece of Allen and a place to gather. Central Drug Store was a landmark ran by a popular pharmacist named Otho Butler. Otho was a civic leader whose wife was the church pianist down at the First Baptist Church. Otho was also a citizen soldier.

Commanding officer of Company G, of the 180th Infantry Regiment, 45th Division (Thunderbird) U. S. Army, Captain Butler probably didn't plan on actually going to war nor did the other Allen men of Company G. But they did. Called up to active duty before the Japs attacked Pearl Harbor, the Company was sent to Texas for advanced combat training. Eventually they would all wind up on an Island called Sicily—the toe of Italy. A famous general named Patton was charged with clearing the island of its occupiers—the Germans—and that's what he did. But it came with a cost—a horrible cost.

On July 25, 1943, on a hillside near Palermo, Sicily, General Patton's advance was slowed by some German machine-gun-nests. Patton ordered the guns taken out and the order went down the line and landed in the lap of one Captain named Butler and his Company G—a unit made up mostly of Allen area soldiers. They were pinned down, and I imagine the Allen guys had already given moments such as this some thought—"How do I leave a secure place, stand up and charge a machine gun emplacement that's already shooting at me?"

Captain Butler was a leader. That's why he was where he was and he made his plans, picked his men and they went over the top, and after a few minutes General Patton had been notified that the hill had been cleared off—but it had been a hard fight. Captain Otho Butler,

Pharmacist and part time soldier now lay dead on the side of a now forgotten hillside in Sicily. For his heroism, Butler was awarded the Silver Star. It was well deserved.

As far as I know, Otho and his wife, Lola Dell Butler, had a daughter, Bonita. Lola Dell sold the store to Bill and Liberty Orick and they continued to operate it for many years under the name "The Central Store." Lola Dell continued to help out with her piano duties and worked as a teller at The Farmer's State Bank before she retired and passed away. And yes, he is the same Captain Otho Butler whose name is on the highway signs between Ada and Calvin. I'm glad his name is there as I don't want the people of this area to ever forget him and the men of Allen who marched off to war a long time ago.

The Allen band under the capable direction of Spencer Cody played several pieces at Monday's Veteran's Day salute to our veterans. Sometimes these programs are boring to kids but not this time. After Rio Jones led our Pledge of Allegiance and the band had finished its medley of music honoring the services, guest speaker Will Maxwell shared with stunning clarity his experiences in Iraq. Will held the kids spellbound with his eye-witness accounts and his declarations of patriotism. A highlight was the presentation of a high school diploma by Supt. Harman and high school Principal Ward to Mr. Calvin Thomas. Thomas fought in Korea—entering service before he could earn his diploma. Congratulations to Calvin and thanks for your service to your country.

Thanks to my readers for writing. I enjoy hearing from you and enjoy reading the stories many of you send. Have a good week and if you enjoy your freedom, thank a veteran. And be sure and go to church this Sunday.

Wayne Bullard, DPh
waynebullard@sbcglobal.net

Christmas on Drip Gas

It was Christmastime in Centrahoma and the year was 1943. World War II continued on but it was our family tradition to get up Christmas Morning and go to Grandma's house at the foot of Wolf Mountain in Leflore County. There was a hitch: Gasoline was severely rationed in 1943 and we had the low priority "A' Sticker on our windshield. We couldn't buy much gas for the 1935 Ford that served as our family car. It was a 200 + mile roundtrip. We needed a full tank, dad said to go there and get back. Luckily we had a friend—Mr. Shoppe who had his own little "drip" station. "Drip is made from the condensate of natural gas which then can serve as a low grade of gasoline. This stuff made your engine knock and smell funny but by adding a little "Ethyl" to cool it down a little we had a full tank of gas.

We left early Christmas morning. We were well on our way when the little Ford started fuming and sputtering. Of course, the manifold heater leaked Carbon monoxide into the car and kept the six of us coughing and wheezing teary-eyed. Dad, scanning his instruments made note that we sure were burning gas up but he thought it was due to the quality of the drip. As the day got light he had a revelation: Mom had pulled out the choke on the dash to make a place to hang her purse. Dad snatched it off and pushed the choke back in. Mom affected a look of innocence as dad rambled on, giving us updates on what he felt our fate might be—thanks to mom's inconsiderate act. We made it.

Later on at Wolf Mountain the day didn't get any better. Some of us came running inside to announce the news that it was getting colder and now was sleeting and snowing. Dad decided to head for Centrahoma. He checked his gas again and it was still less than a half tank. I guess he had been praying for someone to slip around and add some. But there just wasn't any gas available around those parts on that cold, windy and snowy Christmas afternoon. But dad had an ace up his sleeve. He knew the guy who operated the big Tony's Gas

House on HW-270 in McAlester. If he could just spare one gallon or two we could make it just fine.

I don't know what time it was, but we set out for home immediately—with the heater off. Gerald, Sister Sue and myself shared an odiferous but welcome quilt in the backseat. There was a dispute about who sat where and who got how much of the quilt. Linda Kay was a 5 month old baby girl then and shared a lap blanket up front with mom. We hadn't gone far until we were in some heavier sleet and rain—stuff that wanted to stick to the windshield. The roof leaked over the back seat. And dad had to have his window down so he could clear the ice. This terrorized mom and didn't do much for the morale of us 4 kids. We were low on gas when as we huffed our way into McAlester. The guy dad knew at Tony's Gas House was nowhere to be found. No gas. Dad become concerned and was less than Christian-like about the whole snafu as we hit SH-69.

The brisk winds drove the rain, sleet and snow into the dim headlamps of the old Ford as we continued south toward Atoka on the narrow-rough two-lane. But we kept heading home. In fact the old Ford was running smooth and our confidence rose as we neared the Stringtown cutoff to Coalgate, at the large German Prisoner of War Camp. Big illuminated signs reminded us not to pick up hitchhikers and that is exactly where the Ford quit—at the sign. No one would stop. Who would have thought about traffic being so sparse on Christmas night during wartime and in a storm? Luckily, about 5 hours later a local doctor from Coalgate saw us and pulled us all the way to Coalgate, where the all night station was open—and had gas. We still had no stamps. But the good doctor was exempt and could have all he wanted. We filled up. What a serendipity! It ended what had truly been a memorable and somewhat Merry Christmas. Don't forget to go to church Sunday and remember what a blessing it was to win a war, and although it's high priced these days, gas isn't rationed.

Wayne Bullard, DPh

One is enough or is it?

Pearlie Golden, a 93 year old Hearn, Texas resident was made to take a new driver's test. Pearlie failed the test and Roy Jones, her nephew drove her home. Pearly, apparently upset about the loss of her driving rights, decided not to abide by the orders to stop driving her car. The concerned nephew refused to give Ms. Golden her car keys and that's when she drew her .38 pistol and got after a now concerned and terrified nephew. Roy called 911 and Officer Stephen Stem responded. Pearlie opened fire and the officer shot her dead. End of Story? Not hardly.

The black lady had her friends and it turned out that Officer Steve didn't. A gathering of "concerned" black citizens led by something called the Quannel X Black Panther group soon threatened to riot if the City Council didn't fire Steve Stem, a white officer. At first it would seem that Stem had a good case. After all didn't the lady open fire on him? Wasn't his life at risk? Wasn't Pearlie in the wrong? Well it would seem that way but the citizens had another card to play and it was the fact that this wasn't the first person Officer Stem had shot and killed. In fact, Stem answered a call at a car wash in 2012 where a 28 year old black guy named Tederalle Sotchell was shooting a gun out a car window. When the police officer (Stephen Stem) arrived and tried to defuse the situation he came under fire and in the resulting shootout, killed the offender.

Steve Stem was fired from his job in Bryan, Texas but he was never charged with a crime since the offender was firing shots at not only him, but anyone he saw. Thus the shots were fired in his own self-defense as well as in the line of duty. Officer Stem was then offered a job in Hearn and sometime later he met up with the 93 year old Pearlie Golden—whom he shot. I guess the moral of this story is that you might get by with one shoot-out that results in the death of a minority member but you better not go for two. Especially if it's a female and she is 93 years old. Perhaps you should duck and run or just "bite the bullet." But enough about that.

My niece, Melinda Powell of Mitchell, Nebraska got a real nice snow over the weekend—if there is such a thing as a real nice snow in the middle of May. But Roz Bullard who lives up in Gillette, Wyoming said the snow storm missed them but they had a lot of bad winds. I wonder how high the winds have to get in windy Gillette before they are classified as bad. You have to be tough to live in Gillette. As a matter of fact I'm beginning to think you have to be tough to live in Oklahoma, what with the bad weather we've had here.

The recent concern that lined the faces of worshipers at First Baptist church was not so much concern for the lost sinners in their community as it was for their own well-being. I promised that I was finished with the squirrel stories at church and I am. This is it. But I couldn't help but notice that the good crowd of worshipers on Mother's Day were keeping an eye on the upper reaches of the auditorium. You never know just what might jump out and get in your hair. But I think the distractions are all gone now and this morning I will check the squirrel trap for the last time (I hope) and let the issue drift off into the past. Just another memory of many in the tradition-rich 112 year old church. Be sure and go to your church next Sunday. I think it's safe. And have a good weekend.

Wayne Bullard, DPh.

waynebullard@sbcglobal.net

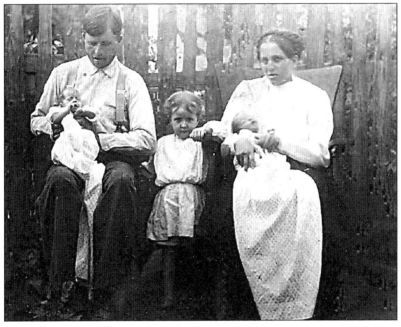

George and Julia Boyd
Twins: Dora (left) and Cora "Jane" (right)
Lora in center

Dora Gets Her Driver's license

When my Grandma Julia Armstrong came down with cancer she needed lots of attention and care. It was a death sentence--a sentence it took several months to get carried out. Mom needed to be over there as much as possible but she didn't drive. We lived in Centrahoma. Pastor Brother Job had an old 32 Chevy Coupe and he said he could take her over there for a dollar. We did that a time or two, but he had this big fat wife who sat up front, the place that I felt I should be, but that's neither here nor there Mom, my baby sister Mana Sue sat in the tiny back seat. I felt that a dollar was pretty high for a trip to Lula and I think mom did too.

One night she grabbed Gerald (8 going on 9) and took him to the old 35 Ford we owned. Between the two of us, we gave her a 5 minute lesson on the gears and ran her through a quick course of using your clutch. She then started and drove the old car back and forth a few times before saying, "I'm ready." For what, my brother exclaimed? In the morning I'm driving to Lula. And she did. She never got out of 2nd that day, going, but on the way home we coaxed her into 3rd gear--a sort of futile move on our part as she never got over 12MPH. Gerald rode on the running board to assist.

But mother was ambitious. If driving was this easy, she wanted to spread her wings and get a license. After all, you can't do too much shopping in Lula, and mom liked to go shopping. And driving. She always took me along to hold my sister. That way she didn't have to worry about someone keeping the kids. There were expressions of skepticism up and down the streets around Centrahoma that day in 1940 that mom announced her intention to license up. Several unkind remarks and cruel jokes made it around our grocery store about her already well-told driving stories and skills. Mom forged ahead.

Sue and I came to know exactly where the Wig-Wam Theater was because it was right next to the driver's license office--across the road from Hudson's Big Country Store. Mom was pretty nonchalant about driving safely, and didn't know the laws applied to her. She told the officer it didn't matter because "I'll just be on country roads most of the time." He thought different and failed her. It was just the beginning of a series of ordeals for several hapless drivers license guys.

Some of you may not know that in 1940 there were offices in Wewoka, Holdenville, Ada and Coalgate that come to mind. We made 'em all. I don't think dad was aware of the intensity of her quest as she warned me to keep quiet. We came full circle one morning. In Coalgate. She had passed her written but couldn't seem to master driving--you know stopping at stop signs, signaling with her arm; her intentions about turning and giving the hand signal for stopping. I'm not sure she ever could have. This particular day the man watched as mom got me and Sue out of the car, seated us in the office and told the patrolman, "Let's go."

He said, put your kids back in, I'm giving you your license. And he did. Local wags in Centrahoma speculated that he was too scared to ride with her again--I don't know. Mom was a liberated woman, leaving a legend of driving incidents behind when she finally gave me her keys after she was well up in her 90s and in a nursing home. Mom lived to be nearly 98, and besides often speculating about buying herself a car and start driving again, she spent a lot of time with her wheelchair parked next to Ruby Kidwell Yount and the two of them filled their days with plots of escape--like two POWs in a Stalag. Well, anyway mom, thanks for all the rides. Maybe we can take another good ride one of these days in a land far-a-way.

Wayne Bullard, DPh
waynebullard@sbcglobal.net

Twin Sisters: Dora Bullard and Jane Ray

**Grandma Boyd holding Gerald
Oma Armstrong and J.C. Armstrong**

Gerald and the 1941 Nash

Pontiacs

It was 1941when the new Pontiac drove around me as I walked down the hot sandy road — barefoot. I can still remember the heat and the dust and the car — a magnificent and brand-new-Pontiac, going along its way and looking great. The thought that I had to have one of those when I'm grown up lingered on in my mind as I walked on in the heat.

My family lived on Highway 3 and my brother and I often watched cars go by, hoping to see a new one — a sight that was unusual in depression-era Centrahoma. Then there was the war.

In February 1942, the government ordered car production to stop and for the auto industry to turn all its resources to making tanks and aircraft. Production of all cars, appliances, radios and other commodities ceased. Millions of young men were drafted into the military and millions more migrated to the cities of America to take jobs producing war goods. Everything changed. People were newly prosperous, but had no way of buying new cars — just used ones. What happened next in August of 1945 at the war's end was just as expected — everyone wanted a new car.

Detroit was eager to help, churning out millions of new Fords, Chevys, Pontiacs and such, but they couldn't meet demand — it was a seller's market. People were "tipping" car salesmen (a hundred buck tip was average) to move their name at the top of the waiting list. When the car became available, you took whatever color it happened to be and options it might have. The heater cost $9.00 and the radio about $12.00 and you were often stuck with those luxury items.

To make matters worse for the Bullard family, dad was "close" with his money and wouldn't bribe a salesman to sell him a car. So we trusted in our old car, a 1941 model Nash. When it broke down it took the Nash garage in Ada two months to get a part — so we walked. When the Nash agency offered us a new Nash, he took it. His name was also on the waiting list for Pontiac, Ford and Chevy but now it was time for fourth choice and he had to buy a "pricey" Nash. The Nash was an Ambassador model, Series 600, that would go 600 miles on its 20 gallon tank.

It was 1948 before the car crazy U.S. public started getting "caught up" on its thirst for new cars. By the mid 50's the U.S. market was invaded by smaller cars from Japan and Germany, our old enemies. The U.S. (in a fit of compassion) had been trying to help them to prosper, so we sent teams of quality control engineers overseas to help them learn how to build and market quality automobiles. I think it worked pretty well. It was only a few years before several brands (Nash, Packard, Hudson and Studebaker) went broke. And the clock had begun to tick for GM, Ford and Chrysler.

I can't imagine an America without Chevys and Fords and Pontiacs. But White House spokesman, Robert Gibbs said "no thanks," proving once more that you can't give away GM stock. Now, GM has submitted a plan which would reduce the number of dealerships from 6,200 to 3,600. GM would sell off Saturn, Saab and Hummer and kill off the beloved Pontiac brand. GM has been using the loyal Pontiac brand for years as a cash cow, importing rebranded Korean (Aveo) Chevrolets and Australian-built Chevys — passing them for genuine Pontiacs.

In spite of this mistreatment, the brand still out-sold the Cadillac brand two to one. But GM WILL allow it to disappear very soon. Pontiacs were first built as carriages in 1893 and the first car (called the Oakland) was marketed in 1907.

GM took over the company in 1920 and its first Pontiac made its appearance in 1926. The six cylinder steel-topped car sold 76,742 units its first year, adopting its Indian head hood ornament in 1928. Now the famous American brand has been consigned to the trash heap along with Oldsmobile. I guess the Indian will go with it.

Have a good weekend and be sure and go to church this Sunday. But if you are going to drive your Pontiac or any other American-made vehicle, I suggest you get your Kodak out and take a picture. It may not be around very much longer.

Wayne Bullard, Pharm. D.

Driving I-20

The noisy interstate suddenly become very quiet except for the cries of the little girl. I had just gently touched her arm when she awakened and cried out. Her world had suddenly changed from a cozy spot in the front seat with her mom, to a nightmare world of pain, confusion and fear. The spot where she sat was a unrecognizable mass of twisted steel and glass splinters. Sabrina Fortier could not move. Her arm was pinned between a seat and the dashboard; her leg was caught in an impossible tangle of steel and motor. Both limbs were broken in several places. I was of little help. Nor was her mama, Jackie Fortier. She wasn't dead, but sure looked like it.

Pat and I saw things going all wrong when a large dump truck zipped by us on I-20 just west of the Mississippi river bridge in Louisiana. We were driving along, making good time in the 70MPH zone. Then a nice looking "sport" black car came by with Jackie and Sabrina catching up to the truck, which stayed doggedly in the left lane. To our surprise, and eventual horror, the giant bed of the truck slowly "raised". In a few long seconds it was almost straight up and made a very strange sight going down the road. I tried to chase it down and signal the driver when an overpass came in view. The results become rather predictable. The front lip of the bed caught on the bridge, sheering it from the truck chassis. The bed was rammed hard into the pavement making for a terrible tool of death. All this was closely followed by the crash of the Fortier vehicle into the truck bed. The car was nearly sliced in half and the passengers were hopelessly broken and pinned. Nearly two hours later, with help from rescue units, ambulance drivers, firemen and a coupla' of prayer meetings held by passing motorists, Jackie and Sabrina were pried and cut out of the tangled mess and transported by ambulance to Vicksburg. We stood in the road knowing the drama was over for us, but I'll remember Sabrina forever. And I guess I will always wonder, as Paul Harvey would say, if we would ever know the rest of the story.

Be careful driving this weekend.
Wayne Bullard, Pharm. D.

Pat, Lou, Wayne, and Freda at Bullard Drug Store in Allen

Lesli Bullard at Bullard Drug

Dora Bullard & son Gerald in Stonewall, 1948

Daily fishing trip for C.D. Bullard and grandson Steven

Courtney Bullard, Meegan, Costner, Steve Bullard, Pat Bullard, Julia Runge, Charlotte Bullard, Wayne Bullard, Lesli Costner, Francesca Bullard, Emilee Costner, Braden Bullard, Lindsey Bullard, Alec Runge and Traci Runge.

Lindsey Bullard (Ron's daughter)

Grandkids - Francesca Pearl Bullard (front).
Julia and Alec Runge and Lindsey and Braden Bullard (seated)

Wayne and Pat

Ron Bullard at Bullard Drug Store in Allen

Francesca Pearl Bullard and Emilee Costner

Barefoot Sue riding a new bike in Stonewall 1948

Jimmy Bullard and Jimmy Bullard

Homecoming Parade 1967

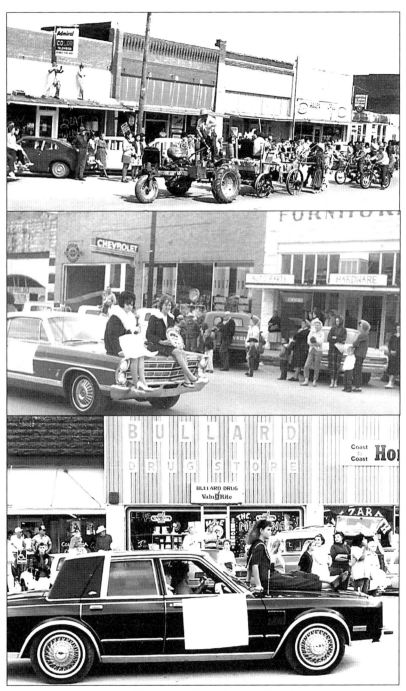

Homecoming Parade 1967

Ellis Family Reunion 2013